Crisis in the Public Sector

Crisis in the Public Sector

A Reader

Reader Editorial Collective:
Kenneth Fox, Mary Jo Hetzel, Thomas Riddell, Nancy Rose,
and Jerry Sazama

Monthly Review Press/
Union for Radical Political Economics

The Union for Radical Political Economics (URPE) is an association of people devoted to the study, development, and application of radical political economics as a tool for building socialism in the United States. It functions as an umbrella organization, providing a forum and focus for people with many different political inclinations who share that common dedication. For further information write: URPE, National Office, 41 Union Square West, Rm 901, New York, N.Y. 10003.

Copyright © by Union for Radical Political Economics
All Rights Reserved

Library of Congress Cataloging in Publication Data
Main entry under title:
Crisis in the public sector.

1. Government spending policy—United States—Addresses, essays, lectures. 2. Economic assistance, Domestic—United States—Addresses, essays, lectures. I. Fox, Kenneth. II. Public Sector Crisis Reader Collective (West Virginia)
HJ7539.C74   336.73   81-11271
ISBN 0-85345-575-9   AACR2

Edited by Martha Cameron

Monthly Review Press
62 West 14th Street, New York, N.Y. 10011
47 The Cut London SE1, 8LL

Manufactured in the United States of America

10   9   8   7   6   5   4   3   2   1

Contents

1. Introduction: The Nature of the Public Sector

Reader Editorial Collective: Ken Fox, Mary Jo Hetzel, Tom Riddell, Nancy Rose, and Jerry Sazama

As the 1980s begin, the public sector in the United States is under severe attack. Many of its activities are threatened by budget cutbacks, tax revolts, and the growing strength of the New Right. Military spending is increasing as public school teachers are laid off, transit systems are allowed to deteriorate, and public-assistance programs for the poor are slashed. This crisis in the public sector began during the 1970s and has been dramatically escalated by the Reagan administration. It is widespread and endangers the well-being and standard of living of millions of Americans.

The "public sector" refers to the array of government programs that serve both the needs of business on the one hand and working people and the poor on the other. Examples of programs that serve business are government subsidies (for example, milk-price supports and government contracts with no cost controls), military expenditures and "economic aid" to protect U.S. investments in Third World countries, tax incentives, transportation systems, and bail-outs of unprofitable corporations (for example, Chrysler and Lockheed). Some of the programs that serve the poor and working people are public assistance, social security, unemployment compensation, minimum-wage and maximum-hour laws, the Occupational Safety and Health Administration (OSHA), and pollution control. These latter programs were not willingly granted by the government but were won by employed and unemployed working people after long periods of struggle.

During the past fifty years the public sector has grown considerably. Today about one-fifth of American workers are directly employed in the public sector, and public sector expenditures account for approximately one-third of the gross national product (total dollar amount of goods and services produced in a year). This increase in public sector expenditures, and the changing amounts spent on social welfare and the military, is shown in the accompanying table.

This Reader deals with the crisis in the public sector—the fact that programs directed at human needs for working people and the poor are being cut in order to aid the private business sector. The goal of this collection of articles is to examine the public sector crisis: to put it into historical perspective, to explore its roots and causes, to spell out some of its effects, and to consider some of the actual and potential reactions to it.

The Crisis of the Public Sector

The public sector crisis is part of the general economic crisis that the United States and other capitalist countries have been experiencing since the early 1970s. This economic crisis is seen in lower rates of economic growth than in the 1950s and 1960s, as well as higher levels of unemployment and lower real wages for workers (wages measured in constant dollars to adjust for the impact of inflation), severe problems in basic industries such as auto and steel, slower rates of productivity growth, accelerating inflation, the energy crisis, and decreasing international military and political power for the United States. Despite the fact that millions of people are suffering from this economic crisis, it is part of the normal functioning of American capitalism. Capitalism is a system that grows in spurts and starts and, from time to time, also suffers major breakdowns. (The last decades of the nineteenth century and the Great Depression of the 1930s were two other periods of economic crisis.)

It is in this context of economic crisis that the crisis of the public sector emerges so forcefully. It appears in many forms. It can be seen in Reagan's efforts to cut back sharply on social-spending programs for various forms of welfare and public services, while greatly increasing the budget to the military, which is euphemistically called "defense." It can also be seen in the tax revolts in localities, in the states, and even at the federal level. In order to protect their standard of living as taxes increase and inflation ac-

The Nature of the Public Sector   3

Table 1-1   *Functional classification of government expenditures as a percentage of GNP, 1927, 1960, and 1977**

Expenditures	Percent of GNP		
	1927	*1960*	*1977*
Military-related†	1.2	10.3	6.7
Social-welfare‡	0.7	4.9	11.4
Other civilian	8.5	11.8	14.8
Total	10.4	27.0	32.9
Federal	2.5	18.4	22.4
State and local	7.9	8.6	10.6

Source: Facts & Figures (Washington, D.C.: Tax Foundation, 1979), p. 33; R. Musgrave and P. Musgrave, *Public Finance* (New York: McGraw-Hill, 1980), p. 148. Because of cutbacks, the U.S. Bureau of Census is no longer publishing regular government financial statistics; hence, 1977 disaggregated figures are the most recently available.

* Includes all levels of government—federal, state, and local.

† Military expenditures include military assistance abroad and veterans benefits and services, but not interest on debt incurred during wars and the space program.

‡ Social-welfare expenditures include social security, welfare, health and hospitals, unemployment compensation, and housing and community development.

celerates, people begin to seek relief. The movement to slow down the growth of taxes or even to decrease them, as in California's Proposition 13 and Massachusetts' Proposition 2½, is partly a reaction to people's economic realities. Working people have less real income and pay a greater portion of this decreasing income in taxes. The movement for tax relief also comes from the widespread feelings that people don't get adequate public services— that they don't get what they pay for.

The tax revolt has been led by the New Right as part of a concerted, organized, and well-financed attack on government at all levels. It is an assault on taxes, on many social-spending programs, and on most government regulations designed to protect workers and their communities. It is an effort to reduce the taxes of the rich and the corporations and to provide less for the rest of us. This attack from the right was clearly seen in the successful presidential campaign of Ronald Reagan.

The public sector crisis also demonstrates itself in the fiscal crises of many local and state governments throughout the United States.

The city of Cleveland was forced to default on some of its bonds, and its progressive mayor, Dennis Kucinich, paid the price to the city's bankers with his job. New York City experienced a budget crisis in the mid-1970s when it almost went into bankruptcy, and since then has had its financial affairs controlled by bankers. In late 1977, Wayne County, Michigan, had to furlough 4000 employees because it didn't have the tax receipts to pay them. The State of Massachusetts was faced with near-bankruptcy in 1975, and the city of Boston threatened to close its schools during the spring of 1981 because of lack of funds. The fragile financial position of many cities and states will undoubtedly become more evident as the Reagan administration cuts back federal aid to state and local governments. The justification for making these and other cutbacks— the need to balance the federal budget—is proven false by the enormous increase in military expenditures.

All of these manifestations of the public sector crisis translate into cutbacks in public services and programs. In particular, they are occurring in those areas that are designed to benefit working people (including the poor)—food stamps, welfare, school lunches, job training, CETA jobs, extended unemployment benefits, OSHA and environmental protection regulations, consumer protection, public transportation, parks and recreation, medical care, and a host of others. These cutbacks in programs will bring further cutbacks in public sector jobs—jobs for teachers, social workers, recreation workers, and even police and fire fighters. The greatest impact of these job cuts will be on national minorities and women, since they have made more gains in employment in the public sector than in industry during the past decade. All these cutbacks will produce a further decline in the standards of living of employed and unemployed working people by forcing them to pay directly for some of these benefits and programs, previously supported through taxes, and to disband others entirely.

We have also seen a dramatic intensification of Cold War propaganda in order to justify large increases in military expenditures. Beginning in the early 1970s, and receiving an enormous boost by the Reagan administration, the Soviet Union has been depicted as an increasing threat to the so-called free world. But the real problem is that the United States is not as powerful as it was in the 1950s and 1960s and can therefore no longer order world affairs. Evidences of this are found in the U.S. defeat in the Vietnam War, the increasing strength of the Organization of Petroleum Exporting

Countries (OPEC), the rise in Third World liberation movements, and the Iranian revolution and the taking of American hostages. The Soviet invasion of Afghanistan and their aid in arming the revolutionaries in Third World countries have been seized upon by the U.S. government to stir up anti-Soviet feelings and therefore validate the decision to greatly increase the military budget. Meanwhile the U.S. government talks about protecting *our* interests in the Persian Gulf and defending our "doorstep" in Latin America from communism, as it sends arms and "advisers" to the repressive junta in El Salvador and tries to coerce Western European countries to install more missiles pointed at the USSR.

The Political Meaning of the Crisis

The public sector crisis, despite its technical, neutral ring, is an intensely political phenomenon. The new conservative ideas, symbols, and policies that have flowed forth since the mid-1970s economic crunch have placed nearly every movement and principle toward liberation on the defensive. It is no longer considered legitimate to care about overcoming poverty or to fight for the rights of working men and women. The new conservative move to cut needed social programs, public sector jobs, and wages is part of a larger political response by business and government leaders to gains made by labor, Blacks, women, and antiwar and poor people's movements in the 1960s and 1970s. In order to turn back that class threat and to resolidify their position of power vis-à-vis competitors from advanced capitalist and Third World countries, U.S. capitalists and their political allies tell us that such social and political activism is a luxury we can no longer afford. We are told that we must avoid the distractions of social justice and learn to accept the "new economic reality of self-sacrifice."

The new conservatives, of both Republican and Democratic stripe, who now dominate the world of government, business, academia, and the media have tried hard to convince the American public that we have no other choice but to accept less—less wages, less basic human services, and less control over the institutions of daily life. We are being told that there is nothing we can do but subordinate ourselves to the new rules of fiscal logic and quietly tighten our belts. We are to be on guard against only one thing:

we must make sure that no fellow workers or citizens gain some-thing at our expense. Austerity is to be the new way of life until sufficient sacrifice of all the "little people" in the nation has again brought us around to our senses and made us realize that our salvation lies in disciplined hard work in the interests of those who employ us, plan and organize our enterprises, and dictate our economic and social policies.

The Goal of the Reader

This Reader is premised on the belief that in one of the most productive countries in the world, founded on liberal democracy and the principles of people's ability to fulfill their potential and control their destiny, we do not have to subordinate ourselves to a capitalist-dictated solution to the public sector crisis. We do not have to sit and watch our jobs cut out from underneath us, our services denied us, our right to self-government stripped away. We do not have to look at our neighbors and co-workers with hostility and fear because they may get something we won't. We need to shift the burden of the crisis onto those who caused it, benefit from it, and wish to perpetuate a system that will be con-tinuously prone to such crises in the future.

This Reader has been developed to help us get off the defensive, and to show why neither the new economic and political conser-vatism nor the old-style liberalism can solve the dilemmas of the 1980s. We reexamine who and what is really to blame for the public sector crisis: "greedy" public workers, "lazy" welfare recip-ients, liberal government "mismanagement," as present leaders would have us believe; or a system of profit-oriented monopoly capitalism, prone to crisis and characterized by extreme inequality reflected in an unfair tax system and distorted spending priorities, as we believe. By understanding the actual sources of the public sector crisis, we are in a much better position to move away from reactive, defensive politics and go on the offensive with a positive program for change.

There are thousands of people written about in this book who do not accept the new conservative view of reality. They have come to realize that the liberal politics of each interest group fighting for its own piece of an expanding pie has become outmoded in the

1980s. It is clear today that as long as we remain content to work within the parameters of the system—that is, to accept the primacy of corporate profit and competitive values, while seeing human needs as a secondary concern—we will continually be on the defensive. We will be helpless when decisions are made to close a factory, cut off a needed service, implement an unfair tax, or put forward an unresponsive candidate for office.

We need to move toward a politics of democratic control over all the institutions of daily life. Our long-term goal is democratic socialism—the ownership and control of the economy and the public sector by working people in the interest of human needs for all, instead of ownership and control by a ruling class of capitalists in the interest of profits for themselves. In building such a movement to take control over economic and political institutions, we need to counter all tendencies that divide us, or else we will forever remain fragmented, fearful, and weak. Thus we need to oppose all forms of oppression aimed at selected groups, specifically at women, gay men, lesbians, Jews, and national minorities, in the United States, as well as the oppression of Third World countries.

The goal of this Reader is to assist the process of organizing a response to the public sector crisis and the current mood of "cutback." This collection of articles is intended to lay the foundation for an understanding of the public sector crisis—its causes, its results, and the reactions to it. We hope that this Reader will help public sector clients, job holders, and beneficiaries to develop further their understanding of the crisis and, based on that understanding, to engage in organized actions to defend and improve public services and public sector jobs, obtain tax relief and reform, and seek progressive social change in the direction of a democratic-socialist society.

The Contents of the Reader

Part I of the Reader puts the public sector crisis into historical and theoretical perspective. The article by Naples et al. argues that the roots of the present crisis can be seen in the postwar domestic and international development of the U.S. economy and discusses the nature of the capitalist state. Other articles in this section interpret the public sector, the role of the state in society, and the place of public employees in the class structure. All of the articles thus define the battleground over the public sector in the 1980s—that is, over taxes, spending programs, and jobs.

Part II focuses on the fiscal effects of the crisis—the taxing and spending dimensions. Some articles are concerned with the overall pattern of taxes and spending, while others concentrate on the specific issues of public pension funds and the fiscal crisis of the cities, as seen in Cleveland.

Part III deals with some of the impact of the crisis on the community—examples of how people in different areas have been affected by recent changes in the public sector and of how they have fought back.

Part IV concerns itself with the controversial issues of public sector unions: their role in the crisis and in defending public programs; strategies they should adopt to defend their interests; their allies and their enemies; and ways that public sector workers can be organized for progressive social change.

Part V deals with some of the direct effects of the crisis on public sector workers and on some of their responses thus far.

The Reader concludes with a section placing the public sector crisis in political perspective. Articles discuss the politics of the New Right and the possibilities for developing a successful progressive movement to combat the crisis in the public sector and in the rest of society.

The Making of the Reader

The Public Sector Crisis Reader Collective was organized at a summer conference of the Union for Radical Political Economics in West Virginia in August 1978. The collective continued meeting regularly from that time until early in 1981 to put the Reader together. Articles were solicited from within and outside of URPE, from people involved in and interested in the public sector. Each article was reviewed by a committee composed of either three members of the collective or, in some cases, an outside reader and two members of the collective. The committees then communicated with the authors to recommend changes, improvements, additions, deletions, and so forth. The final step involved editing and arranging for publication of the Reader.

Many people have aided this effort. Two who were especially helpful were Martha Cameron who edited this reader and provided valuable suggestions and Gary Edelman of URPE's Economic Education Project Board, who provided editorial advice and other assistance to the collective.

It was a lot of work for all involved, and the collective meetings were exercises in social cooperation, comraderie, and good eating.

We would be interested in any comments, criticisms, and feedback on this reader; write to the Public Sector Crisis Reader Collective, URPE, 41 Union Square West, Room 901, New York, N.Y. 10003.

Part I

Understanding the Crisis

2. The Crisis in Perspective

Michele Naples, Tom Riddell, and Nancy Rose

"California Passes Proposition 13—Property Taxes Slashed by $6 Billion." "Cleveland Faces Threat of Default." "New York City Lays Off Hundreds of Fire Fighters and Police." "School Budget Cuts in Columbus—Teachers Laid Off." "Elderly Woman Freezes to Death—Municipal Electric Company Shuts Off Heat—Bills Not Paid."

These familiar headlines of the last few years are symptoms of a crisis in the public sector in the United States. We have seen cities on the verge of bankruptcy. In fiscal year 1975–76, New York City was able to refinance its large deficits with additional loans only after the banks' demands for spending limits, layoffs of city employees, and more business input into city policies were met. In 1979, Cleveland refused to buckle under to the bankers' requirements and defaulted on some of its bonds; but that default has made it much more difficult for Cleveland to finance its budget by loans, and taxes have had to be increased.

For the first time in years, we are seeing major cutbacks in federal social spending. The Carter administration's budget for 1980

Michele Naples teaches economics and women's studies at Douglass College, Rutgers University; Tom Riddell teaches economics at Smith College; Nancy Rose is a Ph.D. candidate at the University of Massachusetts, Amherst. We would like to thank all those who made comments and criticisms of earlier drafts of this paper, notably the Popular Economics Research Group (formerly the Red Cent Collective), including Sam Bowles, Bob Buchelle, Harry Cocaine, Diane Flaherty, Herb Gintis, David Kotz, Karen Pfeifer, Julie Schor, and Steve Shulman; the members of the Public Sector Crisis collective; and Jim Crotty, Paul Luebke, and Nick McConaughy.

called for "austerity" and "restraint" in the provision of government services. While defense spending, social security, and health-care payments were increased (the latter two because the benefits are tied by law to the rate of inflation), other programs were level-funded or cut. The 1981 budget continued these trends, with increases for defense spending and austerity for domestic programs; the Reagan administration's economic program only accelerates these shifts in the public sector. This means layoffs for some government employees and fewer social services for the people.

At the state and local level the crisis appeared in the tax-revolt fever that swept the country in 1978. This was largely a reaction to the increasing economic pinch of rising inflation and rising taxes and to the apparent incompetence or impotence of government. But it was also fueled by right-wing propaganda about the "excesses" of spending on welfare, education, and other public services. In twelve states laws were passed placing limits on the growth of public spending and taxes. The campaign against the public sector has even spawned a national effort to require a balanced federal budget. This tax revolt has directly threatened many needed public services.

As a result of the fiscal crisis, public hospitals have been closed, state universities have doubled tuitions while shutting down buildings they cannot afford to maintain, welfare and food-stamp eligibility requirements have pushed thousands of people off public assistance at a time when the number of unemployed in the economy is increasing. As spending is cut back, class size in public schools increases; and activities that were taken for granted, such as sports, art, and music, disappear. Special programs for children, the aged, and the handicapped are being eliminated. The hours of the town library are reduced, or it is closed. The effects of the cutbacks are visible nationwide, but the extent and degree of these problems vary tremendously in different parts of the country.[1]

These are only some of the dimensions of the crisis of the public sector. As this crisis develops, it affects Americans as public sector workers, as recipients of public services, and as ordinary taxpayers. We are overwhelmed with proposals claiming to solve the crisis by getting *us* to tighten our belts. In order to provide a basis for strategies to deal with this situation, we need to understand the causes of the fiscal crisis in the United States.

The United States is in the midst of a general crisis of capitalism. The economy is a mess, and the state (that is, the government at all levels) is in flux. Economic stagnation, inflation, unemployment, and the structural problems underlying them are the context of the fiscal crisis. But they are also the outcome of U.S. history since World War II. In order to understand where the crisis of the public sector has come from, we need to see why capitalist society goes through cycles of economic crises. And we need to examine the role of the government in such an unstable society. From this examination we can make sense of the history that has brought us to this point, and we can evaluate current proposals for restructuring the state and its role in the economy. Only then can we formulate strategies to fight for changes that will meet *our* needs and protect *our* priorities.[2]

Why Capitalism Has Economic Ups and Downs

We will begin our exploration of the causes of the crisis in the public sector by asking why the "economy" is in crisis.[3]

Capitalism generates crises as a "normal" part of its own growth process. The goal of production under capitalism is *private profit*. Capitalists and corporations organize production, use raw materials, and hire labor in order to produce products that can be sold for a profit. Moreover, capitalists must compete with each other for profits. The competition among capitalists in search of profit can be quite intense; they use past profits to invest in new ventures or in expanding output because they think that they can earn more profits as a result. This process is called capital accumulation. Capitalists have no choice but to participate in this process. If they don't, they will be driven out of business by competitors who expand their markets or invest in new technologies to lower costs and increase profits. The results of the process (when it "works") are investment, growth in output, and, the capitalists hope, more profit.

However, the process of capital accumulation under capitalism has some limitations. First of all, capitalists must employ labor to produce their goods and services. Obviously, capitalists will be able to earn higher profits if they can get workers to work hard for low wages. On the other hand, if workers demand higher wages, safer working conditions, and a slower pace of work, profits won't be as high—and capital accumulation will be more difficult. In other words, class relations between capitalists and workers will affect the ability of capitalism to earn profits and accumulate capital.

Moreover, the capitalist growth process is unstable. It generates both short-term and long-term crises in economic activity. The short-term crises are usually called business cycles or recessions; and the long-term crises are called depressions or structural crises. The current economic crisis can be understood in the context of both short-term and long-term instability in U.S. capitalism.

Let us begin with a description of the way in which the capital accumulation process produces short-term, business-cycle crises. In periods of prosperity, capitalists' expectations of profits encourage an "over-investment" of capital—for example, the building of too many shopping centers. It then becomes difficult for all capitalists to earn the profits that they expect. As a result, they reduce the rate of capital accumulation; that is, they spend less on investment goods, like machinery and equipment. Such a movement causes a decline in business activity—a recession—as production is reduced and workers are laid off. This source of instability is inherent in capitalist production for private profit.

The class conflict between capitalists and workers contains another source of instability. During economic upswings, the rate of unemployment decreases as economic activity increases and more workers are hired. However, this also tends to increase the tightness of labor markets, as well as other resource markets. Labor's bargaining position is strengthened when there are fewer unemployed workers available and when capitalists expect high rates of profit. Therefore, workers can win higher wages and other improvements in the conditions of work (such as increased safety measures, reduced speedup, etc.). But such gains for labor eventually cut into profits, and lower profits lead to reduced capital accumulation. The result is recession: economic activity is once again cut back and unemployment increases.

It is this short-term instability in the capital accumulation process that produces swings, ups and downs, "booms and busts." In the post-World War II period in the United States there have been seven recessions, counting the most recent one in 1979–1980. But in the current context, there are also some long-term problems that further complicate and, in fact, hinder the capital accumulation process. These long-term problems add up to a structural crisis of capitalism.

In order to function well—to be able to earn profits and accumulate capital—capitalism requires certain conditions: a stable international monetary and trading system; access to cheap raw materials (that is, stable relations with the Third World); a "truce" between labor and capital; and some mechanism for regulating the instability produced by capitalists' competition with each other and by the capital accumulation process itself. During periods when these conditions can be secured, capitalism can work relatively well in producing profits, capital accumulation, and economic growth and may only suffer periodic and short-lived recessions. However, when these conditions are absent, capitalism enters a period of long term, structural crisis. Since the 1970s, the United States and other advanced capitalist countries have been in such a structural crisis situation. There have been two other such periods of crisis for U.S. capitalism—the depression of 1873–1898 and the Great Depression, 1929–1941. The causes of the current crisis date back many years.

The Historical Background of the Fiscal Crisis

The Great Depression

Many people remember the 1930s as the Great Depression—as apple-sellers in the streets, soup lines and Hoovervilles, ghostly looking factories, and waves of bank failures. At the bottom of the depression in March 1933, industrial production had fallen 37 percent from the 1929, predepression level, investment had fallen 90 percent, and measured unemployment (counting only married men) stood at 25 percent of the labor force.

Part of the reason for the depth of this depression was the collapse of the international trade and financial system. Great Britain, which had been the major world power through World War I, was no longer in a position to make loans to countries so they could keep paying for their imports. The international imbalance in Europe after the war had never been successfully resolved. This meant that, when the depression hit, every country acted individually to try to defend itself from the worst effects of the downturn. Countries cut their imports but tried to sell more exports in order to prop up their economies. Of course as everyone cut imports, export markets dried up, so that in the United States, for example, exports fell 25 percent from 1929 to 1933. This was equal to one-quarter of the total fall in industrial production.

Of course, capitalists tried to avoid having the effects of this production crisis fall on them by passing them on to the working class—cutting wages and laying people off. But people did not endure the suffering in silence. In the first few years of the depression, eviction blockages and penny auctions (when someone's farm would be foreclosed by a bank, neighbors would bid small amounts for the goods and then turn the property back over to the original owner) successfully prevented many people from being thrown out on the street. Large hunger marches brought the plight of many in the working class to the attention of Washington (there was no federal relief at this time, only state and local resources, which were quickly used up) and provided a feeling of solidarity for the participants. In 1934, the year after Franklin Delano Roosevelt became president, a wave of strikes occurred in which employed and unemployed workers were united, often as the result of efforts by communist organizers. In general there was much turmoil and protest, and to many people capitalism seemed to be on the verge of collapse.

Thus there were four major dimensions to the crisis that capitalism faced: militant action for income and jobs by people in the reserve army of the unemployed or underemployed; the domestic chaos in financial markets; activism by the employed for unions and job guarantees and against speedup (which increased labor costs); and the international instability, which meant no growth in foreign markets for U.S. goods. Basically the New Deal, a set of reforms under President Roosevelt, succeeded in dealing with the first two problems, and the third to a certain extent, and structural changes during and after World War II ultimately resolved the third and fourth problems.

Roosevelt and his advisers went through different phases in the New Deal in their efforts to solve the problems of the Great Depression. What emerged overall was a great increase in the role of the government with respect to both the functioning of the economy, and to the protection of the working class from economic fluctuations and some of the worst abuses of the capitalists.

The New Deal included the Wagner Act, sanctioning labor's right to organize and bargain collectively. This gave legal recognition to the massive organizing efforts of the newly formed Committee for Industrial Organization (CIO). It also included the Social Security Act, providing payments from the government for those who lacked resources to provide for themselves (financed by payroll taxes). At the same time, other more radical solutions to the poverty caused by the depression were proposed but were not adopted. These included Huey Long's Share Our Wealth plan and the Townsend Plan whereby the state would provide a pension of $200 per month for every person over sixty-five years of age.

In addition, the New Deal initiated banking reform to centralize the functions of the Federal Reserve System, holding-company acts to regulate trusts, and direct government investment (instead of only government subsidization of private investment) as in the Tennessee Valley Authority power plants.

These programs resulted in a great increase in government spending and a relatively large federal deficit. And for the first time, in 1938, the government allowed the deficit to get larger, rather than cutting spending to "balance the budget," in order to stimulate economic activity; this was the first time Keynesian economics was used in the United States.

Such New Deal reforms were accompanied by an increase in the power of the executive branch at the expense of the legislative branch of government. This facilitated the centralized coordination needed to carry out the policies of Keynesianism and to deal with the enlarged role of government in the regulation of private enterprise. It also helped to insulate "technical" government policy from the "political" considerations raised by the mass movements of the era.

World War II

By 1941, on the eve of U.S. entry into World War II, although several beneficial changes had been made, the accumulation process still faced severe structural problems, especially regarding organized labor and the international scene. These were not to be successfully dealt with until soon after the war.

World War II was an event that saw a major change in the structure of U.S. society. The fight against fascism united most of the nation for the first time in more than a decade; it was the most popular war in U.S. history. Even the unions just formed in the 1930s pledged not to strike during the war in order to keep up the war effort. And, of course, the war meant that the United States achieved full employment for the first time since the 1920s (the unemployment rate dropped to 1.5 percent, even though thousands of Blacks and women entered the labor force for the first time). This was the basis for a major change in the relationship between unions and companies. Instead of fighting unions tooth and nail, as they always had, many corporations learned from the relative labor peace of the period and adopted a less hostile attitude toward the unions.

Also during the war, the split between internationally oriented corporations and smaller, U.S.-oriented businesses was overcome as everyone agreed to enter the war abroad. The success of the "internationalist" outlook for U.S. foreign policy thrust this country into the lead in building international trade and financial arrangements during the war and the postwar period. Only after this national truce within the capitalist class, built on the structural changes of the New Deal, could the United States begin to play the role, vacated by Great Britain, of the dominant, hegemonic world power.

In fact, World War II also created the space for a dramatic increase in U.S. imperialism. German, British, and French corporations were all absorbed in the war effort, and those economies were very close to demolished by the end of World War II. U.S. corporations were then able to get a foothold in Third World countries that had previously been dominated by European capitalists, such as in Southeast Asia, sub-Saharan Africa, and the Middle East. Even in Europe itself the need to rely on U.S. aid after the war, such as the Marshall Plan, meant using the borrowed dollars to buy imports from the United States. In this way the large European markets opened up to American corporations as they never had before.

Thus, in the period after the war, from the later 1940s to the early 1950s, a new world order emerged, dominated by the United States. Economically, this meant the birth of many American multinational corporations, operating on several continents. In the early 1950s many corporations "ran away" from newly unionized, higher-wage areas of the United States to the new frontiers like Taiwan, Hong Kong, Korea, and South Africa. Politically, this meant that the United States had to take on the role of police force for the world, in order to prevent any threats to the profits of these multinational corporations by expanding U.S. imperialism and supporting "friendly" governments. As a result, military spending in the United States, although somewhat lower than during the war, stayed higher than ever before in peacetime (from less than 2 percent of GNP to about 10 percent of GNP). A large part of the Marshall Plan was military aid, including money to build military bases the United States would have access to. The Central Intelligence Agency (CIA) and the Pentagon grew dramatically, as the United States prepared to intervene in conflicts in other parts of the world on the side of governments it favored—Indochina in the late 1940s, South Korea, Lebanon, and Iran in the early 1950s, the Dominican Republic in 1965, and so forth.

The main enemies of this extended U.S. imperialism were, of course, socialist and communist movements. The USSR had proven its economic and military strength in defeating the Germans; and after the war many more countries discarded capitalism and started to build their own brand of socialism, including Yugoslavia, the countries of Eastern Europe, and the People's Republic of China. Even in France and Italy, the Communist parties were very popular because of their central role in the resistance against the fascists.

Thus the increase in U.S. imperialism after the war and higher peacetime levels of military spending went hand in hand with anticommunism abroad and at home. The Communist Party had also become popular here because of its activity in organizing unemployed councils and union drives in the 1930s and backing the war effort after 1941. But the Red Scare, the McCarthy witch hunts, and the Taft-Hartley Labor Act of 1947 were successful in undermining militance in the unions and in smashing most of the left-led, progressive unions, as well as in supporting the high levels of military expenditure. This was the price the unions paid for their newly found financial security and legitimacy.

While the shape of the unions in the postwar period was being influenced by these government policies, other trends and government programs were undermining working people's belief that they needed unions to make economic gains. The GI Bill enabled many veterans to obtain a college education they otherwise could not have afforded. With the sustained growth of the late 1940s and 1950s, many college graduates were able to find middle-level white-collar jobs. Also, government-subsidized home mortgages and the federal highway program spurred the move to expanding suburbs. These trends reinforced an individualist ethic. The possibility for social mobility pushed people to turn to making it on their own by leaving the factory, rather than staying and struggling to change conditions there.

About half of World War II had been paid for by raising taxes, and the other half paid for by loans—war bonds—from private individuals and institutions. Because of the war's popularity, many war bonds had been bought by working people who had the cost deducted little by little from their paychecks. Before the war only the very wealthy paid income tax, but during and after the war the government expanded the income tax base. At the same time withholding of income taxes from workers' pay packets was instituted by the government. This increased revenue was needed not only to pay the war debt but also to pay for the military budget. Over time—after the successful creation of political and economic conditions favoring capital accumulation—the tax structure became more and more regressive, taking less from the corporations and the rich and more from everyone else, especially middle-income people. From 1954 to 1975 the effective tax rate on corporate profits fell from 43 percent to 30 percent. Meanwhile, individuals were pushed into higher tax brackets as a result of inflation. In the 1960s the "average" marginal tax bracket rate was 22 percent; by the late 1970s it was 30 percent.

Thus postwar prosperity was tied to U.S. imperialism (and cheap imports) and a large military force, as well as to nonmilitant unions. It built on people's renewed confidence in the government, their faith that depressions could be avoided in the future, and that the government would alleviate the worst effects of poverty. Capitalists invested heavily, secure that the government would follow foreign policies that would support a profitable international environment, that the banking system was solid and virtually independent of pressures from elected officials, and that the unions were busier purging communists and competing with each other than struggling for better working conditions or higher wages.

In all of these fundamental changes in the structure of U.S. capitalism, the role of the state, in intervening between capitalists and the working class and for capitalists on a world scale, had been greatly expanded. These solutions to the crisis of capitalism in the Great Depression not only created the foundation for postwar American prosperity but also laid the basis for the current fiscal crisis.

This can be seen in two ways. First, the state has expanded in order to help establish the conditions necessary for a period of extended capital accumulation. Some of these state activities, such as changes in the tax structure, defense spending, federal support of research and development, highway construction, and promotion of nuclear power, directly assist the capital accumulation process. Federal policies to stabilize the economy—and prevent depressions—serve to smooth out the extremes of capitalist instability. Second, the state has expanded in certain areas, such as welfare, social security, health care, education, unemployment compensation, and occupational safety, to maintain the class relations of capitalism. The economic position of the working class is improved through many government programs. Without these the working class would be much worse off—and possibly more militant. While these functions of the state serve to legitimate capitalism, many of these government programs were, in fact, adopted as a result of political and economic struggles on the part of working people to improve their lot under U.S. capitalism. Some of these struggles can be seen in the history of the late 1950s through the 1970s. Such struggles challenge capitalism, its class relations, and the capital accumulation process.

The Postwar Period

In the immediate postwar period, many sectors of the working class were left out of the emerging prosperity, especially Blacks. In the 1950s, a movement began for civil rights for Blacks, against segregation, and for voting rights and decent education. This movement grew slowly but steadily; by the 1960s it developed several different trends, raising the question of equal access to economic opportunities as well as to the political system, and ultimately demanding economic rights to employment, promotion, housing, health care, and so forth. Sometimes the movement took the form of nonviolent demonstrations and freedom marches, sometimes less organized and more spontaneous urban riots. Several groups worked on particular reforms, such as welfare rights, public housing, and affirmative action. Others in the Black Power movement worked toward a broader goal, ultimately struggling against capitalism as well as against white supremacy.

While the fight for political and economic rights for Blacks was the major political movement in the United States in the late 1950s and early 1960s, the beginning of direct U.S. intervention in the Vietnamese civil war gave birth to an additional broad-based movement: the movement against the war. Most of the protestors were students who, after 1968, were also subject to the draft. But there were others as well who challenged this imperialist intervention and worked to help Americans understand both what the war meant to the Vietnamese and how its drain on economic resources would harm the U.S. economy. Even a few labor unions became involved in the efforts to get the United States out of Vietnam. This was one of the first times since World War II that any unions were openly critical of the U.S. government's foreign policy.

A third major political movement that began toward the end of the 1960s and gained momentum in the 1970s was the movement to save the environment. Although at first this was also primarily a student movement, many white-collar workers joined in the fight against pollution, from factories as well as from automobiles. And workers in all sectors of the economy raised questions of human pollution—of safety and health on the job. One of the few political movements of the early 1950s, the fight against nuclear weapons, united the antiwar movement and the environmental movement against nuclear energy.

So the prosperity of the postwar era came back to haunt both the corporations and the government as more and more people became politicized and demanded that many of the not-so-visible but still harmful outcomes of the prosperous years, such as imperialism and an unhealthy environment, be changed. The fight for political rights for Blacks was one thing; but when Blacks started demanding economic rights, and students and other young people demanded an end to imperialism and refused to fight, and environmentalists demanded regulations that would increase costs, corporations saw their profits being directly threatened. Many capitalists favored action by the government to meet some of the demands and to repress others in order to quiet the political agitation. One key to the current fiscal crisis is the government's response to the political movements of the last twenty-five years.

The early government answer to Black demands for political rights was legislation and court rulings for desegregation of schools and public facilities. The struggle for equal economic opportunity was met by more legislation, like affirmative action, and by new government programs and money for job training, welfare, and a general "war on poverty." On the other hand, cities and the federal government spent more money on police forces to repress urban violence and on the Federal Bureau of Investigation (FBI) to hunt down more radical elements in all political movements, including the Black Panther Party and Students for a Democratic Society (SDS).

The federal government also increased spending on higher education dramatically in the 1960s to try to pacify minority group demands for economic opportunity. In general, government spending on social services rose, as did transfer payments through medicare, medicaid, and social security. This led to major increases in employment in the government and to public sector workers' unwillingness to see their wages stay way behind those in private business. The organizing drives among public sector workers began in the mid-1960s, for city welfare workers, state university employees, and federal postal workers. In most states it was against the law for public workers to bargain collectively or to strike. Despite this, risking heavy fines and jail sentences, school teachers, sanitation workers, and even police and fire fighters struck for union recognition and for better pay and working conditions. The success of these strikes also drove government spending up.

Because the Vietnam War (which was never officially declared by Congress) was so unpopular, the government couldn't pay for it by raising taxes, even though federal spending on the war rose to $30 billion per year. Instead, most of the war was financed through private institutions. This led to inflation, as more people were employed in military-related jobs but not enough resources went to produce the necessities of life. By borrowing to pay for the war, the government was only postponing the issue of who would end up paying; by inflating the economy, it was masking the reality of too many resources going to the war and not enough to the home economy.

Finally, the government also responded to the environmental movement by increasing government regulation of the economy and spending money on agencies to enforce the regulations. The Occupational Safety and Health Act, pollution emission standards, and nuclear plant licensing regulations were passed in the early 1970s, and many government employees took seriously the effort to ensure pure food, safe waste disposal, and clean air.

Almost all of these government actions to appease the mass-based political movements resulted in increased government spending at all levels, while the antiwar movement made it difficult to raise federal taxes. The long economic upswing of the 1960s reduced unemployment to the lowest levels since World War II. But it also allowed people the time and resources to struggle for better wages and working conditions. This, combined with the effects of other political movements, meant that profit rates were squeezed by higher real wages and other government-regulated costs, even though the effective tax rate on corporate profits decreased during the 1960s and the 1970s.

In addition to downward pressures on profits at home, the success of the Vietnamese people in defeating a demoralized U.S. army added fuel to other Third World liberation movements, as in Laos and Cambodia, Central America, South Africa, Guinea-Bissau, Mozambique, and Angola. So many U.S. resources were tied up in the war that it became more and more difficult for the government to fulfill its role as the hegemonic world power. It was not possible for the United States to slow down the economy in 1967–1968 (although the monetary authorities tried to) and still continue to supply the needs of the war in Vietnam. It became more and more difficult to keep other currencies, like the German mark and the Japanese yen, from growing stronger and the dollar from weakening, as German and Japanese capitalists made headway in international trade. To be the world's banker in the late 1960s would have meant following different policies from those of the world's police force. The result was that the United States' dominant position in world trade and finance was continuously being eroded.

The OPEC oil-price increase in 1973 and the gradual devaluation of the dollar by 20 percent in the early 1970s signaled the breakdown in the international financial system. The understandings and agreements reached by the end of World War II were no longer working. As if that were not enough, the Watergate scandal, which broke out in 1973, dealt a devastating blow to the American people's faith in the government. All of these trends combined led to the beginnings of the recession in 1974; corporations cut back investment plans because of the unstable national and international economic and political situation. In fact, industrial production fell 25 percent from October 1974 to February 1975, and the official unemployment rate reached 9 percent in May 1975. The economy might even have plummeted further had it not been for the tax cut quickly passed by Congress to put more money into consumers' hands and by a major expansion in the money supply and credit.

Although the unemployment rate fell and the economy expanded somewhat after 1975, the prosperity of the 1960s did not return. The U.S. economy stagnated in the late 1970s, with the unemployment rate rarely falling below 6 percent and inflation running as high as 13 percent. This long period of economic crisis is the context of the current fiscal crisis of the state.

As described earlier, government spending on the war, social services, and regulatory agencies grew dramatically in the 1960s, and was paid for *not* by higher taxes but by inflation and debt. When the recession came in 1974–1975, government spending on unemployment compensation and welfare had to actually increase while tax receipts decreased (people had lower incomes and so paid lower federal, state, and local taxes). Then, with the 1975 tax cut, the government deficit rose even more, reaching almost $70 billion. The financial crisis in some cities, such as New York, became evident then, as banks and institutions who were owed money by governments became afraid that the cities would never be able to pay them back. Corporations argued that federal borrowing was pushing interest rates too high and called for cutbacks in government spending, especially on social services and welfare, which were least important to them.

Into the later 1970s, as employment picked up somewhat and inflation accelerated, some areas found themselves in another dilemma: inflation of real estate prices was pushing property taxes through the ceiling. The state of California actually had a tax surplus. Some businesses spearheaded a revolt against high taxes, leading to the successful passage of Proposition 13 in California and similar tax revolts in other states.

Since the 1970s, especially in the North and on the West Coast, people's real income has fallen as prices have risen, especially the price of oil and other imports. In many families two breadwinners are needed to bring home what one breadwinner could earn in the prosperous 1960s. Most people would like to see less money taken out of their paychecks for taxes that get spent on things they seem to have no control over.

In fact, the pressure to cut back government spending has hit certain parts of the population critically. Cutbacks in higher education have forced working-class families to pay higher tuition and have greatly reduced the quality and quantity of public education in general. The failure of social security payments to keep up with inflation has pushed many elderly people to the brink of starvation. The cutbacks in CETA training programs, which if nothing else had offered people temporary employment, increased the number of unemployed Blacks and Hispanics. Not only have hospital closings, welfare cuts, and reduced funds for public housing lowered the already marginal standard of living for the poor, but the disappearance of those public jobs have thrown a large number of skilled minority people and women back onto the unemployment rolls. These manifestations of the public sector crisis are fundamentally related to the current economic crisis of American capitalism.[4]

Finally, state regulation of capitalism's instability is proving increasingly problematic. The government has been trying to create a "good business climate," mostly through various types of corporate tax breaks, to induce capitalists to invest. But they are not taking the bait. As long as expectations of future profits are "too low," as they have been during the past few years, capitalists won't invest. From 1959 to 1968, corporate profits were 12.3 percent of national income; in 1969–1973, they were 9.4 percent; and in the 1974–1978 period they were 8.8 percent. In 1978, corporate profits had rebounded somewhat and comprised 9.4 percent of national income. (For *some* corporations, notably the oil companies, profits have increased phenomenally in recent years.) It is not that corporate profits do not exist, nor is it that they have not increased during the recent recovery from 1975 to 1979. Rather, the corporate profit picture is less rosy than it was in previous periods during the last thirty years of postwar prosperity. From 1955 to 1961, the rate of return on depreciable assets for nonfinancial corporations in the United States was 12.7 percent; from 1962 to 1966, it was 14.7 percent; from 1955 to 1970, it was 13.0 percent; but in the 1970s, it has dropped to about 10 percent.

The result of the long-term structural crisis of American capitalism is that the economy cannot expand its real output of goods and services as fast as it could in the quarter-century following World War II. This is both a cause and an effect of the crisis—of the raging rates of inflation, the relatively high rates of unemployment, and the slowed productivity growth. The pie isn't expanding as fast as before. Now, as in the Great Depression, the crisis will force a redefinition of the role of the state in American society.

The Implications of the Economic Crisis for the State

This generalized crisis in the economy requires new efforts by the federal government to reformulate the rules of the game in order to create a more profitable environment for business. The state is the social institution that has the formal, legal power to establish the rules and regulations governing all behavior. It tries to set up the general framework governing the functioning of all other institutions, like the family, the corporation, and the labor union. These "rules of the game" only hold, of course, if people and institutions actually follow them and believe them to be legitimate. In addition, the state also has available to it certain police and coercive powers to enforce the rules of the game.

If the state is to succeed in reproducing capitalist society, it must facilitate economic growth and mute class conflict so that capitalists can obtain maximum profits. In the past this has meant direct assistance from the state to corporations through subsidies, land grants, development of the infrastructure (transportation and communication), and a monetary system. In addition, it has established regulatory laws and agencies, like the Food and Drug Administration, OSHA, and the Environmental Protection Agency. It has also provided social services and income-support programs in an effort to meet some of the demands of various political movements, while leaving intact the basic structure and class relationships of capitalist society. By 1973 the role of the government was so extensive that about one out of five employed people worked for the federal, state, or local governments.

Thus the role of the state in capitalist society is shaped by the structural requirements of that society. The state defends private property (which means the existing distribution of property) and constitutional freedoms (if they are convenient), but above all the freedom to buy and sell. The history of capitalist society to date means that the people employed in various levels of government have to function within this framework. But at the same time political and economic struggles by working-class people, including state workers and the poor, can "stretch the boundaries" of the legal system. Although the role of the state in capitalism is constrained by the need to facilitate investment and to reproduce class relations, when push comes to shove, class struggle and demands on the state can make it impossible for the state to do both. In this case the whole role of the state comes into question.

Most traditional liberal analyses of the state view it as a neutral arena in which any interest group can put forward its demands. The state is seen as a referee, impartially judging what will happen based on the arguments of the various groups. It is often admitted that some groups, for example, oil companies, have more power than other groups, for example, the poor. But the essentially neutral nature of the state is still asserted. Marxists, on the other hand, disagree with this analysis. The society is a class society, and the state does as much as possible to maintain the status quo. Capitalists dominate the society by virtue of their ownership of the means of production and therefore also dominate the state. There are limits to what the state can do—limits prescribed by the power of capital. Notably, if capitalists become too displeased with the actions of the state, they can stage an investment strike: they can cut back or refuse to invest. Thus the state is *not* neutral and is *not* free to do as it pleases.

In the 1970s and 1980s, the state itself is in crisis. The fiscal crisis of the state has three dimensions: economic, political, and ideological. Economically, there are fewer resources in U.S. society than in the 1960s. Since people's real incomes have fallen and unemployment is high, total tax revenues are not sufficient, and most government administrations find that revenues are now below expenditures. Also, the fact of economic stagnation has reduced the rate of growth of the total pie. Pressure is increasing to reduce taxes in order to give people more disposable income. At the same time, the poor and many of the employed want to increase government spending on health, education, unemployment compensation, food stamps, and social security. On the other hand, many multinational corporations want to increase defense spending, as a show of force to the world in general and to the USSR in particular; they also want funds for planning boards, like the Energy Security Corporation and the Energy Mobilization Board President Carter proposed in July 1979. But most corporations also want their taxes cut and are calling for drastic cutbacks in spending on social services to reduce total government spending.

These different political conflicts over how to restructure government spending and taxes mean a lot of struggle over national priorities. As if this political controversy were not enough, people have become more and more disillusioned with the government itself. The Vietnam War encouraged people to question the U.S. role in world politics. The Watergate break-in, investigation, jail sentences, and the eventual resignation of President Nixon confirmed people's distrust of politicians and politics.

The long period of stagnation has undermined people's confidence in the government. And recent events have caused people to feel that the United States is less and less democratic, more and more controlled by big business: the wage-and-price controls, which tried to hold wages below the rate at which companies raised prices; the federal government's careless handling of the Three Mile Island nuclear accident; its continued promotion of nuclear power; its policy of decontrolling gasoline prices without enacting a windfall-profits tax with teeth.

What all this means is that the state is in crisis; fundamental questions are being raised about the structure of government in the future. In order to get the economy going again—in order for business to invest—this crisis must be resolved, especially if the state is going to have the legitimacy necessary for it to restructure society and the economy and to get people to agree to follow the new rules of the game—like austerity.

Future Directions of the Crisis

How is the crisis likely to proceed? We can expect a continuation of current economic trends: slowed rates of growth throughout the capitalist countries resulting from insufficient investment; instability of the dollar on the international money markets; and inflation and relatively high levels of unemployment in the United States. We will feel the effects more deeply as the standard of living of lower- and middle-income people continues to fall and social services are cut back further, while "tax relief" goes primarily to wealthy individuals and to corporations in the form of tax breaks, relaxation of environmental controls, and probusiness legislation. Accompanying this we can expect stepped-up attacks by the right on gains that we have won in the past.

A solution to the crisis in the interests of the capitalist class, that is, the re-creation of the conditions for expanded capital accumulation, would most probably involve four components.

The first would be some form of economic planning on a national level, analogous to the Energy Mobilization Board and the Energy Security Corporation. As the capitalist class as a whole finds it increasingly problematic to leave investment decisions to individual capitalists, it will likely try to take over more and more of these decisions. This would probably be done via the federal government acting in the interests of the capitalist class. But (as discussed earlier) there is room for working people to make their demands felt on this level. The capitalists cannot do exactly as they please, and even if they could, they would have to reach a consensus among the various factions of the capitalist class. This, too, is proving quite difficult.

The second component entails the capitalist class internationally working out an agreement among themselves to stabilize the international monetary system and thereby provide a more predictable climate for investment and growth on the part of individual capitalist countries. This is already evident in the Trilateral Commission and the various economic summits that are being held. This is no easy task. World leaders generally want first and foremost to protect the interests of their own countries and don't want to concede too much to obtain a workable system as a whole. And many capitalists in the home countries are dubious or downright hostile toward these internationalist solutions.

The third component thus involves the attempt to reassert U.S. control over the Third World, and hence over unlimited supplies of cheap raw materials. Clearly, the United States is unable to intervene in the affairs of Third World countries as it has in the past (as, for example, the case of Iran and the growing strength of OPEC). Successful liberation struggles in Third World countries have been taking more and more territory out of the arena of capitalist exploitation, thereby narrowing the area that capitalist countries can use to solve their problems. However, the United States is seeking to reestablish its dominance in the world through a renewed military build-up—especially in the context of the challenges of Iran, Nicaragua, and Afghanistan.

The fourth component would involve an alliance between the capitalist class and elements of the working class to channel workers' demands along economistic lines and to contain forms of protest within institutional limits that are compatible with capitalist development. This would likely entail a combination of co-optation, conciliation, and repression of the movements that began developing in the 1960s—rank-and-file movements, movements of national minorities, women, gays, and public sector employee unions.

In the 1980s under the Reagan administration, the state has accelerated the change in priorities away from social programs and toward military spending, as well as slowing the growth of the public sector through tax cuts. Put simply, resources are to be reallocated to the corporations and the rich, and state supports for the poor will be severely restricted. Supposedly, given enough time, this strategy will produce increased economic growth. However, the results of this "recovery program" are by no means certain, and the immediate burden is unfairly placed on those most in need in our society. Increased inflation may result from increased spending and government deficits. And there is no assurance that corporations and the rich will use their increased profits and money for productive investment, or that they will invest in the United

States. Consequently, there will be continued debate about methods of resolving the economic crisis.

Clearly, none of these alternative solutions is very good for the working class. However, workers cannot simply adopt a defensive stance against the attacks from conservatives and liberals alike. The capitalists know exactly what they want—a social structure that provides a good environment for profits and growth. We need to be clear about this, and we need to organize for what we want, too—a democratically run society that is organized to meet people's needs, not to maximize profits. We can learn from history how to take the offensive, not only in fighting against the abuses of capitalism but also in building a socialist alternative.

Notes

1. In parts of the South (for example, the Raleigh–Durham area in North Carolina; Jackson, Mississippi; and Houston, Texas) the local and state effects of the fiscal crisis have not been felt. This is a result of the South's relative underdevelopment compared to the North. The South has generally had lower tax rates, fewer social services, and relatively little public sector union organizing. This latter aspect follows largely from the anti-union practices that exist in many Southern states, notably right-to-work (open-shop) laws and the prohibition of strikes and collective bargaining by public sector employees. Such practices have been a major factor in making the South so attractive to firms who "run away" from the North. These movements have increased the taxes collected, as well as the level of employment in many areas of the South, and have therefore greatly lessened the effects of the economic crisis.
2. Our interpretation of the economic crisis and of the public sector crisis is obviously not the only one. For alternative conceptions, see James O'Connor, *The Fiscal Crisis of the State* (New York: St. Martin's, 1973); Union for Radical Political Economics, *U.S. Capitalism in Crisis* (New York: URPE, 1978); Paul Baran and Paul Sweezy, *Monopoly Capital*, (New York: Monthly Review Press, 1968); and Ian Gough, "State Expenditures and Advanced Capitalism," *New Left Review* (July–August 1975). On the tax revolts of the late 1970s, see Robert Kuttner, *The Revolt of the Haves* (New York: Simon & Schuster, 1980).
3. For a collection of descriptions and analyses of this crisis, see *U.S. Capitalism in Crisis*, op. cit.
4. See "The Shrinking Standard of Living," *Business Week*, Jan. 28, 1980, pp. 72–78.

3. The Accumulation Crisis and Service Professionals

Dale L. Johnson and Christine O'Donnell

The United States is plagued by an economic crunch that is likely to deepen in the decade of the 1980s. The post-World War II era of unparalleled economic growth has been superseded by frequent sharp recessions and steady inflation, which economists call "stagflation." The general economic situation is apparently getting worse: persistent high levels of unemployment, declining levels of real income for growing sectors of the labor force, a shrinking dollar, spiraling energy costs. The deteriorating economic situation at home is associated with crumbling American military, economic, and political power abroad. The economic crunch is more than that; it is an incipient crisis of industrial capitalism.

This crisis carries its social and political consequences: the country is suffering from a process of social degeneration in the form of crime and other social problems; people feel the declining quality of life; a rampant narcissism is rupturing social bonds; antagonism is increasing between races, classes, generations, and people in general—on the street, at work, and in homes; a dangerously aggressive foreign policy has been revived. At the same time there has been a precipitous decline in the American people's faith in their institutions and in their government's ability to solve problems.

Dale Johnson is associate professor of sociology at Rutgers, The State University of New Jersey. Christine O'Donnell is assistant professor of sociology at Manhattanville College, Purchase, N.Y. Some of the ideas expressed in this chapter are more fully developed in Johnson's forthcoming book, *Social Class and Social Development*.

The crisis of the public sector is but one facet of the larger economic, social, and political demise of the great American celebration that began to falter well before our bicentennial ceremonies.

In this chapter we will examine the situation of a particular segment of state employees: the professionals who supply social services to the community at large. We will develop an historical and dialectical perspective, one that requires an analytic conception of polarized class relations and a focus on capital accumulation as a process of class formation and changing forms of conflict relations between classes. We will first analyze the position of the middle class as a whole in class relations and the historical formation of the occupational groups that make up the class. The analysis then turns to the service professionals as a distinct segment of the middle class.

The Determination of the Middle Class

Professionals employed by the state are part of a larger social collectivity—a segment of the middle class—which is composed of scientists, engineers, technicians, administrators, professionals, and semiprofessionals. The middle class today encompasses some 20 percent of the population in the United States. The diverse occupational groups that coalesce into the middle class comprise neither productive workers nor bosses: middle-class employees do not, in the main, directly produce values that are appropriated as profit by capital; nor do they control the means of production.

The place of the middle class in the social relations of capitalism has to be understood in the context of a structurally polarized social order. Capitalist societies are divided into two fundamental classes, capitalists and workers, each with a determined place in social relations and function in the economic process. Historically, capital has achieved control of the accumulation and labor processes. Workers, on the other hand, sell their labor power and produce value that is appropriated by the controlling employer class. The basic social relation of capitalism is the appropriation by one class of a proportion of the value produced by the labor power of the other class. While this is a commonplace assertion, what is not so easily understood is the place of the intermediate classes, the petty

bourgeoisie and salaried middle classes, in these structurally polarized relations.

In this respect, it should be immediately noted that exploitative
social relations necessarily require social means of enforcement,
reinforcement, and reproduction over time. A panoply of related
forms of oppression, suppression, and repression evolve as means
that facilitate exploitation. In their totality, these forms can be
conceptualized as a system of exploitation and class domination.

The determination of the salaried middle class as a class formed
in the monopoly stage of development requires an examination of
the place and activities of different segments of the professional,
technical, and administrative labor force in the historically shifting
social relations of exploitation and domination. Some of the occupations were formed historically to administer the relations of
domination within the corporate enterprise and on behalf of agencies of the state. As the growth and concentration of the economy
proceeded, other segments were formed to assume coordinative
and technical tasks in an increasingly complex, differentiated, and
integrated social and technical division of labor. The middle class
was formed historically of those elements whose labor is purchased
in whole or in part, not to produce surplus value, as in the case
of workers, but to assist capital and the state in the control, overall
management, planning, and coordinative functions of capital. At
the same time, the middle class is not simply composed of the
administrative and technical agents of the capitalist class. They
exist in antagonism to the capitalist class because their labor power
is purchased, its use value is appropriated by capital, and they are
subordinated to the despotism of capital in the labor process.

Capital Accumulation and the Formation of the Middle Class

The principal driving force in the historical formation of the professional, technical, and administrative labor force that forms a large
segment of the middle class has resided in the process of capital
accumulation. The opening of new avenues of capital accumulation
had a profound effect on the social structure, the social conditions
of the population, and the social struggles accompanying capitalist
development; they precipitated basic structural changes in eco-

nomic organization, in markets, in technology, in the labor process, and in institutions such as the family and the state.

The historical avenues of accumulation are quite diverse. Analysts of Western capitalism generally place a particular emphasis on "epoch-making" innovations: the inventions of the industrial revolution and, in the United States, developments of vast consequences such as the assembly line, railroads, and the automobile. A good deal of attention has also been given to colonialism and imperialism as principal sources of accumulation in the development of Western capitalism: much of the world was first pillaged of visible wealth, then colonized and subjected to relations of unequal exchange between primary exports and manufactured imports. Finally, in the postcolonial period, Third World regions became integrated into a subordinate position in an international economy in which transnational corporations became the leading productive forces on a world scale.

Here we examine four sources of capital accumulation and their impact upon the formation of the middle class. First, while there are different sources of accumulation, it should always be kept in mind that, in the final analysis, all rest upon changing social relations. For example, in the United States after 1870, an ever increasing proportion of the population became initiated into the wage labor-to-capital social relation. This permitted the appropriation of surplus previously produced outside the sphere of capital by small independent producers. In the twentieth century, accumulation proceeded more and more on the basis of the transformation of the population into a dependent mass of wage workers who remain, on the one hand, in the employment of capital and, on the other hand, consumers of marketed commodities. Family production for people's own use declined; and most production became commodified in the age of what Harry Braverman terms "universal markets."[1] Historically, this was mainly accomplished in two ways: by dispossessing self-employed farm families, businesspeople, and workers and converting them into wage workers, and by the incorporation of large numbers of immigrants and women into the working class. The new middle class of professionals was formed in this context. The productivity of the mass of workers, employed in ever expanding areas of production, was constantly augmented by the activities of expanding groups of scientists, engineers, and organizational experts; control of the extended and complicated labor process required layer upon layer of supervisors; and the reproduction of the growing labor force was technically managed by an ever growing number of professionals.

As the twentieth century progressed the average family became more and more dependent on commodified relations and less and less dependent on communal exchanges. Self-sufficient families and communities, which produced their own food, shelter, clothing, tools, home remedies, education, and leisure were forced into the public realm as wage laborers. Middle-class professionals penetrated the life cycle of the average American in the most intimate spheres of private life, from the slap of the doctor's hand at birth to the grooming of the mortician's hand at death. In most aspects of life middle-class professionals supervised and managed people's lives.

The incorporation of vast numbers of people into the wage labor–capital relation depended upon opening up new areas of large-scale investments. The second source of capital accumulation is precisely what so many historians have emphasized: in the twentieth century, automobiles, electronics, cheap energy, and computers revolutionized the world of work and, with it, the social structure and social relations. In the wake of large-scale capital expansion into new areas, new occupations opened up for both the working class and the middle class. The organizational and technical aspects of these developments required large numbers of qualified employees, who thus formed a sizable segment of the newly constituted middle class. This class was set squarely between the polarizing relations of increasingly concentrated and centralized capital and the growing mass of proletarianized workers.

Third, the internationalization of U.S. capital as a principal source of accumulation also carried with it a changing social structure at home. The establishment of the United States in the post-World War II period as the technological and administrative center of transnational capital and the "free world" empire caused a considerable expansion of the middle class, a strengthening of corporate capital, and a change in the composition of the American working class. While the postwar forms of the internationalization of capital greatly extended conflict on a world scale, to a certain degree the consequent social developments internal to the United States mitigated the antagonisms between capital and labor at home. It was in this period that the American middle class became the bastion of social and political stability.

Lastly, the nature of the modern state is shaped by the processes of accumulation and class formation. Because of the increased level and complexity of social struggle and periodic crises accompanying capitalist development, the state greatly enlarged its scope of activity and expanded enormously, in order to facilitate accumulation, manage repression on domestic and foreign fronts, assume overall responsibility for reproduction of the social order, and provide for social needs that could not otherwise be met in the new social conditions of industrialism and urbanism. The ranks of the middle class swelled accordingly as it came to inhabit all the interstices of the imperial welfare-warfare state.

Historically, each of the principal sources of accumulation—the incorporation of most of the population into wage labor, the great technological and organizational innovations, the internationalization of capital, and the growth and proliferation of functions of the capitalist state—has increased the numbers of professional, administrative, scientific, and technical employees. This segment of the labor force increased at a much faster rate than any other, especially from 1945 to 1970, by which time it included 17 million employees, or one-fifth of the labor force.

In recent years, most of the forms of capital accumulation that once swelled the middle class have nearly reached the limits of their expansion. New technological accomplishments are not significantly revamping the labor process in such a way as to rapidly expand new middle-class occupations. In fact, the overall impact of the latest technological innovation—computers—has been to rationalize the labor process so as to eliminate or reorganize and downgrade technical, professional, and administrative work. In addition, the United States is no longer the exclusive administrative center of international economic activity: the American administrative apparatus of world empire is largely consolidated—even in decline; transnational corporations are moving many of their operations overseas; U.S. exports are losing out to Japanese and European competition; and the international economy faces incipient crisis. Finally, the historical expansion of state activity and of middle-class employment in public-service activities is receding under structural, fiscal, and political constraints.

However, the incorporation of increasing sectors of the population into the wage labor–capital nexus, has not entirely reached its limits. Over the last decade in the United States, women accounted for nearly three-fifths of the increase in the civilian work force, but half of working-age women are still not employed. More-over, there is an inexhaustible supply of surplus population in the periphery, such as the Latin American and Caribbean immigrants to the United States. But the incorporation of new producers of surplus value depends upon the development of technological in-novations or other sources of accumulation that, in the present phase of crisis, do not appear on the horizon.

It now appears that, at least in the United States, the very processes of capital accumulation that formed the middle class are constrained or no longer operating, precipitating a crisis in the class situation of this heretofore rapidly expanding and socially privileged group. A college degree is no longer a ticket to a secure, comfortable, middle-level sinecure in a corporate or administrative hierarchy. Public sector budget reductions raise the specter of unemployment for large numbers of established professionals. In-comes that used to outpace inflation now often lag behind the cost of living. Maintenance of a middle-class family life-style now re-quires two incomes—and women have entered the labor market in unprecedented numbers. While they are important indicators of the depth of crisis, these effects are not as significant as the implications of the changing place of the middle class in the larger context of antagonistic class relations.

The Service Professionals

While all those pursuits conventionally termed "the professions" form part of the middle class, the service professions—social work, education, counseling, religion, and salaried sectors of such fields as medicine, art, and entertainment—occupy a distinct place in the relations of exploitation and class domination. They constitute a separate fraction of the middle class who command a rapidly increasing work force of office workers and technicians in the service institutions.[2] The service professionals are mainly employees of the state. In 1970, the last census for which data are complete, there were 4.3 million salaried professionals in the United States, or 5.4 percent of the labor force. (An additional 500,000, mainly doctors and dentists, were self-employed practitioners.) Of the salaried groupings, 3 million were employed by federal, state, or municipal governments. Salaried professionals constituted more than one-fourth of all the scientific, technical, administrative, and professional persons who make up the rather substantial American middle class.

The work activity of most salaried professionals, especially those employed by the state, the social relations in which they are enmeshed, and their place in the social order are different from those of the administrative, scientific, technical, and self-employed fractions of the middle class. Gelvin Stevenson notes:

> Human service industries differ in several important ways from manufacturing and extractive industries. First, in human service industries production and consumption occur simultaneously. They are part of the same act. The product is nothing material, but rather a form of interaction between two or more people and a change in one or both of them. It is intangible. Therefore nothing is produced unless it is also consumed.[3]

Paul Halmos has pointed to the distinctive character of this form of service labor: "Professions whose principal function is to bring change in the body or personality of the client are the personal service professions."[4] Bennett and Hokenstad refer to "people workers."[5] While these conceptions state a defining characteristic of professional activity in contemporary capitalist society—direct servicing of individual need—these and other authors who have examined the differences between traditional professions (such as law and engineering) and the newer human-service professions (such as social work, education, and counseling) have not done so in terms of the historical forces propelling their rapid development, nor in terms of class relations or the class position of professionals.[6] Here an effort is made to develop (in a preliminary and incomplete manner) a dialectical analysis of the service professions.

The proliferation of the service professions in recent decades in the United States and Europe is a result of the extension of the capitalist division of labor into every intimate area of economic and social life and of the dire social consequences of industrialism. These developments have created the conditions for new forms of social struggle. From this perspective, the development of the welfare state (the main employer of service professionals) is an outcome of the dialectic between economic and social transformations, propelled by the accumulation process, the adverse social conditions faced by people located and relocated into social classes in formation, and the associated social struggles. The service professionals can be viewed as agents of a welfare state that is at one and the same time a social gain of popular movements and an instrument of domination over the people. The class determination of service professionals emerges not only from the performance of specialized functions in an industrial division of labor that are necessary to social production and reproduction, but also from their special place in the social relations of popular struggle against oppression and the forces of this oppression. There is, in addition, dialectical movement at a higher level of historical change: service professionals engage in the socialized production of use values (that is, they produce socially necessary services rather than marketed commodities); this production carries implicitly within it the germ of a new society, one which is organized to collectively produce, distribute, and consume use values in a humane, rational, and egalitarian form.[7]

Historical Formation of the Service Profession Fraction

The historical roots of the growth of social services can be traced to the main features of development in the twentieth century. Capitalist development creates the conditions for both the historical increase in the need for social services and their eventual socialization in the form of state activity. This is a development of twentieth-century monopoly capitalism, especially of the post-World War II period. During the stage of nineteenth-century competitive capitalism the economy was decentralized and the majority of the population lived in rural areas or smaller communities. There was less need for services (higher education, welfare, mental health, social insurance), and necessary social services could be provided for communally, that is, by families, by community cooperation, by folk practitioners of social arts (healing, midwifery, entertainment), or by individual professionals (doctors, lawyers, ministers) living as part of the people, not as a distinct social group.

During the course of the twentieth century, the basis of family production for consumption was eliminated. The family as a basic social unit suffered disintegration.[8] There remained no basis for cooperative community efforts involving unpaid labor. The competence of people to provide for themselves outside the market atrophied or was destroyed by the professionalization of services previously provided by the people themselves, as in health services.[9]

What the people lost the professionals gained, as they became a distinct and privileged social group. The entire population turned to the market for the satisfaction of need.[10] In the initial stages, some services necessary for the satisfaction of these individual and social needs became commodified—they could only be purchased for a fee. In these activities, commodification of the servicing of human need by the destruction of the communal basis of production of use values presented opportunities for professionals to become successful independent practitioners. But since the market did not extend to the provision of an increasing range of essential services, and since people could not afford to purchase them on a market, the state stepped in to provide them. This had the effects of socializing the production and distribution of an increasing range of services and of creating an expanding group of salaried service professionals recruited into state agencies or tax-supported institutions. As the twentieth century progressed, the need for social services grew almost geometrically with industrialization, urbanization, technological sophistication, and especially with the formation of modern class structures. In urban industrial societies individuals, particularly those in the marginal sectors of the working class and the aged and infirm, became almost unable to provide for themselves. A proliferation of governmental and private charitable agencies grew up to minister to a dependent population.

State assumption of a wide range of service activities was the outcome of a dialectical process. Capitalist development destroyed the communal life of the previous era and it also formed a dependent, fragmented, and atomized working class—but one that was also self-conscious to some degree and always combative. Small farmers and independent producers protested and rebelled as their way of life was destroyed and they became reduced to selling their labor power. In the United States in particular, the working class was formed of socially and geographically uprooted, ethnically divided, and atomized individuals forced to fend for themselves. This working class nevertheless unionized and engaged in fierce struggles for amelioration of the emerging oppressive conditions of industrialism. Capitalist development thus created severe deprivation of the most elementary needs, while simultaneously raising the level of antagonistic social relations in all spheres. As Stevenson puts it, this process raises two sets of demands that emerge in fierce social struggle: "Those of the ruling class to keep the expanded and heightened antagonisms in check; and those of the working classes to provide needed public services, such as education, medicine, and protection."[11] This is the meat of the social history of twentieth-century America.

Class struggle is too often thought of as industrial conflict; but the principal forms have always involved protests against oppressive *social* conditions. Among the main demands of progressive social struggles are those that ameliorate the conditions of deprivation and promote social justice by decommodifying and socializing the production of vital services and goods. In Western capitalism many of these demands were attained. Growing perceptions of social need and increased demand for decommodification resulted in wider areas of production, especially in the human services, being organized around politically determined use values rather than exchange values. At the same time, the state—acting as an expression of the unequal power relations of class forces—satisfied the demands of the bourgeoisie by administering needed social services as new forms of social control over the working class and general population.

Service Professionals and Class Relations in the Recent Period

State-administered services developed dialectically: on the one hand, they were pushed from below by the popular demand of the people for adequate servicing of human needs laid bare by development; on the other hand, they were promoted from above by the desires of the dominant class for social control of the population. The struggle over social services reached its maturity in the 1960s. A "war on poverty" was declared, and the decade was a period of conflict over whether these services were to be strictly control-oriented, as in prior years, or to be more widely and equitably available, genuinely service-oriented, and subject to community control. The outcomes of the social struggles since the 1960s have come down heavily on the side of social services as a means to reinforce, reproduce, and expand the system of exploitation and domination.

Social welfare is now organized "to regulate the poor."[12] Social control of the poor is implemented through the welfare and criminal-justice bureaucracies. By means of the expansion and contraction of the welfare rolls and prison and probation populations, surplus labor is absorbed, monitored, and controlled—or "freed"—for the dynamics of the market economy. Public education, which in legitimating ideology exists to afford equal opportunity to all regardless of class background, sex, or race, in reality reproduces existing social inequalities and according to Larkin absorbs surplus labor that cannot be gainfully employed.[13] In addition, as Bowles and Gintis note, education works according to the "correspondence principle"; that is, attempts are made to gear schools to the labor needs of business, to ideological indoctrination, and to the creation of a disciplined and docile labor force.[14]

Social services are couched by the state in terms of professionals as agents of social control. Today social services are organized bureaucratically, with elite professionals commanding a labor force of technicians and office workers. A needy consumer must face the bureaucracy and enter into a subservient relation with the service provider.

The situation is at its worst in the area of health care, the area that has been least subject to decommodification and socialization in the United States. Perhaps the epitome of the commodification of human need is exemplified by the popular joke in which the patient asks the physician, "How serious do you think it is, Doctor?" The doctor responds, "About $400 worth." And within that commodified relationship, the relationship between doctor and patient is rich in messages of dominance and submission.[15] The relationship is typically one of expertise and dependency, of impersonalized intimacy and unquestionable authority, between an ordinary person and (usually) a white male expert who makes more money than the patient could ever dream of earning.

Where services have been fully socialized, professionals work in bureaucratic structures that have the coercive power to enforce the professional's decision vis-à-vis his or her client. Professional expertise and largesse are reinforced and constrained by bureaucratic power. State-organized production of human services produces not only the needed service but the mode of the objective and subjective dimensions of its consumption as well. Concretely, in the day-to-day contacts between ordinary people and professionals, the objective structures of social relations are those of marked dependent inequality: social worker to client, teacher to student, doctor to patient, bureaucrat to applicant, and so on. The client's subjective response may be one of submissive deference to what may appear as the natural order of the social world or of hostile acquiescence to authority. The professional's attitude may be one of professional (often patronizing) concern or of elitist arrogance and contempt for dependence and ignorance. In either case, the social relations are those of latent or manifest antagonism.

The Middle Class and Crisis in the 1980s

The main point developed so far can be succinctly stated: the professionals who work in service agencies are caught in a deep contradiction. On the one hand, they are expressions of a potential for a new order—generated by the dialectic between the imperatives of capitalist development and the social demands of oppressed people—which is organized to produce use values and service social needs. On the other hand, their defined roles in the existing order—reinforced in the bureaucratically structured everyday relations between professionals and clients—are to buttress and reproduce the system of exploitation and class domination. Until now the defined roles have predominated. In the context of this contradiction of the actual and the potential, the concrete social relations involve a three-way antagonism:

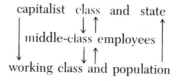

Figure 3-1   Three-way class antagonism

What then is the dynamic of this expression of antagonistic class relations in the context of an incipient, generalized crisis of capital accumulation in the 1980s?

The cutbacks in state-provided social services are one aspect of the strategy employed by the capitalist class and the state. These cutbacks fly in the face of escalating needs for social services as the crisis deepens and social demands for necessary services escalate. But both public revenues and political commitment by the capitalist state to redress these needs contract. The service professionals are caught squarely in the middle of this contradiction, which reveals in ever-clearer terms, to the professionals as well as to the needy supplicants to bureaucratic largesse, the contradiction between the actuality and the potential. Moreover, the careers, economic position, and social privileges of increasing sectors of service professionals are eroded as the fiscal crisis deepens and the state managers turn upon the professionals as well as their clients. Yet cutbacks are but one aspect of a broader crisis-management strategy. Perhaps more significant for the escalation of social struggle in the 1980s is the coordinated push by both corporate capital and the state to reorganize the social division of labor as it affects the place of the middle class as a whole.

The labor process has undergone significant change in the 1970s that will likely continue with full fury in the 1980s. The principle change is an acceleration in the pace of rationalization of the labor process, such that previously complex technical and skilled mental-labor functions in the division of labor are simplified, routinized, and deskilled. Following Braverman and his pioneer work on the labor process and the formation of the working class in the United States, this may be referred to as a process of labor "dequalification." The root of dequalification of labor power resides in the accumulation process, since capital is accumulated only through the appropriation of surplus labor of workers, not by employing huge numbers of unproductive agents of capital. Corporations strive to reduce the range of activities devoted to performance of the functions of capital and enlarge the proportion of the labor force engaged in activities that permit the appropriation of surplus labor. To accomplish this, managerial tasks previously delegated to middle-class functionaries are proletarianized as much as advances in the technical division of labor permit. In this manner, more can be produced at less cost, and control can be more centralized at the top.

In short, in the latest phase in the development of monopoly capitalism, the functions of capital are themselves subject to rationalization and the cost of carrying out these functions cheapened. The complex functions of control and coordination are divided, subdivided, and codified; the labor required is dequalified, the work is routinized and degraded. The state emulates the corporate sector in rationalizing the labor process within those agencies that facilitate accumulation, manage repression, and provide social service. The conditions of work in those sectors of the middle class subject to dequalification of labor power change from relative independence to dependence, from employment as educated and skilled mental labor to underemployment in terms of education and skill levels attained, and from economic well-being to relatively reduced levels of income. As a consequence, the class position and class privilege of sectors of the middle class are eroded. They become less management's agents and more like workers as their work is stripped of its control, coordinative, or creative functions, and their salaries held down commensurate with their new functions as detail workers collectively engaged in facilitating the production of use value or exchange and surplus value.

Labor dequalification can only be affected by assertion of firm managerial control over the labor process. At the institutional level of power and decision-making, centralization has recently tended to supersede the relatively decentralized organization of the previous phase of development. The hand of the managers in the spheres of corporate capital, the state, and other institutions has been considerably strengthened at the expense of the preexisting work autonomy of wide sectors of the professional, technical-scientific, and administrative employees.

The theses of the dequalification of labor and institutional centralization are diametrically opposed to the main thrust of the literature in the sociology of occupations.[16] For example, a number of authors subscribing to the "postindustrial society" notion have suggested that craft forms of organization are reemerging in a wide variety of occupations as alternatives to the administrative rationalization of the industrial capitalist era. Eliot Friedson states: "It seems to be implicit in discussions of the prototypical worker of the postindustrial society that knowledge-based work, the work of middle class experts, professionals and technicians, is by its very nature *not* amenable to the mechanization and rationalization which industrial production and commerce have undergone over the past century."[17] "Bureaucratization" and "professionalization," Friedson suggests, are two different modes of organizing the division of labor. Occupations monopolizing specialized knowledge and technical skills in postindustrial society are usurping the power of capital.

This thesis is not borne out by the actual trends in the latest phase of monopoly capitalism. As Haug suggests, "deprofessionalization, rather than professionalization, is the trend of the future. Deprofessionalization is defined as a loss to professional occupations of their unique qualities, particularly their monopoly over knowledge, public belief in their service ethos, and expectations of work autonomy and authority over the client."[18]

In the 1970s, as the division of labor in service institutions became more rationalized, narrow technicians and paraprofessionals assumed many of the functions of professionals. In part, this reflects a socially progressive development: large numbers of working-class women have become teacher's aides; former addicts are drug counselors; secretaries have become legal assistants; colleges are developing physician's assistant programs; paraprofessionals are being introduced into a wide variety of fields. Perhaps in the future physicians' assistants will record patient symptoms into the computer for diagnosis; legal assistants will instruct the machine to locate precedents; teaching assistants will sit students in front of teaching machines, etc. Computers can also be used in systems of professional accountability to check whatever judgments professionals still are allowed to make, in the exercise of the more artful side of their fading craft, against standardized norms and procedures.

The forces reshaping the labor process move unevenly and at varying rates within different service institutions and scientific and technical occupations. Elsewhere we have examined this process in a range of professional occupations.[19] In concluding, consider the contradictory position of teachers today. They are wage workers performing socially necessary productive labor insofar as their activities increase the skill levels and productivity of the labor force, without at the same time being engaged directly in capitalist relations of production. They carry out reproductive functions that are universal to any form of complex society, capitalist or socialist, by producing essential use values within institutions that are socialized means of production. The social conditions of their work are subject to deterioration with each phase in the development of monopoly capitalism: they face the effects of the class structure, particularly dramatic in the current period of crisis, on a day-to-day basis in the classroom; they are increasingly subject to degradation and devaluation of their labor power as education is rationalized and teachers' work is transformed from a respected, salaried profession into a wage trade, with effective control of the educational process outside their purview. Insofar as they impart critical abilities to youthful workers they are key elements in the struggle to transform society. In other words, the forces of class determination are beginning to affect the class situation of teachers in much the same way as they do for most workers. At the same

time, much of the activity of teachers remains "guard" and super-
visory labor. Their subsistence is derived from redistributed surplus
appropriated through the tax system from the general population.
While they share with other workers the experience of class oppression, they do not experience direct exploitation. As controlled
agents of the state, their defined role is principally to buttress the
social conditions of exploitation and class oppression through in-
culcation of ideologies of domination and habits of discipline among
youth.

Teachers are an important sector of the service-profession fraction
of the middle class; their jobs and lives are highly affected by the
contradictory forces determining their class position and class situation. In the recent period their defined role as agents of domination has predominated in day-to-day activities; yet the contradictory place of teachers and of other service professionals also
sharply conditions their antagonistic relations with institutional
managers and the dominant social interests as a whole.

The growth of unions and cultural and political radicalization
since the 1960s among a wide range of professional employees in
the United States and Europe are manifestations of their contradictory locations and the conflictive relations in which they are
enmeshed. The days of compliant acting out of defined roles may
be nearing an end for increasing sectors of professionals. Popular
movements will likely rise again to challenge the "cult of expertise"
and raise demands for accountability to clients and citizens. But
professionals are experiencing the greatest pressure from the
state—the institutional managers and the dominant class. Their
work situations are being fundamentally altered and their social
privileges threatened.

The implications of the trends discussed in this paper for the
broad spectrum of class relations in the 1980s are considerable.
Dequalification of professional labor and the accompanying institutional centralization of power means that sizable segments of the
middle class are being pushed in the direction of the working class;
the boundary between the managers and middle-class employees
is more clearly demarcated and the relations between them more
antagonistic. As the position of the managers is strengthened by
centralization of institutional power, it becomes more integrated
with the core fraction of the dominant class, corporate-finance capital, and in a greater degree of structural antagonism with all other
classes. Meanwhile, the middle class is increasingly bifurcated into

two strata that have less and less in common. The upper strata of technocrats, middle managers, and elite professionals become more closely tied to the higher-level managers; these elements become the staff and line personnel of the managers. The lower strata is composed of technical and administrative employees and paraprofessionals whose labor is increasingly subordinated and dequalified, whose security is constantly threatened, and whose place in the social order is downgraded.

The internal structure of the lower strata of the middle class also changes as the sexual and social composition of the labor force in these sectors shifts. Technical and administrative vocations are no longer bastions of white male privilege. The continuing expansion of lower-level technical, administrative, and paraprofessional employment seems to be related to the increasing participation of women in the labor force and to a diffusion of minorities in the occupational structure. We have not yet been able to thoroughly investigate the degree to which the hiring of women and minorities in technical and paraprofessional activities is a definite social concomitant of the labor-dequalification process, but preliminary work suggests that it is.

We do not know, of course, what impact these objective changes will have in the long run on the subjective conditions within the middle class. The consciousness of many may be more than ever caught up in status panic, in racist and sexist responses to dequalification, in fiercely competitive intraclass scrambles and in right-wing politics. An overtly fascist potential may indeed exist that could mobilize significant numbers of pressured middle-class employees. But conditions in the United States of the 1980s are significantly different from the prefascist and fascist periods in Europe. Moreover, it is as yet unclear whether the incipient crisis of the present will become an *organic* crisis in the 1980s—that is, a crisis in which the capital accumulation process grinds to a halt and the level of class struggle attains unprecedented heights. It is clear, though, that the objective basis for the polarization of class relations is developing. To the degree that this objective polarization translates into overt social struggle, the middle class is not likely to remain the stabilizing middle force it has been in the past. The dominant corporate fraction of capital and its partners, the higher-level managers, will likely be able to count on most of the technocrats and elite professionals who are being separated out and elevated from the rest of the middle class by the rationalization of the labor process. On the other side of this struggle is a vast, stratified working class, at present unprepared and unorganized for the onslaught of the 1980s; yet this class is likely to find new allies in the increasingly female and minority-group proletarianized lower strata of the middle class and in a minority of the elite professionals who may become the "organic intellectuals" of a broadly based movement to eliminate the contradiction between the dismal actual and the real potential for a new America.

Notes

1. Harry Braverman, *Labor and Monopoly Capital: The Degradation of Work in the Twentieth Century* (New York: Monthly Review Press, 1974).
2. "Fraction" is a technical term for a sector or segment of a class. It denotes a particular positioning within the social relations of exploitation and domination.
3. Gelvin Stevenson, "Social Relations and Production and Consumption in the Human Service Occupations," *Monthly Review*, 28 (1976): 82.
4. Paul Halmos, *The Personal Service Society* (New York: Schocken, 1970), p. 22.
5. Willian S. Bennett, Jr. and Merle C. Hokenstad, Jr., "Full-time People Workers and Conceptions of the Professional," in *Professionalization and Social Change*, ed. Paul Halmos, The Sociological Review Monograph, No. 20 (England: University of Keele, 1973), pp. 21–46.
6. An exception to this is Pat Walker, ed., *Between Capital and Labor* (Boston: South End Press, 1979).
7. This dialectic should be stated with due caution: a historical process, decommodification and the socialized production of use values that meet the needs of individuals and collective social needs represent one basis for the birth of a new society within the old society. Capitalism creates incipient forms of socialism, understood as a society that suppresses private accumulation and organizes the economic and social order to produce, distribute, and consume use values in an egalitarian form. By no means does this mean that incremental social gains in decommodification of the means of satisfying human need and the socialization of social services and necessary social reproduction will one day add up to socialism. A socialist society does not emerge as the end result of an evolutionary process out of the welfare state. It certainly does not mean that the professionals who provide social services are the harbingers of the new socialist order.

8. Christopher Lasch, *Haven in the Heartless World: The Family Beseiged* (New York: Basic Books, 1977); Eli Zaretsky, *Capitalism, the Family, and Personal Life* (New York: Harper & Row, 1976).
9. John Ehrenreich, ed., *The Cultural Crisis of Modern Medicine* (New York: Monthly Review Press, 1978); Barbara Ehrenreich and Deirdre English, *Witches, Midwives, and Nurses: A History of Women Healers* (Old Westbury, N.Y.: Feminist Press, 1973).
10. Harry Braverman, op. cit., chap. 13.
11. Gelvin Stevenson, op. cit., p. 79.
12. Frances Fox Piven and Richard A. Cloward, *Regulating the Poor* (New York: Pantheon, 1971).
13. Ralph Larkin, *Suburban Youth in Cultural Crisis* (New York: Oxford University Press, 1979).
14. Samuel Bowles and Gerbert Gintis, *Schooling in Capitalist America: Educational Reform and the Contradictions of Economic Life* (New York: Basic Books, 1976).
15. John Ehrenreich, op. cit.
16. These theses are more fully developed in D. L. Johnson, M. Openheimer, and C. O'Donnell, "The Dequalification of Professional, Technical, and Administrative Labor," *Social Class and Social Development: Comparative Studies of Class Relations and the Middle Classes,* ed. D. L. Johnson. (In preparation.)
17. Eliot Friedson, "Professionalization and the Organization of Middle Class Labour in Post-Industrial Society," *Professionalization and Social Change,* op. cit., p. 55.
18. Marie R. Haug, "Deprofessionalization: An Alternate Hypothesis for the Future," *Professionalization and Social Change,* op. cit., p. 197.
19. D. L. Johnson, op. cit.

4. A Class Analysis of State Workers

J. Gregg Robinson

Social critics, especially those who have been involved with popular issues, have argued for years that a theoretical understanding of class position is absolutely essential for the comprehension of the practical aspects of crises and conflicts. Like all pat formulas of this sort, someone must sooner or later call the question. These analysts must show that their abstract speculations have some foundation in the real world and, in particular, a real world in which the practicalities of political change are central. In the following discussion I will attempt just such a task; but before I do this, there are two questions that I think must be answered. First, what is class analysis? Second, why is it important for the current crisis facing the state?

Class analysis is based on the simple notion that conflict between those who hold power and those who are subjected to it is one of the central features of social life. More precisely, class analysis revolves around the examination of groups that hold different amounts and kinds of economic power. Put simply, the analysis of class is the recognition that, in order to know how a game is played, you must understand who the players are *and* how much power they have to make the rules of the game. The use of economic power is one of the more important ways in which any social "game" can be influenced.

An analysis of economic power can help us understand how different occupational groups in the state sector will be affected by the economic cuts now under way. The fiscal crisis will affect different state jobs (for example, low-level clerical versus high-level administrative) in very different ways, and an economic class analysis can explain how this takes place. The real payoff with this type of analysis, however, lies in a more practical area. It provides a guide to developing alliances and coalitions to resist and redirect these fiscal cuts. To understand which groups share similar economic positions is to understand which are one's allies and which are one's enemies. This concern with alliances and practical responses to the fiscal crisis will be a consistent focus of this paper.

There are two main sections to this essay. The first section outlines the relevant structural constraints on class formation in the state. The second section relates this analysis to issues of political and economic organizing among state workers. This analysis will be confined to an examination of what may be called the "progressive classes," that is, those groups that will play some kind of positive role in the process of social transformation.

These progressive classes are composed of two groups: working-class occupations and semiprofessionals. Examples of the first group are road-maintenance personnel, trash collectors, janitors, and low-level clerks and secretaries. Examples of the second are teachers, nurses, social workers, and to some degree, police and fire fighters. In addition, there are two issues that are of particular significance to contemporary political conflict. The first is the immediate struggle taking place around the fiscal crisis of the state. In essence, this involves the fight against cutbacks in progressive social services. The second is the contribution groups may make to the longer-term general transformation of society. The issue that is key here is the emergence of an alternative to the contemporary form of social organization. The present crisis, both in its social and economic aspects, has brought home once again some of the limitations of a society that bases its whole meaning on the search for profit. To truly confront this crisis will mean confronting the dilemmas that this form of social organization has forced on us.

These two issues are obviously connected, but they will be considered separately, as they presuppose different time frames and levels of political analysis.

The central point of the essay is that the key group in the struggle around the fiscal crisis is that of the semiprofessionals; while in the movement for long-term change the working class may be expected to be of greater importance. To understand the implications of this statement it is necessary to pursue a more detailed analysis of these occupational groups.

Preliminary Definitions

Class membership is defined here by the relationship to the means of production: specifically, whether one has control over the production process or is controlled by it. It is subjugation to the process of production that is the central element of this definition. Workers are defined as those who must sell their labor to an employer, and who have no control over either the production process, or the final commodity they produce. Workers put in their time in an institution which is controlled and operated by someone else. They must face an owner or supervisor who tells them what to do, when to do it, and what will be done with their product or service afterward. People in this class situation are viewed by those in control, and often view themselves, as "commodities" necessary to the production process.

Semiprofessionals, on the other hand, occupy middle-strata positions which have a relatively privileged status in the process of production. While they are usually subjected to a set of authority relations which are somewhat similar to those which confront workers (that is, they have supervisors, managers, etc.), they nevertheless have a significant degree of control over the production process. Wright[1] has seen this group inhabiting a "contradictory class position," located halfway between the working class and the traditional petty bourgeoisie.

Teachers, for example, must work in an educational bureaucracy in which the long-term goals of the institution are set by principals, boards of education, and high-level administrators. Yet, in the classroom they have immediate control over the day-to-day practice of education. They give assignments, grade papers, and evaluate students. Teachers may *take* orders from administrators, but they also *give* them—at least to students.

The Structure of Production

It is a basic tenet of class analysis that our comprehension of class must be grounded in an understanding of the evolution of work and the division of labor in production. Recently, analysts following in the footsteps of the late Harry Braverman[2] have explored these processes. Looking largely at the activities in the private sector, they have documented how capitalism degrades and fractionalizes work. They argue that the specific form of the division of labor found in capitalist enterprises must be understood as serving two goals: (1) the separation of workers from control of production, in order to maximize capitalist domination of this process; and (2) the guarantee of maximum profit returns on the labor performed by means of the "simplification" or degradation of that labor. Conflict over the process of work reorganization constitutes the main field of class struggle in capitalist society. Capitalists face workers in the "contested terrain" of the shop floor: the former push for changes that will increase their power and profits; the latter seek to maintain their work autonomy and buying power.

The question we must ask is whether a similar dynamic of work degradation has been taking place in the state. It takes no great insight to realize that many state-sector occupations have changed considerably over the years. Clerks who seventy-five years ago might have been in charge of an entire department now do no more than stuff files. Accountants who used to oversee the transactions of an entire branch of government service now find themselves tied to a computer terminal. The changes can't be denied; the remaining question is, Why?

The answer is not as easy as it may first seem. In the private sector, the motivation for work organization is clear to both sides of the conflict. Profit is the dominant factor and is recognized as such by all participants. But what happens to work when there is no immediate profit attached to production, as is the case in state production? In such a situation can we really speak of a capitalist form of work organization? The answer, I believe, is a *qualified* yes. State sector production resembles capitalist production in structure, but it is also shaped by the specific structural needs of a capitalist *state*. Let me explain this point.

The state is obviously not an island unto itself. It sits in the midst of a capitalist society which influences its basic structure, as well as any policies it may pursue. It is to this surrounding environment that we must look for the origin of capitalist forms of work organization in the state. The state is not forced to turn a profit on each service it performs, but it *is* constrained to act "efficiently" and responsibly with tax monies. Given the ideological hegemony of capitalism in our society, this means the use of the most "profitable" forms of production available. State managers imitate the forms of production found in private enterprise, because they appear to be the most efficient. The state imports capitalist production techniques from private industry. Capitalist work control and labor organization come to the state in second-hand form, but they are present nonetheless.

This process of imitation is more than just a vague and haphazard tendency for state sector production to adopt capitalist methods. There are specific forms which this imitation takes—two in particular. First, a state agency can imitate *specific work technologies* found in the private sector; second, the state can attempt a more general imitation of the *conditions* under which capitalist production is possible. In the first case, we have the simple transfer of production techniques from private production to the public sector. For example, if General Motors finds a way to computerize the work formerly done by accountants, and thereby reduce its overhead costs, the state can little afford to ignore this innovation. Within a relatively short time the technique will become a part of public sector production. To ignore it would be an affront to the sense of fiscal responsibility of state managers or would open the agency to accusations of profligacy.

In the second case, vast portions of state production are reorganized so as to resemble profit-making organizations. Most often this involves the creation of market conditions for the disposal of state goods and services. The best-known example of this process was Nixon's reform of the post office. Here a state agency was turned into a "corporation" by making it dependent on the fees charged for services. In the last few years, more complex reforms have also been initiated. Social services, which are impossible to put on a fee-for-service basis (for example, welfare and unemployment insurance), have been turned into ersatz corporations, where outputs are quantified and fictitious prices attached to them in order to estimate "production efficiency." The essential point regarding these reorganizations is that an agency is remade in the image of private sector production by introducing some form of pseudomarket. It is not a specific technique, but the market conditions under which capitalist production takes place, that is imitated.

I will label the first form of imitation "technique-specific imitation," and the second, "systematic imitation." I think it is important to realize that these two forms have *not* occurred with equal frequency in the history of state production. It has been the first form—technique-specific imitation—that has been most common. Only in the last few years, with the increasing fiscal crisis and general economic downturn, has systematic imitation come into greater use. These efforts are still largely experimental, but their importance grows with each budget cutback.

Until the early 1970s, then, technique-specific forms of imitation were dominant. Such imitation is most effective if there is some kind of work analog in private enterprise, that is, a model which can be imitated. What about those public occupations which have no analog? What are the forces which shape them? How does the state find occupational models for activities such as education and social work, which are unique to the public sector?

In these cases, more general constraints on work organization exist. Like any other occupation in a capitalist society, they must conform to general guidelines of "efficiency" and "rational" work organization; but the specifics of these constraints are much looser. General technologies are available: bureaucracies can be set up and work tasks divided. But these moves do not guarantee the kind of minutely detailed division of labor found in occupations with direct analogs. Teachers, social workers, librarians, and police are groups for whom a division of labor exists, but not so extensively as to fully "degrade" the profession. Strikingly, it is in these non-analogous services that we find the greatest number of semi-professionals.

There are, then, two very different labor situations in state employment. On the one hand, there are occupations whose resemblance to jobs in the private sector keeps them directly tied to the pace of development in work organization found in that sphere. On the other hand, there are occupations whose specificity to the state sector has given them relative autonomy from the pressures of ongoing job rationalization. The first group I term "analogous" occupations, and the second, "nonanalogous."

Semiprofessionals

The Fiscal Crisis

The most obvious change which the current fiscal crisis and general economic downturn is bringing to the state is constriction of funds. Money and jobs are increasingly hard to come by. Gone is the era of Keynesian affluence when state policy and economic planning coincided in a philosophy of "more": more state jobs, more public spending, more taxes. The years in which state spending and public sector jobs were the fastest growing areas of the economy now seem a distant memory. In their place is the era of limits. This has meant both cutbacks in the services offered and greater reliance on systematic imitation of private sector production (that is, the attempt to turn whole social agencies into pseudocorporations). These days every public bureaucrat with career aspirations is busy figuring out ways in which public services can be put on a "profit-oriented" basis.

To understand the specific impact of this on semiprofessionals, we must look to their class situation. As I noted earlier, semiprofessionals inhabit a contradictory class position, which combines significant degrees of autonomy and control in the work situation with subjection to bureaucratic authority structures. As a result, they are acutely aware of any possible infringement on their occupational rights. They are highly conscious of the need to defend themselves from occupational degradation, precisely because their work privilege is so problematic. This sensitivity has produced a strong sense of group identity and corporate self-interest.

A second consequence of this contradictory occupational status is that semiprofessionals tend to identify their interests with the immediate services they perform, rather than with the organizations in which they serve. Some analysts who have correctly recognized the relative occupational privilege that these professions possess have made the mistake of assuming that as a consequence there is a straightforward identification with the organization in which they work. But the situation is more complicated than this. It is true that semiprofessionals tend to identify with, and have a proprietary interest in, their jobs, but this does *not* imply that such feelings extend to the organization as a whole. Because their occupational privilege is only partial, and because they must take orders from a supervisor who represents the long-term goals of the organization, there is a tendency for them to identify their interests with work they perform and not with the organization in which they perform it.

Take, for example, education. Teachers view themselves first as educators, with a tie to students, and only secondarily as representatives of the school board. Administrators and board members are often seen as having no real concern for the actual job of education; they are viewed as disciplinarians, technical managers, or mere politicians, with no real understanding of the day-to-day activities of teaching.

Finally, as I mentioned previously, the majority of state semi-professionals are in nonanalogous occupations, that is, occupations which have no counterpart in the private sector. In the past this has meant that these occupations were shielded from strong, direct pressure for job rationalization. When combined with the self-conscious resistance of these groups to rationalization, this has produced occupations of remarkable continuity and stability. In contrast to both the working class in general and semiprofessionals in the private sector (for example, engineers or lab technicians), the nature of work and division of labor have remained constant over a long period of time for state sector semiprofessionals.

With the fiscal crisis, however, this stability is under attack. The move to rely increasingly on systematic forms of imitation has produced a corresponding threat to the autonomy of these occupations. The efforts to make education, welfare, and even police work more "profitable" operations poses the possibility of occupational degradation for a large number of semiprofessionals. For example, if education is farmed out to the private sector (as is now being threatened in California) or if teacher competency is evaluated and rewarded on the basis of student scores on examinations (as has been proposed in a number of school districts throughout the country), occupational autonomy can only decline. Salaries will inevitably decline and class sizes increase (at least for all but the wealthiest schools) as the ability of teachers to bargain collectively is severely jeopardized by the increased number of separate bargaining agents; and teacher control over classroom activities will be weakened as educational administrators move to standardize curricula and methods of instruction.

The combination of all these factors leads me to believe that semiprofessionals will play a very important role in the current crisis. What is at stake is not merely the standard of living of these people, or even the loss of jobs, but rather the basic nature of their occupations. Their occupational autonomy is on the line, which means that the interests of the group *as a whole* are at issue. It is not one faction or area that is threatened, but entire occupations. Since it is their interest as an occupation that is in jeopardy, we can expect them to respond as an occupation as well.

The resistance to cutbacks has, in fact, already begun. The groups which have been most militant and vocal in opposition to fiscal cuts and service decline have been semiprofessionals. For reasons which

I will explore shortly, working-class groups have been much more quiescent. In the New York crisis of 1975, while blue-collar public-service unions bit the bullet, teachers threatened a strike if their services were touched. In city after city, it has been teachers, nurses, social workers, librarians, and even cops who have been the first to hit the picket line, while working-class employees have been more restrained. No other group of state workers has the personal and occupational interest that would motivate such a spirited defense of services. Because they are fighting against their own occupational degradation, because they identify so strongly with their service activity, and because service cutbacks increase their work load, semiprofessionals are a key factor in the opposition to cutbacks.

Implications for Short-Term Organizing

Granted that there will be resistance to cutbacks among semi-professionals, the question is, What are the implications of this for the conflict currently taking place around the welfare state? Before we can estimate this, we must first know a little more about the nature of the conflict. At present we are witnessing an attack on the state that is, at least in part, an attempt to systematically roll back the progressive victories of the poor and the working classes that were won in the 1930s and 1940s. The major corporations of this country are taking the current economic downturn as an opportune moment to push for a reorganized state that is more to their liking. Industry regulation, legal wage guarantees (social security, the minimum wage, collective bargaining laws, etc.), social insurance measures (medical aid, aid to the handicapped and elderly, unemployment insurance), and social services in general are all under attack. The common denominator of these attacks is the corporate struggle to increase its portion of the real social product. This move has been labeled by some as a rollback in the social wage.[3]

The social wage is the total income paid all workers in society and consists of direct money wages *plus* indirect income such as government services and tax redistribution (for example, social security, unemployment insurance, etc.). It is the weakening of this social wage that is at the center of the corporate offensive against the state. The goal is to redirect funds from social-wage expenses into corporate coffers by way of either reoriented state expenditures

(investment in military hardware, subsidization of private investment) or simply by allowing corporate taxes to fall and profits to
rise (for example, by deregulation of oil).

How do semiprofessionals relate to this development? As wage
earners they are themselves, of course, directly affected by this,
but their importance goes beyond this. In particular, their opposition to service cutbacks can be an important element in the
opposition to the decline in the social wage. Because a large portion
of social services that have become part of the social wage are in
the nonanalogous sphere of state production, resistance to cutbacks
in these services is a resistance to a drop in the social wage. There
is, then, a broad area of common interest between those who want
decent work and pay (semiprofessionals) and those who want decent
services.

The most obvious response to this identity of interests would be
a coalition around the defense of the social wage. Such a coalition
would not only help defend the services that are important to both
semiprofessionals and the general working population, but would
constitute a significant blow against the corporate-sponsored reorganization of the state. This kind of tactic was experimented with
in the late 1960s and early 1970s and was effective. Welfare-rights
organizations were one outgrowth of this process. This form of
coalition could be even more effective in the 1980s, when semiprofessional personnel will most certainly be threatened by cutbacks.

Long-Term Social Change

The very reasons which make semiprofessionals such a good bet
for short-term issues make them a more uncertain quantity for full-
scale social transformation. Their structural position (half professional and half worker) pulls them in contradictory directions. No-
tions of general equality, democratic control over production, and
an end to hierarchies of production are threats, at least in part,
to their own semiprivileged occupational status. The corporate self-
interest of these groups, which was so important in pushing them
toward militant opposition to attacks on the welfare state, stands
in the way of any genuinely progressive reorganization of production. People who have spent years in school to gain access to their
positions, and whose own social status rests upon their superiority
to occupational groups below them, may see the idea of general

social and productive equality as more than a little disquieting. The ideology of the meritocracy and "professional" privilege is firmly rooted within their ranks.

On the other hand, there are forces which drive them in the opposite direction. They are themselves, we must remember, exposed to an authority hierarchy which they resent. They must take orders from superiors and for this reason may be open to arguments for the abolition of these kinds of hierarchies. Thus, semiprofessionals are anxious to maintain their own privileged status, but they also yearn to be free of the dominance to which they are subjected.

A class analysis cannot go beyond the recognition of this structural ambivalence. Possibilities may be seen and examples cited in support of both alternatives. Final determination will be a function of factors other than strict class position or the forces associated with the form of class struggle that operates internal to this area. Cultural, ideological, and political elements may be expected to play their part. In particular, the kind of political education that takes place within their ranks will be of crucial importance. If in the preceding period the kind of coalition around the defense of the social wage has developed, it can be expected that this will play an important role in broadening the definition of the issues involved. A second and possibly more important element is the fact that a very large portion of these semiprofessionals are women. The growth of feminism in their ranks over the last few years and in the years to come could have a decisive impact on the understanding of the reasons behind these conflicts.

Some of the implications for practical politics can be summed up as follows:

1. One of the most immediate tasks of any progressive response to the fiscal crisis is the defense of social services which compose part of the social wage. Here semiprofessionals may be expected to play a vital role. To defend their own occupational power against degradation means to fight against both general cutbacks of services and attempts to rationalize production. No other group in the state is likely to be as militant in opposition to cutbacks, because no other group's interests are tied so intimately to the delivery of these services.

2. Coalitions involving both semiprofessionals and service consumers, oriented toward the defense of the social wage, would

seem to be real possibilities. These coalitions are an exciting political possibility, not just because they offer the opportunity to halt the decline in social services but because they can form part of a larger defense against the corporate-sponsored effort at government reorganization.

3. The structural interests of these groups make their allegiance to larger issues ambivalent. They are conservative to the degree that they have a position of relative privilege to defend, but progressive to the degree that they themselves are subjected to an authority hierarchy. Their occupational position can lead either to an identification with proponents of a meritocracy and a technological hierarchy or to sympathy with those fighting for a liberated society in which all are guaranteed full and rewarding work. Structurally, there is no way to choose between these two possibilities; the weight of determination will rest upon other factors. The organization, education, and politicization of these groups will be crucial.

Working-Class Occupations

The most important point about working-class occupations in state production is that they are largely analogous occupations; that is, these occupations have nearly identical counterparts in private industry. Consequently, their occupational fate is tied to developments in that sphere. It is this commonality of fates that is a key to understanding the options open to public sector workers, both in the short term and in the long term.

The Fiscal Crisis

State workers will pay the price of the fiscal crisis in layoffs, declining salaries, and worsening job conditions. But I believe the immediate response to this will not be, and certainly has not been to date, as militant or as massive as that found in the semiprofessions. The reasons for this lie both in the structural similarity of public and private sector working-class jobs and in conditions unique to the public sector. There are three specific ways in which this works. First, no matter how dramatic these cutbacks may be, they will not affect the nature of the occupations the way they do in the semiprofessions. There is no occupational change waiting in the wings that would have the impact of a fall from semiprofessional to proletarian status. The changes will be quantitative, not qualitative. As unfortunate as it may sound, declining salaries and worsening job conditions do not constitute dramatic changes in these occupations. The threat of job degradation, however real, is nothing new for these workers.

The most dramatic change in public sector working conditions is the increasing possibility of layoffs. But this merely serves to increase the structural similarity between private and public work environments; it is *not* a qualitative change. Until the early 1960s, it was a truism of public sector work that pay was poor, but job security excellent. With civil-service protections, it was a standard joke that the only way to get someone out of a job was to kick them upstairs or carry them out feet first. But during the 1960s this situation changed. Public sector unions emerged and pushed aggressively for the kind of salary benefits that their private sector counterparts (specifically in the monopoly sector) enjoyed. It was consciously argued that those who perform the same work deserve the same pay. This strategy was more or less successful, and public sector pay came to resemble that in the monopoly sector. But there was no corresponding reduction in the job security of public employment. Public workers as late as the early 1970s faced no serious threats to their jobs.

The fiscal crisis has changed all this. Public employees are now facing massive layoffs and reductions in rank. But this only brings them into line with the private sector, and most employees are aware of this. The logical implication of the demand for parity is that it should apply to risks as well as to benefits. The erosion of their relative advantage may be bemoaned, but it is unlikely to produce fierce opposition. The analogous nature of their jobs would render illegitimate any claims to greater job security than that of their private sector counterparts.

The second point is related to the first and involves the nature of American trade unionism. The working-class occupations of the state, and in particular blue-collar jobs, are those which are the most heavily unionized (trash collectors, transportation workers, custodial staff, etc.). Therefore, if we are to understand their attitudes toward the current economic problems affecting them, we must look at the nature of the bargain around labor conditions that American unions have struck.

Unfortunately, issues such as layoffs, job losses, and work speedup have not been major concerns of U.S. trade unions. Instead the focus has been on wages. Unions in this country have been militant in pursuing cash benefits for *employed* members, but not in fighting for jobs for unemployed ones. The rules of the game have allowed companies to control the process of production, with the right to install whatever productivity improvements they see fit, so long as those who remain employed are well compensated. Companies and unions have cooperated in trading productivity increases for higher salaries.

What this means for public sector employees is that little sustained opposition to the current fiscal crisis can be expected on the part of their trade unions. Union leaders may decry layoffs, and progressive union locals may resist them, but basically the changes occurring are within the rules of the game. The losses involved are indeed a bitter pill to swallow, and public sector union leaders may personally prefer to avoid them, but there are few options open to them. The logic of their own history compels them to recognize the right of the employer both to reorganize production and to discharge employees thereby rendered unnecessary.

The third point has to do with factors that are peculiar to state production. Foremost is the fact that the wages of state workers come out of tax monies. This means that any wage increases, cost-of-living clauses, or fringe benefits are immediately political phenomena. Generally, the public sector is not able to pass on cost increases by tacking them onto the price of goods and services, since their products are not distributed in a traditional market. Public sector union negotiations are under intense scrutiny, not just by state managers but by all those who pay taxes as well. Given the stagnating economy and the fact that the bulk of taxes come from the wages of the working class, this is an increasingly tenuous situation. Any state wage increase which threatens to raise taxes must be justified to this beleaguered source of tax revenues.

Another complicating factor is the nature of production that occurs in the state. Predominately, it is service production and has a comparatively slow rate of productivity increase. Service work, while capable of being rationalized, does so at a slower rate than that found in commodity production. Even services in the private sector (secretarial work, plant maintenance, etc.) have been slower to be mechanized than strictly production jobs. What this means for state service workers is that productivity-wage trade-offs are on shaky grounds. There will be productivity improvements, but it is doubtful that they will finance much in the way of wage increases.

Given these three factors there are two possible courses of action for state workers under current conditions. The first and most likely is that they will admit defeat and retreat to a purely defensive posture. This will mean knuckling under, not only to job losses and layoffs but to a fall in real wages as well. At best, what can be expected is that the difference between wages in the private and public sectors will not widen too much. At worst, state workers and their unions will be forced to retreat from any labor activism and will quickly fall into a struggle merely to survive.

The second possibility is that individual unions and groups of state workers may fight to resist wage cuts and layoffs or even attempt to improve their income. Unions would resort to traditional wage demands and union tactics. Strikes over better pay and against layoffs can and will take place in individual areas, and they may even be won, but the possibility for this succeeding in the public sector as a whole is slim. The most likely outcome of this kind of resistance is growing public hostility and general isolation from the rest of the American labor movement.

Thus, it appears unlikely that public sector workers will engage in sustained opposition to the current decline in public services. To do so on a systematic basis would invite organizational suicide for their unions *if* the rules of the game as currently defined are accepted. A purely economic struggle by public unions in the present economic environment would appear irresponsible, selfish, and money-hungry. If private sector unions are being forced to accept layoffs and wage demands that are pegged to productivity improvements, why shouldn't public unions do the same?

Long-Term Social Change

The previous section left us with the conclusion that for these workers, there is little hope that they will be able to play the traditional game of bread-and-butter unionism. The middle course, in which productivity is traded for wages, will simply not be open to them. Options will be limited to either extreme quiescence or a kind of traditional labor activity that would be but a shortcut to defeat. There is, however, a third alternative: a break with traditional unionism. It means recognizing the political nature of economic decisions in the state sector. Realistically, there are no improvements for labor in the state sector that do not come out of somebody's pocket. The question is, *Whose pocket* and *for what purposes?* These questions, of course, can only be addressed by a *political* form of unionism, a unionism that recognizes that economic issues for public workers can *only* be justified politically, a unionism that sees the importance of justice, both in wage demands and in the search for sources to satisfy them.

The only real solution to the problem of declining wages for state workers lies in turning to those who can afford to pay, because those who cannot have already been bled dry. Rather than allow tax monies to be taken from whoever is least able to resist it (the poor, those who work for a living), it must become a specific part of union demands that oil corporations, large manufacturers, and the corporate rich be made to pay their share. State workers who wish to save jobs and fight declining wages in the face of a stagnating economy will have to raise an issue that has been long forgotten by U.S. trade unions: the issue of social justice.

Justice in this case means more than simply a demand for progressive taxation; it includes as well the demand that all those who live in this society have a say over the institutions that shape their work and lives. This may begin with public institutions, but it will have to go beyond them as well. The lines which divide public and private institutions are themselves part of the problem to be overcome. The fiscal crisis itself is a result of the economic contradictions facing capitalist society today. The tables will have to be turned on corporate decision-makers. The corporate attempt to reorganize the state may yet prove to be the first step in reorganizing and democratizing these reorganizers. This kind of struggle involves the return to the *political* unionism of sixty years ago—a return to the traditions of democratic-socialist unionism, which is the first and most vital step toward revitalizing the state sector union movement in the 1980s.

Conclusion

The discussions of both semiprofessional and working-class occupations have concluded on a similar note: the centrality of activism and political work by those of us in the state sector for the development of progressive alternatives. This, I think, is the most important point of this paper. Structural analysis merely gives us a set of abstract possibilities. Turning them into concrete movements takes the efforts of the women and men who work in these occupations. Those of us who are active in these areas, occupationally and politically, have an obligation to make sure that these possibilities become realities. We can serve as an important link with the progressive potential of these public sector occupations. The state sector can be the place where, in the 1980s, labor activism is renewed; or it can be a scene of defeat and accommodation. The decision is ours.

Notes

1. Erik Olin Wright, "Class, Crisis, and the State," *New Left Review* (1978).
2. Harry Braverman, *Labor and Monopoly Capital* (New York: Monthly Review Press, 1974).
3. Stanley Aronowitz, "State Workers and the Social Wage" (paper delivered to the New American Movement 1979 annual convention).

5. The Tax System and the Tax Revolt

Jerry Sazama

Taxation and Tax Revolts

The current tax revolt is part of a long tradition of tax revolts in the United States. Many of the battles about restructuring the economy and the public sector were fought around tax issues. The left now has an excellent organizing opportunity to follow in this tradition.

The struggle against unfair taxes was basic to the American Revolution. The Boston Tea Party was directed against the British Townshend Acts, an import tax. Around the slogan of "no taxation without representation," the colonial assemblies pushed Britain for control over the spending of revenue raised here. This was no simple political rebellion: it resulted in the creation of the first bourgeois national democracy. There is the famous Whiskey Rebellion of 1794 in Pennsylvania, which was part of the struggle over the nature of the political economy in this new country. The independent landholders fought against taxes imposed on them by national merchant capitalists, who were pushing a strong federal government over decentralized, locally controlled governments.

After the Civil War the economy was industrializing rapidly and the industrial capitalist class of the North dominated the federal government. From 1868 to 1913 excise taxes on liquor and tobacco hit the people least able to pay. These taxes were the source of about 90 percent of federal domestic revenue. As the pressures of the industrial revolution became unbearable, the populist and so-

Jerry Sazama is associate professor of economics at the University of Connecticut.

73

cialist movements grew stronger. Emotional battles were fought around the ratification of the Sixteenth Amendment, which authorized a personal income tax. Because of socialist and progressive efforts, the corporate and personal income tax laws were passed along with antitrust legislation and basic labor laws.

During the 1920s conservatism reigned, and some earlier gains were reversed. The next big pressure to tax the rich came during the Great Depression, but it was largely unsuccessful. Then, to finance World War II, the personal income tax was transformed from a tax on the rich, paid by a small fraction of income recipients, to a mass tax paid by all income earners, thus rendering it a less progressive instrument. After the war the progressive tax system was further eroded with each new "reform." The 1978 changes in the federal income and payroll taxes further accelerated the inequity of the tax structure. Capital gains were taxed more lightly under the personal income tax, while rates were increased on wages and salaries below certain maximums. The Reagan proposals, with their concern for "encouraging savings," will increase the inequities even more by favoring income from capital over income from wages and salaries.

Now the tax revolt is in full swing. It is more than justified, since average tax rates on income for all taxes taken together are highest among the middle-income groups. Average tax rates decrease as wealth increases. This, together with the current squeeze on the living standard of most middle- and low-income groups, and the popular perception that big business benefits most from government, provides good reason for the tax revolt.

One response to this frustration has been the movement to cut taxes, thereby implying cuts in expenditures. The right has used this movement as a wedge to cut business taxes and taxes for the wealthy, as well as social services. An alternative response could be a restructuring of taxes and expenditures. Such reform implies fundamental change in the way the economy is organized and how the government is run. It would raise questions about the validity of the government and the groups that it benefits. Thus far, however, tax cuts have resulted in spending cuts on social services, instead of cuts in defense, corporate subsidies, or police. Socialist and progressive organizing will therefore have to confront taxes and expenditures as a combined issue. They need to ensure that regressive taxes are replaced by genuinely progressive taxes, such as a net-wealth tax, and that service cuts for capital replace service cuts for the poor or working class.[1]

The Current Tax Structure

Background and Concepts

Major federal taxes include personal income tax, payroll taxes used to finance unemployment insurance, social security, etc., and corporate income tax. On the state level, while personal and corporate income taxes play some role, general and specific sales taxes are most important, while at the local level the property tax is the mainstay. Table 5-1 shows the relative importance of the major taxes in the total tax system. Total tax revenue for 1978 amounted to $660.4 billion.

Effective or average tax rates for an income group are the taxes paid by the group divided by the income received by the group. This sounds straightforward enough, but it is difficult to get a precise measurement of income and a consensus on which income groups really bear the burden of some of the taxes. Determining which income groups pay how much of total taxes involves applying economic theory to each of the separate taxes to estimate which groups are most likely to pay the tax. For the personal income, payroll, sales, and property taxes, the orthodox economic assumptions can be used.

Assigning the burden of the corporate income tax is the most controversial calculation, however. If the corporate income tax is absorbed by workers and consumers, it rests primarily on low- and moderate-income groups. If it is absorbed by stockholders or capital owners, it rests primarily on the highest income groups. On the

Table 5-1   Total government revenue from taxes, 1978

Tax	Percent
Personal income	33.7
Payroll	24.9
Sales and excise	13.6
Corporate income	12.7
Property	9.6
Other	5.5
Total	100.0

Source: U.S. Department of Commerce, *Survey of Current Business*, April 1979.

basis of a political economic theory of differing market power of firms and the relative strength of labor in various industries to resist wage decreases, I have assigned the burden of the corporate income tax 50 percent to consumers (price increases), 25 percent to labor income (delayed wage increases), 12.5 percent to dividend recipients, and 12.5 percent to capital owners in general.

As for the measurements of income, the estimates of researchers at the Brookings Institution, a private, foundation-financed economic think tank, were used, together with other sources of income, which I have added, including trust income, the many free business privileges that high-income people receive (such as the company car), and gifts, and bequests. All are income according to the commonly accepted public-finance definition used to measure ability to pay taxes. These additions are important because they provide a truer picture of the income of the rich.[2] They increase the income of millionaires by 94 percent, while that of the lowest tax group ($0–$3,000) is increased by only 7 percent. Since effective rates of a group are determined by taxes over income, by including all sources of income of the rich we see that they are really paying lower effective rates than is frequently claimed.

The final background concepts are the definitions of "progressive" and "regressive" taxes. A tax is progressive if its rate increases as income increases, that is, if one pays a higher percent of taxes as one's income goes up. It is regressive if the rate decreases as income increases, that is, the percent of tax paid goes down as income goes up. In Table 5-2, tax A is progressive and tax B is regressive. Notice that with tax B, Jack can be paying more money than Jane or Jim, but the tax still is a lower percent of his income, and therefore regressive.

Table 5-2   Progressive and regressive taxes

Individual	Income	Progressive tax A		Regressive tax B	
		Amount	Rate (%)	Amount	Rate (%)
Jim	$ 5000	$ 500	10	$ 500	10
Jane	$ 20,000	$ 3000	15	$1000	5
Jack	$100,000	$20,000	20	$2000	2

Now let's look at the separate taxes to see if they are progressive or regressive.

Effective Tax Rates of the Major Taxes

Table 5-3 contains the effective rates for the major taxes. The rates were calculated on 1970 income data, which is the latest available. However, the structure of the various taxes and their incidence have not changed enough since that time to negate the impression given by Table 5-3. The relative movement of the rates would be the same. Income has doubled since 1970 because of inflation; consequently, the position of the $20,000 income group today is similar to that of the $10,000 group in 1970.

The most progressive tax in the system is supposedly the personal income tax. But even with this tax the super-rich—those receiving more than $1 million in annual income—pay a lower rate than those with incomes of $100,000.

Only the corporate income tax is moderately progressive. If we assumed 100 percent incidence on consumption, it would become regressive, like sales and excise taxes. Also, these are averages for all sizes of farms and all industries.

Payroll taxes (FICA) finance social security, medicare, and unemployment compensation. These are income-redistribution programs to ease problems that are the outcome of the total economic system. Yet they are charged only on wages and salaries and only below a fixed maximum. Notice how regressive this tax is as it is now financed. Social security and unemployment compensation are reforms that alleviate problems of the system but in no way alter the class structure. They are taxes on the employed working class to pay for the retired and unemployed working class, not taxes on the rich who benefit more from the total system.

Sales and property taxes are the bulwark of the state and local tax system. State and local governments deliver the bulk of our day-to-day government services, from garbage collection to schools. But these services are financed by the most regressive, feastlike taxes. No wonder these services are pushed so hard for cutbacks. The tax system is rigged against these most vital expenditures.

Table 5-3 shows the effective rates for the total tax system. The data show clearly that the U.S. tax system makes the poor pay relatively more taxes and the rich pay relatively less. It is shocking to see that the effective tax rate for a millionaire is just over half

Table 5-3 Effective tax rates for the major taxes as a percentage of total income, 1970

Adjusted family income	Payroll taxes	Sales & excise	Property	Corporate income*	Personal income*	Total rate†
$0–$3000	3.7	8.5	8.1	4.0	4.1	29.1
$ 3000–$5000	3.5	6.2	5.6	2.9	3.2	22.1
$ 5000–$10,000	5.2	6.4	4.1	2.8	4.6	23.5
$ 10,000–$15,000	5.8	5.9	3.5	2.9	6.8	25.1
$ 15,000–$20,000	5.3	5.2	3.2	2.8	8.1	25.0
$ 20,000–$25,000	4.8	4.6	2.8	2.5	9.1	24.0
$ 25,000–$30,000	4.2	4.2	2.7	2.3	9.8	23.4
$ 30,000–$50,000	3.1	3.4	2.7	2.4	10.8	22.5
$ 50,000–$100,000	1.5	2.3	2.9	2.3	12.6	21.8
$100,000–$500,000	0.5	1.2	2.7	2.8	12.5	19.8
$500,000–$1,000,000	0.3	0.8	1.1	2.8	13.6	19.6
Over $1,000,000	0.2	0.7	0.6	4.2	11.0	16.7

Source: J. Sazama (see fn. 2), and "Appendix E, 1970," 1977, unpublished update of J. A. Pechman and B. A. Okner (see fn. 5).
* Includes federal, state, and local income taxes.
† Total rate includes major taxes and a few minor miscellaneous taxes.

that for someone with $3000. Only the middle-income groups ($5000–$20,000 in 1970) have a rising tax rate with rising income.

The Total Tax System

Things are getting worse all the time. Table 5-3 is a static snapshot of one year; remember that payroll taxes have become relatively more important through time. They increased from 9 percent of revenue in 1947 to 24.9 percent in 1978. At the same time the corporate income tax, which is mildly progressive, is becoming relatively less important. It dropped from 19 percent of revenue in 1947 to 12.7 percent in 1978. A sharply regressive tax is replacing a mildly progressive one, as is clearly evident in Figure 5-1.

This trend is not stopping. The 1979 increases in the payroll tax further increase the relative importance of this tax. At the same time, Congress just passed more cuts in the personal and the corporate income tax, the two most "progressive" forms of taxation.

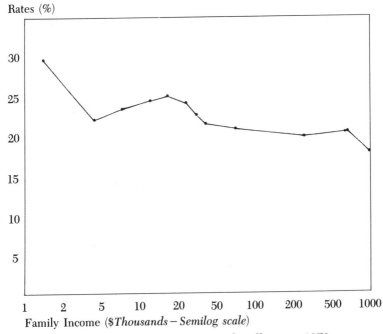

Figure 5-1   Effective tax rates for all taxes, 1970

Also, the effective rates cited in Table 5-3 are being eroded as more tax breaks for upper-income groups are written into the structure of the separate "progressive" taxes.[3]

The federal personal income tax improved slightly in progressivity in 1975 and 1976, but again in 1978 Congress and Carter went back to giving a disproportionate amount of the cuts to upper-income groups. Carter's campaign promised tax reform. The law that was passed closed a few small symbolic loopholes, like treating a yacht as a business expense, while it opened wide new ones, like reducing the maximum rate on capital gains from 35 percent to 28 percent. For a married couple with two dependents earning $8000, the personal income tax cut was 0.72 percent of income; it was 1.25 percent for the same family with $80,000 income—a 58 percent larger tax cut than for the lower-income family![4]

This cut, combined with the social-security tax increase, meant that many middle-income people received virtually no net tax cuts. At the same time, high-income people kept their larger personal income tax cuts and paid virtually none of the payroll tax increase since their incomes were above the taxable income ceiling, and they received much more of their income in nontaxable forms.

Effective Tax Rates on Wealth

Income is unequally distributed. The poorest 20 percent of families receive 3.7 percent of pretax income, while the top 1 percent receive 10.5 percent of the income. The highest income group is one-twentieth of the number of families of the low-income group, yet they have three times more income.[5]

But wealth is even more inequitably distributed than income. Personal wealth is the net value of assets people own—the value of what they own minus any debts or mortgages they have. If you own your house, its net value is its market value minus the balance due on your mortgage. Homes, cars, small business and professional assets (for example, the dental chair or the small grocer's inventory) comprise 56 percent of total personal wealth. Another 18 percent of wealth is in bank accounts, U.S. bonds, and personal trusts. Finally, a crucial 33 percent of wealth is in investment assets, that is, marketable securities, investment real estate, and mortgages.[6]

In Table 5-4 we see that the bottom quarter of families has only 0.4 percent of personally held wealth, while the top 1.3 percent of families has 35 percent of such wealth. (The government does not regularly collect wealth statistics, hence the latest wealth distribution statistics available from private or special government studies is 1966.)

Income measures our capacity to consume and save. But the mere ability to buy things, or the small capacity that most of us have to accumulate savings, is not economic power. It does not give us substantial control over our lives and the nature of the society in which we live. Wealth gives power to determine what our nation does with its basic resources, to determine what we will produce and how it will be produced. Wealth means power to outlast strikes, to hold firm positions. Wealth gives social status and political influence. It provides the means to finance campaigns, influence elections, and shape legislation.

The ownership of corporate stock is even more concentrated than that of wealth. While the top 6.1 percent of the families controls 25 percent of income and 55 percent of wealth, they own a full 89 percent of corporate stock. The notion that working people have a substantial financial interest in corporations is absurd. There is no such thing as "people's capitalism."

Such a concentration of economic power seriously threatens, if not eliminates, the viability of political democracy. Politics and economics go together—you can't have one without the other.

Table 5-4   Effective tax rates as a percentage of wealth, 1966

Adjusted family income	Percent of families	Percent of wealth	Effective tax rates as a percent of wealth
$0–$5000	24.9	0.4	97.3
$ 5000–$10,000	28.2	5.0	27.8
$10,000–$15,000	23.5	15.0	15.7
$15,000–$25,000	17.2	25.0	9.0
$25,000–$50,000	4.8	30.0	5.1
Over $50,000	1.3	35.0	2.4

Source: J. Sazama (see fn. 2).

Measuring taxes against wealth seriously challenges the maldistribution of economic power. A strong wealth tax would strike at the very core of capitalism, since the essence of capitalism is private profit and private capital accumulation. Therefore the capitalist system will never tax wealth of its own accord. That will happen only when pushed by the workers—the real producers trying to reclaim more of the fruits of their labor.

Taxation of Personal Wealth

There are many ways of taxing personal wealth: the property tax, inheritance and gift taxes, and net-wealth taxes. The role of each in the existing U.S. tax structure will be discussed in turn.

Capital Income in the Personal Income Tax

Many provisions in the personal income tax laws grant special privileges to income earned from capital as compared to income earned from labor. The principal privileged item is capital gains. Annual capital gains are the increase on the market value during a year. They are realized capital gains if the asset is sold. For instance, if a stock certificate bought last year for $500 is worth $600 this year the owner received $100 of capital-gains income, which could be realized if he or she sold the stock.

According to orthodox tax theory, income is an increase in a person's power to purchase goods and services; hence, full capital gains should be part of taxable income. Yet according to the tax law only 40 percent of realized capital gains are subject to the tax. Since 70 percent is the highest tax bracket, capital gains above the maximum bracket pay a true maximum rate of 28 percent (70 percent × 40 percent).

The capital gains column of Table 5-5 shows the reduction in average tax rates for different income groups caused by the capital gains provisions effective in 1973. Until 1978 half of realized gains were taxed, resulting in a maximum rate of 35 percent. The 1978 "tax reform" reduced the maximum from 35 percent to 28 percent, so that the existing privilege is now larger.

More important than the exemption of 60 percent of capital gains is the difference between realized and unrealized capital gains.

Table 5-5 Revenue lost from capital income privileges in the personal income tax as a percent of Adjusted base income of various income classes, 1973

Adjusted base income	Individual capital gains	Special provisions for housing, farming, timber, minerals	Interest on life insurance	Investment credit and dividend exclusion	Interest on state and local bonds	Total
$0–$3000	.12	.11	.06	.01	.03	.33
$ 3000–$10,000	.18	.16	.10	.11	.002	.55
$10,000–$20,000	.20	.12	.10	.12	.01	.55
$20,000–$50,000	.75	.26	.12	.19	.07	1.39
$50,000–$100,000	3.00	.64	.36	.28	1.04	4.32
Over $100,000	6.38	.44	.21	1.40	.81	9.24
Total in millions of dollar of revenue lost*	$7000	$1690	$1200	$1050	$1000	$12,040

Source: Michael Mogavero, Ph.D. thesis, University of Connecticut, 1979, Table 6, Variant III, and Appendix to Table 1.
* Yield of the federal personal income tax in 1973 was $103,246 million.

Unrealized gains occur when the asset is not sold. Unrealized gains are income, but only 40 percent of realized gains are included in the tax base. The unrealized annual increases in the value of assets has been estimated to be six times larger than realized capital gains.[7] Taking account of both the 28 percent maximum and the restriction of taxes to only realized gains, this privilege is more than six times more lucrative than indicated by the data in Table 5-5.

The remaining columns of Table 5-5 list other important ways that income from capital is treated in a privileged way under the personal income tax. Similar privileges are also available under the corporate income tax, but they are not included in the table. The net result of these provisions is a substantial reduction in the average rate of taxation for owning capital. As can be seen from the last column, these provisions mean much larger tax reductions for the highest income group.

Table 5-6 shows the effect of these special privileges for capital income in another way. Effective tax rates are much lower on income from capital than they are on income from wages and salaries, even for high-income persons with the same income (see also Table 5-5). If you were a millionaire and earned primarily capital income, your tax rate would be 18.1 percent, but if you earned income primarily from working it would be 46.6 percent. The personal income tax doesn't just favor the rich; it especially favors the rich who earn income from owning capital. As a result of this distinction in source of income, the class structure is rein-

Table 5-6   Effective tax rates on capital income and labor income of the federal personal income tax

Selected income classes	Capital income* (%)	Labor income (%)
$0–$5000	0.7	3.8
$20,000–$25,000	5.6	9.5
$50,000–$100,000	13.2	18.3
Over $1,000,000	18.1	46.6

Source: J. Peckman, *Journal of Finance*, May 27, 1972, pp. 179–91.

* From privately owned wealth (interest, dividends, capital gains, parts of proprietor's income, etc.).

forced: the income of a star athlete or entertainer is taxed away, while the Rockefellers of the country remain captains of industry.

Property Taxation

While the personal income tax is principally a federal and, somewhat, a state tax, the property tax is 98 percent local. It provides 78 percent of local tax revenue. It finances education, police, fire, parks, hospitals, and roads, interest on local debt, etc.

The property tax taxes wealth held in the form of real estate (about 84 percent of the tax base) and part of personal property such as cars and boats in some states (2 percent of the base). The balance of the tax base, 14 percent, is from farms and businesses. The real estate includes owner-occupied homes and rental homes (50 percent), the buildings and land of businesses and farms (29 percent), and utility real estate (5 percent).[8]

The tax is the mill rate times the assessed value. For example, if a house is assessed at $20,000 and the mill rate is 60, your property tax bill would be $1200. A 60 mill rate is the same as $60 per $1000 of assessed value, or 6 percent of assessed value.

Perhaps the only virtue of the property tax is its easy collectability by local governments. In Table 5-3 we saw that this tax is very regressive, having an effective rate of 8.1 percent for the lowest income class and 0.6 percent for the highest income class. Some of the worst inequities of the property tax come from the differences in rates among different tax jurisdictions.

Central cities have high costs because they support economic and cultural activities used by the entire metropolitan area. The poor are concentrated in the cities. Low- and middle-income suburbs have low property value per person, while high-income suburbs have high property value per person. This means that the poor of central cities have very high tax rates and poor services. The low- and middle-income suburbs have high rates and moderate levels of service, while the rich suburbs have low rates and excellent services (see Table 5-7). The better-off suburbs try to preserve these fiscal disparities through such things as zoning by large minimum-lot sizes and restrictions on apartments, which effectively keep out low- and middle-income families.

The effective tax rate is affected not only by the tax jurisdiction in which a person lives but also by substantial inequities within

*Table 5-7   Comparison of richest and poorest towns
in Connecticut, 1972*

	Effective school tax rate on property (%)	Property wealth per pupil	Operating expense per pupil	State aid per pupil
Richest 5 towns	7.0	$127,300	$1,189	$287
Poorest 5 towns	30.0	19,594	864	254

Source: W. A. McEachern and J. Sazama, *Fiscal Crisis in Connecticut*, Connecticut Conference of Municipalities, New Haven, 1975, p. 57.

tax jurisdictions. Taxes are paid on assessed values. Yet within the same jurisdiction houses are assessed at different percentages of market value. In neighborhood X, a $40,000 house may be assessed at $20,000, in neighborhood Y, at $10,000. The home owner in neighborhood X pays twice as much property tax as the owner in neighborhood Y, even though they have the same value home and live in the same town.

The assessment ratio is the assessed value divided by the market value. For the person in neighborhood Y, the ratio would be 0.25 (assessed value divided by market value). For taxes to be fair within a jurisdiction, all assessment ratios should be the same. Yet the U.S. Census Bureau found that 70 percent of the tax jurisdictions in the country did not get most of their assessment ratios within 20 percent of the average ratio.

Further studies showed that assessment ratios were higher, and thus effective tax rates were higher, on new homes, on less expensive homes, and in Black neighborhoods. Also, assessment ratios are usually lower on commercial and industrial property than on residential property.[9]

If the property tax was true to its name, it would tax all property; but many types of property are exempt from taxation by legal and illegal means. A study in 1968 estimated the total property value in the country to be $7 trillion, yet only $1.4 trillion of this was included in the property tax base. The rest was lost in loopholes, which were getting bigger and bigger. If all property was taxed in 1968, property tax rates on the average could have been only one-fifth as large as they actually were in order to produce the same income.

The largest part of untaxed property is intangible property, paper wealth such as stocks, bonds, etc. A full 56 percent of all property is intangible and only a small fraction of it is included in the tax base.[10] Tangible property has physical characteristics like land, buildings, machinery, boats, furniture, etc. About 40 percent of tangible property is exempt. The property of charitable organizations and governments are exempt. Also businesses receive many special exemptions in the form of tax freeze, leased-back government land, exemption of personal property in many states, and underassessment. Because central cities are the commercial, governmental, and cultural centers of a region, the burden of these exemptions falls heaviest on taxpayers living there. Of course they are mostly lower-income people.

In summary the property tax is not only a very regressive tax, it is also an arbitrary and capricious tax, once again favoring the powerful and the wealthy. However, because it is a local tax, it is especially susceptible to local organizing efforts.

Inheritance, Estate, and Gift Taxes

The purpose of inheritance and estate taxes is to tax all personally held wealth when the owner dies. Estate taxes are largely federal and tax the net value of the estate of the decedent. Inheritance taxes exist in most states; some have estate taxes instead. The inheritance tax covers the net value of assets that a person inherits. For example, the inheritance tax is on each child's portion, the estate tax on the total before distribution. The gift tax is a tax on large gifts, designed to prevent wealth from being given away just before death to avoid estate and inheritance taxes.

The ostensible purpose of these taxes is to break up large estates, to provide equality of opportunity in a competitive capitalist system. The statutory rates are awesome: 70 percent of estates over $5 million. In spite of this, these taxes yield only about 1 percent of government revenue.

The value of gross estates on taxable federal returns in 1973 was $33.3 billion. Exemptions and deductions written into the law reduced this amount by more than 50 percent, leaving $15.8 billion subject to taxation. But the $33.3 billion gross base does not include the wealth that never showed up in the tax returns as value of gross estates.

The most important reason for this escape is that very large amounts of wealth are held in institutional form. The Rockefeller group legally owns small portions of the Chase Manhattan Bank and Exxon. However, by the means of owning controlling stocks, holding companies, conglomerates, and positions on boards of directors, they control and benefit from substantially more wealth than they legally own for tax purposes.

Within the tax itself, the use of special trusts, splitting of estates with one's spouse, and charitable contributions without limit are special structural problems which further erode the tax and make it impossible to do what it was theoretically set up to do, namely, redistribute large fortunes. In fact, the tax has had the reverse effect. The need to pay the tax frequently forces medium-sized, family-owned businesses and farms to sell to larger businesses.

All this prompted a noted expert on estate taxation to write: "In sum, because estate tax avoidance is such a successful and yet wasteful process, one suspects that the present estate and gift tax serves no purpose other than to give reassurance to the millions of unwealthy that entrenched wealth is being attacked. The attack however is more cosmetic than real."[11]

Net-Wealth Taxes

A net-wealth tax annually taxes the net value of a person's assets (gross assets after subtracting all debts, mortgages, and other liabilities). The tax rate is a flat percent of the value of the wealth, in other words, a progressive rate. The highest rate is 2.5 percent in Sweden. The United States does not have such a tax. However, it is found in eight European countries and several underdeveloped countries. Nowhere does it yield more than 2 or 3 percent of a country's revenue.

Wealth owners would have to draw up an annual balance sheet on their net assets similar to the one the executor of an estate does at the time of an individual's death. Small estates, which include only housing and cars, and very small businesses could be exempt, thereby eliminating 90 percent of the population.

Such a tax can be argued for on grounds of equity, precedence, and usefulness in catching revenue lost through loopholes in the income tax. But, more importantly, it would raise issues concerning the concentration of wealth and the capitalist accumulation process.

Conclusion and Strategies

The mismatch between who benefits from government and who pays for it is the cause of the tax revolt. It is a crucial link in the fiscal crisis of the state. As private business for profit has grown from small local industries to the large multinationals and conglomerates, the public sector—the state—has been called on to provide more and more new services to assure profits for the rich. These services range from transport systems to military intervention for foreign markets, from subsidized sewerage systems to tough national labor laws.

An important source of the money to pay for all this *should* be profits, the income of the rich and powerful. But they will not tax themselves: that would contradict the profit-accumulating rules of the game, which keep them on top in the first place. This is the fundamental cause of the high tax rates on low- and middle-income groups that we saw in Table 5-3.

As this profit-oriented economic system comes under more and more pressure—from its own inefficiencies, from the energy crunch, from the collapse of the dollar in international money markets, and from underdeveloped countries—the rich call more and more on the government to protect their profits. But the middle- and low-income groups are now waking up to the situation; they refuse to pay more taxes for government programs that do not benefit them. A *Washington Post* national survey found that one out of three people favored tax cuts. At the same time however, two out of three surveyed said they would prefer to keep taxes at the present levels if only government could be made to work.[12]

In some places the tax revolt has been successful in cutting taxes, as in California's Proposition 13. However, when the dust settles we find that the tax cuts disproportionately benefit the high-income groups, and the resulting drop in revenues lead to cutbacks of expenditures benefiting low- and middle-income groups.

There is an important contradiction that people need to deal with: this country is *not* run democratically. The state has been using the tax revolt to do just what capitalism needs at this point, to push back the working class and give more breaks and privileges to capital. Even if people force government to cut taxes, they can only ensure that the net effect is not regressive if they see that truly progressive taxes are substituted for reduced regressive taxes, and that if services are cut, they are services for capital not services for the poor and the working class.

Such a strategy would deepen the fiscal crisis and the general crisis in capitalism. If pressures to enact these policies became strong, the capitalist state would try to deflect it by putting in sham taxes on capital or token expenditure cuts, with all sorts of fanfare. Just witness what has happened to the "progressive" income tax and the estate tax. But the possibilities of co-optation and deflection have always existed; it just means that diligence and fortitude are necessary.

The tax revolt is real. It need not just provide opportunities for the right. The battle to restructure government taxes and expenditures is a battle for fundamental change in the system. Tax reform can be used to raise larger questions, such as who benefits and who pays for this system. It is a struggle for popular control of our fiscal institutions, which, if successful would harm the private capital accumulation process and provide opportunities for popularly controlled capital accumulation.

Proposing a net-wealth tax can be an integral part of this strategy. Truly progressive taxes need to be substituted for regressive ones. The income tax is full of loopholes and held in disrespect: income-tax reform is a tired issue. Increasing the corporate income tax raises tricky questions about who pays the tax. It is very likely that most of an increase in the corporate income tax would be quickly passed on to consumers and workers. On the other hand, the net-wealth tax is a direct attack on privately held wealth. Proposing the tax immediately raises discussion about the unbalanced distribution of wealth and economic power under capitalism.

Obtaining a net-wealth tax does not mean socialism. It does mean, however, a heightening of the contradictions in the capitalist system, and it would raise issues about the system's true nature. It is a viable strategy in today's political climate. The working class and poor want government expenditures that benefit them, and they want to pay less taxes. Struggling for a net-wealth tax could be an important part of the total struggle on the fiscal crisis.[13]

Notes

1. These are the best sources on how to use the tax issues for organizing purposes: Elliot Sclar, Ted Behr, Raymond Torto, and Maralyn Edid, "Taxes, Taxpayers and Social Change," *Review of Radical Political Economics,* 6(1974):134–53; Robert Brandon, Jonathan Rowe, and Thomas H. Santon, *Tax Politics* (New York: Pantheon, 1976), a Nader-group source which contains a list of tax-change organizations.
2. J. Sazama, "Effective Tax Rates on Income and Wealth," mimeographed (Storrs: University of Connecticut, 1979).
3. Teri Erickson and John D. Helmburger, "The Changing Distribution of Federal Income Taxes," mimeographed (St. Paul: University of Minnesota, Department of Agriculture and Applied Economics, 1975).
4. *Wall Street Journal,* Oct. 16, 1978.
5. J. A. Pechman and B. A. Ockner, *Who Bears the Tax Burden?* (Washington, D.C.: Brookings Institution, 1974), p. 48.
6. D. S. Projector and G. S. Weiss, *Survey of Financial Characteristics of Consumers* (New York: Board of Governors of the Federal Reserve System, 1966), p. 21.
7. John G. Gurley, "Federal Tax Policy: A Review Article," *National Tax Journal,* 20(1967):319–27.
8. Robert M. Brandon et al., op. cit., p. 144.
9. Massachusetts Public Finance Policy, *The Rich Get Richer and the Rest Pay Taxes* (Lynn, Mass.: Lynn Economic Opportunity, Inc., 1974). This short book, which can be obtained from the publisher, 360 Washington Avenue, Lynn, Mass. 01901, looks at Massachusetts state and local tax structure for organizing purposes.
10. Brandon et al., op. cit., pp. 146–54.
11. George Cooper, *A Voluntary Tax?* (Washington, D.C.: Brookings Institution, 1979), p. 82.
12. *Boston Globe,* Oct. 6, 1978.
13. These are some socialist and progressive sources for additional information on the tax system and governmental fiscal activities: Massachusetts Public Finance Project, op. cit.; J. O'Connor, *Fiscal Crisis of the State* (New York: St. Martin's Press, 1973), on the theory of big government in a big-business economy; Jerry Sazama, "A Theory of Fiscal Crisis Applied to Connecticut," *New England Journal of Business and Economics,* 3(1977):1–16, an O'Connor-type analysis applied to Connecticut state and local finance; Jerry Sazama, *Taxes for the Rich and the Rest* (New York: Union for Radical Political Economics, 1979); and Dean Tipps and Lee Webb, eds., *State and Local Tax Revolt: The Progressive Challenge* (Washington, D.C.: Conference on Alternative State and Local Policies, 1979), an information-

packed reader on the state and local tax system, analyzing specific taxes as well as total tax system change proposals.

The best liberal sources describing and analyzing our nation's tax system are: J. A. Pechman, op. cit.; and James Maxwell and J. Richard Aronson, *Financing State and Local Governments* (Washington, D.C.: Brookings Institution, 1977).

The best sources of statistics on federal, state, and local governments are the Census of Governments, U.S. Bureau of Census, U.S. Department of Commerce and the U.S. Advisory Commission on Intergovernmental Relations. There is a full census of governments every five years and the annual "Government Finance" series is excellent. The Advisory Commission's annual series, *State and Local Finances, Significant Features,* is also especially helpful.

6. The Great Tax Revolt

Popular Economics Research Group

The year 1978 has been labeled the year of the great tax revolt—and it isn't over yet. Many working people, squeezed in a vice between deteriorating purchasing power and rising tax bills, have joined the revolt. But it is doubtful that they will see any economic relief at all. In fact, it is as inevitable as "death and taxes" that the corporations and the rich will use the tax revolt to foist their costs onto the rest of us.

The Revolt at the State and Local Levels

California's Proposition 13, fathered by millionaire Howard Jarvis and the state's real estate industry, cut property taxes by 60 percent. But two-thirds of the tax savings have gone to landlords, corporations, and commercial interests—a small fraction of the population. Virtually none of the savings have been passed on to the public in lower rents or prices.

With reduced revenues, local governments in California have been forced to cut back on education, libraries, parks, and recreational services. More serious cuts, sure to fall most heavily on

The Popular Economics Research Group (formerly the Red Cent Collective) is comprised of economists who work and study at the University of Massachusetts, Amherst. This paper is an updated version of an article that originally appeared in the April 1979 issue of *New Unity*, a community labor newspaper located at P.O. Box 891, Springfield, MA 01101.

those who are weakest and most in need, have been forestalled only by the existence of a $5 billion surplus in state funds.

Proposition 13 thus provides the model for the current tax revolt. The rich use the anger and insecurity of an increasingly threatened working class to create a movement that lets them line their pockets at our expense.

Proposition 13 spawned a movement of imitators across the United States in 1978. In twelve states, taxes were reduced and limits were placed on the growth of state and local spending.

Cuts at the Federal Level

The tax revolt has encouraged efforts to control federal spending. During the last three years, twenty-seven state legislatures passed resolutions calling for a constitutional amendment that would require a balanced federal budget. Only seven more states are required before Congress must set up a constitutional convention to draft such an amendment.

In this environment, it is likely that the tax revolt, which began in 1978, will continue in the early 1980s, as people press their demands for tax relief, and politicians attempt to implement and exploit those demands.

Prospects for the Tax Revolt

Given the tax-revolt frenzy, whipped up in part by the rich and the right-wing, further tax cuts and spending limitations are inevitable. The measures might provide some minor, short-term relief for working people. But the lion's share of relief will continue to be grabbed by the wealthy.

The spending cuts that will occur—in education, welfare, health, social security, public-service jobs, aid to cities—will cut services for the working class at all levels of income.

Ordinary taxpayers tire of paying unfair taxes and watching tax relief go to the rich and the corporations, while they themselves get very little for their money. Jason Boe, president of the Oregon State Senate and head of the National Conference of State Legislatures, has said, "Within the next six years, the revolt against businesses will make Proposition 13 look like a kindergarten."

But such a development in the tax revolt still requires a more critical, pro-working-class analysis and leadership to provide relief to the needy instead of the greedy. Without organizations and leaders of and for the working class—both middle-income and poor—and against the rich and the powerful, we can expect more of the same: an economic system and taxing structure that benefits a handful at the expense of the majority.

If the tax revolt is to improve the position of working people, we will need our own critical examination of taxation and spending at all levels of government. We will need a radical overhaul of the system. And the leadership of the revolt will have to be wrested away from right-wing fakers.

The Tax Revolt—Why Now?

The tax revolt is a protest against paying more and more and not getting much in return. Our purchasing power has been assaulted by inflation, increasing taxes, and a tax system that rewards the rich and punishes the rest.

Based on government statistics, which don't even take full account of the total tax bite, real take-home pay for the average worker was no larger in 1977 than in 1967. Taxes have been an increasing percentage of the total gross national product since the 1950s: state, local, and federal tax receipts were 20 percent of GNP in 1950, 26 percent in 1960, and 30 percent in 1970.

Social-security taxes, local property taxes, and state sales, income, and excise taxes have all been on the increase for the last two decades. In part, the tax revolt has been directed toward this increasing tax bite—especially in the context of hard times.

The total size of the tax burden might not be too bad if it were fairly distributed. But it isn't, and people know it.

Prior to World War II, the vast majority of people in the United States didn't pay income taxes. To finance the war, the federal income tax was transformed from a tax on the rich into a tax on everybody. In 1939, 7 million taxpayers, about 12 percent of the total labor force, paid income tax. In 1945, the tax was collected (by withholding from paychecks) from 50 million—over 90 percent of the labor force. The income tax accounted for 17 percent of federal revenues in 1939 and 49 percent in 1945!

While individual taxes have been shifted from the rich to the rest of us, corporate taxes have been reduced in importance as a source of revenue. In 1945, corporate income taxes made up 40 percent of federal revenues; by 1976, they provided only 15 percent, and by 1979, the figure was 14 percent.

Meanwhile, social security and sales taxes take a much larger bite from working-class Americans than from the 10 percent who make over $25,000 a year.

Then there are the tax loopholes: 53 percent of all tax breaks in 1973 went to the top 15 percent of all taxpayers; 622 individuals who earned over $100,000 paid no federal income tax at all.

According to the Tax Reform Research Group in Washington, D.C., between 1953 and 1974, the federal, state, and local tax burden on the high-income American family ($50,000 and up in 1974) rose 45 percent compared to the burden on the average-income family ($14,000), which jumped 98 percent.

Loopholes for the Corporations

In 1973, ten corporations with combined profits of $1 billion paid no income taxes. Another twenty companies paid 1 percent to 10 percent in taxes on $5 billion of profits. And twenty oil companies with profits of almost $20 billion paid an average of 6.5 percent.

In 1976, seventeen corporations with combined profits of $2.5 billion paid no income taxes. The effective rate for 168 major corporations surveyed by Rep. Charles Vanick was only 13 percent, roughly equal to what a family of four earning $20,500 would pay.

And Congress approved lowering the corporate income tax rate from 48 percent to 44 percent by 1980. Representative Vanick warned that this "could possibly result in exempting almost one-third of America's major corporations from federal income taxation."

In February, the Coalition of American Public Employees—a union-based organization—argued that Americans are not rebelling against taxes and spending for public services, but rather against an unfair distribution of the tax burden.

Welfare for the Rich

Through the tax revolt, the rich are manipulating for an even larger share of wealth and income for their class. For instance, more gouging of the working class was the substance of the so-called tax cut at the federal level in 1978. Congress and Carter served up corporate income-tax reductions, increased investment credits for business, and reductions in capital-gains taxes for the rich.

There were also reductions in the individual income tax. But when they are compared to the 1979 increase in the social security tax and the effect of higher wages pushing people into higher tax brackets, the 47 percent of people who fall in the $10,000–$50,000 range ended up paying *more* 1979 federal taxes. Meanwhile, families in the over–$100,000 group averaged tax reductions in excess of $5,000. Some tax revolt! The result merely transfers income from us to the well-to-do.

Working people also know that a large part of public spending doesn't benefit us at all. Subsidies go to the wealthy and to the large corporations. Defense spending protects a global empire and gives profits to the largest corporations. The social services that are provided to the public are often woefully inadequate, bureaucratic, or failures.

Spending for health, education, welfare, recreation, urban development, and so on are certainly sizable and are essential to tens of millions of working-class Americans at all income levels. But even in these areas, spending patterns often reflect unfairness. More money is spent to educate the rich, collect the garbage in the suburbs, transport cars on highways rather than to develop mass transit, etc.

Reagan's new budget accentuates the bias in public spending, as it inflates the defense budget at the expense of public services. Such priorities spell extreme economic distress for millions of people. Only a *real* tax revolt can relieve that distress.

7. Pension Power and the Public Sector

Laura Katz Olson

The contradictions of monopoly capitalism have caused state and local budgets to provide ever-increasing revenues for welfare, unemployment, health needs of the poor and dependent aged, public housing, and a wide range of social services, as well as urban-renewal projects, transportation, public utilities, and other infrastructural services. The corresponding growth of public sector employment at the state and local levels, which increased by 20 percent from 1970 to 1976 alone, has had a substantial impact on public budgets. Since state and local governments increasingly absorb needs generated by monopoly capitalism, while profits continue to be expropriated privately, and traditional means for increasing revenues have become politically and economically inaccessible, these public sector entities are faced with a potential (and, in some cases, real) fiscal crisis. However, budgets, revenues, and deficits reveal only the more visible aspects of government activities; these indicators fail to expose the hidden dimension of public-pension obligations, without which the extent of the crisis cannot be fully appreciated.

The rapid growth of state and local retirement systems has mirrored the enormous expansion of the public sector in recent years. There are approximately 6630 state and local retirement systems covering 10.4 million employees and providing benefits to 2.3 million retirees. While these pension trusts, which are increasing

Laura Katz Olson teaches political science at Lehigh University in Bethlehem, Pa. She is currently completing a book entitled *Public Policy and Aging: A Critical Approach,* which will include portions of this paper.

at a rate of 12 to 15 percent annually, had amassed assets totaling $148.5 billion by the end of 1978, state and local governments are simultaneously facing growing pension obligations and pressing social needs that are outpacing available revenues.

Pensions and the Fiscal Crisis

The extensive growth of costly state and local retirement systems is attributable to several factors. In reaction to demands for higher wages and widespread pressure to limit immediate tax increases and budget deficits, public employers turned increasingly toward deferred benefits involving long-term obligations that could be financed by future generations. Consequently, most retirement systems either had inadequate funds or utilized a pay-as-you-go funding method. Pension programs were also viewed as a means of enhancing labor efficiency, lowering total wages, and alleviating unemployment by simultaneously attracting and retaining proficient workers and mandating the retirement of older (and more highly paid) employees. In addition, potential dependency on state and local resources would be reduced through pension savings for old age.

An admixture of increasing public sector employment, improved benefits and eligibility provisions, rampant inflation, and a larger percentage of retirees relative to active workers in the 1970s has resulted in both higher current pension costs and growing accrued liabilities. The latter refers to the expected cost of pensions that have already been promised and that cannot be met through current contribution rates. Thus state and local governments must raise sufficient revenues to fulfill pension obligations that reached $7.3 billion a year by 1975 and are rising by 16 percent annually.[1] These units of government face an enormous growth of unfunded pension liabilities (future obligations for which no money has been set aside) that is estimated at between $150 and $175 billion.[2] In the Illinois Public Retirement System, for example, the unfunded liability rose 10 percent over the last two years, reaching $7.7 billion in 1979. California's aggregate unfunded liability of $4.5 billion is considerably greater than its general-obligation debt.[3]

Local governments are already using a high proportion of property taxes for fringe benefits. Nearly 30 percent of Chicago's and

46 percent of Los Angeles's property taxes have been used to fund pension systems. In 1977, for every $1 in pay, municipalities provided 42.7 cents for fringe benefits, with retirement systems accounting for the largest expense. Higher taxes at the state and local levels, where tax structures tend to be highly regressive, would place growing public-pension burdens primarily on low- and middle-income families who are already providing substantial and increasing payroll taxes to support the federal social security programs. Moreover, since increased state and local taxes and higher general-debt obligations are not politically or economically viable alternatives, mounting pension obligations are competing more and more with scarce revenues for social programs and projects. Significantly, many states and localities are even utilizing revenue-sharing funds to meet retirement obligations, instead of enhancing services or developing local economies.[4] The General Accounting Office recently found that federal revenue-sharing funds are being used increasingly to fund pension systems. In 1977, for example, Delaware placed its entire revenue-sharing sum into the state employees' system.[5]

In order to cut pension costs, two important trends have emerged in recent years. First, a number of state and local governments have begun to revise retirement systems by lowering benefits and increasing mandatory employee-contribution levels. As noted by a 1978 government study of public-pension systems, "it is clear that even state governments can and will renege on present or future pension commitments when pension costs become too burdensome or threaten the governmental unit's fiscal stability."[6] In fact, *Pensions and Investments* reported that in thirty-five states benefit accruals based on prospective service could be legally reduced, even for present members.[7] Approximately 8 percent of plans, covering 18 percent of active participants, have been amended to reduce the value of past or future benefits in the last ten years.[8] The $800 million San Francisco City and County Retirement System has recently initiated a new pension plan offering lower benefits and providing for greater employee-payroll taxes. In Los Angeles, pension revisions for new workers raised employee contributions by 50 percent, while simultaneously lowering early-retirement benefits by 23 percent and annual cost-of-living adjustments from 3 to 2 percent. In March 1979, the Maryland legislature established new pension schemes for all future teachers and state employees that reduced benefits by approximately 20 percent and placed a 3-percent cap on cost-of-living increases for retirees. Massachusetts enacted a five-year program to fund its retirement system and increased employee contributions from 5 to 7 percent.

Current Investment Practices

A second movement for restoring fiscal solvency has been the gradual shift from pay-as-you-go to partially funded systems, along with new investment practices focused on increasing the rate of return. A major impetus for these changes is to reduce employer costs by covering greater percentages of current annuities through investment earnings. Consequently, the assets of state and local retirement trusts steadily increased from less than $2 billion in 1940 to $20 billion in 1960 to $58 billion ten years later; at the end of 1978, they had reached $148.5 billion, an increase of 13.5 percent from 1977. These retirement systems have thus become a significant and growing source of funds available for capital investment.

During the 1950s and 1960s public-system investments tended to be legally restricted to certain types of fixed-income securities, particularly public sector obligations and bonds. As late as 1961 stocks accounted for only 3 percent ($.6 billion) and corporate bonds 39 percent ($8.5 billion) of total portfolios, while public securities represented nearly half ($10 billion) of investments. In the mid-1960s corporate bonds and stocks actually surpassed public issues. By 1976, the former accounted for 74 percent while public sector obligations represented only 11 percent of total state and local retirement trust portfolios. Investments presently include: corporate stock, 22 percent; corporate bonds, 52 percent; state and local securities, 3 percent; federal securities, 8 percent; mortgages, 7 percent; cash and deposits, 1 percent; real estate, 1 percent; and foreign and other investments, 6 percent. Moreover, state and local retirement systems have been increasing holdings of corporate stock at a faster rate than other institutional investors. From 1970 to 1978, corporate stock investments alone increased from 13 to 22 percent, representing approximately $31 billion.

The transformations suggested above have been made at the expense of capital that could have been available for investments in state and local programs, promoting both direct and indirect benefits to plan participants and public treasuries. Instead of utilizing these growing assets for job creation, neighborhood revitalization, and other socially desirable projects, they are, instead, contributing substantially to corporate capital markets and private accumulation. Given the fiscal crisis and shortage of revenue available for pressing state and local needs on the one hand, and the generation of huge pools of investment capital by public governments on the other, it is ironic that worker pension funds are invested primarily in major corporate enterprises. Further, it has been shown that investments in corporate stocks and bonds have produced extremely poor financial returns. "In fact, public pension funds are earning overall far less on their monies than either a passbook savings account, Treasury securities, or the average home mortgage."[9] Between 1965 and 1975, Treasury securities yielded higher investment returns than corporate bonds, and the latter outperformed equities. Only 4 percent of the total pension-equity portfolios were able to outperform the Standard and Poor's index during the last fifteen years.[10]

In addition to diverting potential capital from public programs to private accumulation, current investment practices contribute to the sustenance of corporations that thwart major worker and community interests and goals, including firms that pollute the environment, flagrantly violate civil rights or labor-relations laws, provide unhealthy industrial working environments, and engage in other socially injurious practices. For example, a 1979 study by Corporate Data Exchange reviewed the stock portfolios of the twenty largest public pension trusts (as well as those of 122 major private schemes) in order to assess the extent of investments in ninety-nine target companies that (1) are predominantly nonunionized, (2) have a poor record in the field of occupational health and safety, (3) fail to meet equal-employment-opportunity guidelines, or (4) are major investors in or lenders to South Africa.[11] Out of $16.6 billion in common stock held by these twenty public plans, 26 percent was invested in fifty companies that were nonunionized, 7 percent in fourteen firms with serious health and other hazards, 8 percent in twenty-six firms that violated equal-employment-opportunity standards, and 20 percent in thirty companies with significant activities in South Africa. Thus, 44 percent of the total equities held by the largest public pension systems "support firms that practice discrimination and fail to protect their employees."[12]

Moreover, as persuasively argued by Jeremy Rifkin and Randy Barber in *The North Will Rise Again*, rather than invest in local industries and the communities from which pension assets are derived, trust managers are directing worker funds toward stocks and bonds of the largest corporate enterprises, which are deserting the North and Midwest—the so-called Graybelt area. This flight of firms and capital to the Sunbelt and to other nations is contributing to the fiscal crisis, the dearth of employment opportunities, and the pressures on services in the industrialized Northern states and localities.[13] As Rifkin and Barber note, "In city after city along an industrial corridor stretching from Back Bay in Boston to Chicago's lake front, factories are being padlocked and boarded up as company after company takes off for new industrial parks both overseas and in the nation's emerging Sunbelt. . . . The only condition for becoming a part of this grand new corporate South is an antiunion loyalty pledge. In other words, corporations are moving South for three reasons: no unions, no strikes, and cheap wages."[14] Over 90 percent of the equities held by the Ohio public funds, for example, are "out of state, out of the region and out of the country."[15] In addition, pension-fund investment trends appear to be headed toward greater involvement in international securities. In February 1979, the Alaska legislature considered a bill that would allow its retirement fund to invest up to 25 percent of assets in foreign-currency time deposits and another 15 percent in foreign-currency securities. Although it was not enacted, it is possible that it will pass in the near future. International investing of pension assets will increase considerably during the 1980s with substantial negative impacts for U.S. labor and American communities.

Investment Alternatives: The Issue of Social Investing

Concomitant with concerns aimed at lowering pension costs, reducing the growing pension debt, and increasing investment profitability has been a growing awareness among workers, political leaders, community activists, and the general public of the adverse impact of certain types of investment and the potential of pension funds to move the political economy in new directions. A recent study of 400 participants in the Wisconsin public-retirement system, jointly financed through the Wisconsin State Employees

Union and the American Federation of State, County, and Municipal Employees, revealed that two-thirds of the respondents were concerned with how fund investments affected their jobs, unions in general, and other public-policy issues. The study concluded that "by sizable margins, the employees want to be involved in the investment policy, particularly from the standpoint of social and economic matters."[16]

There are several alternative ways to advance institutional change through pension power. First, pension investments could be restricted to socially desirable programs and projects, as well as to firms that provide greater employment opportunities and adhere to socially desirable guidelines developed by fund members. For example, the Conference on Alternative State and Local Policies proposed myriad innovative pension-fund investment possibilities for constructive social change. Although not an exhaustive list, these include general neighborhood revitalization; enhanced old-age homes and retirement communities; development of community-controlled services such as health care, day-care centers, and other enterprises; expansion and rehabilitation of low- and moderate-income housing; loans for employee purchase of factories facing shutdown, co-ops, energy conservation and alternative energy sources, pollution control, college tuition for low- and moderate-income students, and the development and expansion of small and minority-owned businesses.[17]

Second, public-retirement systems could either withdraw trust assets from bank pension managers who fail to support community interests through their commercial and trust departments or divest the funds of stocks and bonds of firms engaging in socially undesirable practices. Alternatively, pension fund contributors could pressure corporations and financial institutions into moving toward new social and economic goals by threatening to withdraw capital from current commitments. Since actual massive withdrawal of funds from selected large-scale enterprises would depress the value of the firm's stock considerably, the threat of divestiture alone places enormous pressure on corporate boards to alter their policies and priorities.[18]

Third, stock voting rights could be utilized to promote significant changes in corporate activities, as well as to place employee and consumer representatives on corporate boards. The Corporate Data Exchange study discussed earlier noted that private and public retirement funds together account for 5 percent or more of the outstanding stock of over half of the ninety-nine target companies analyzed.[19] State pension funds alone presently hold over 5 percent of the stock of at least eighteen major companies.[20] It is generally agreed that holdings of as little as 2 percent in a corporation can result in significant influence over its policies.

Partly in response to the current questionable investment practices of pension funds raised by Rifkin and Barber, a growing number of public retirement systems have begun to seriously entertain alternative investment opportunities. For example, the Massachusetts Social and Economic Opportunity Council has assessed the possibility of investing some of its $1.2 billion state employees' and teachers' funds in state economic growth activities. Similarly, the treasurer of Rhode Island has suggested that a portion of its $300 million retirement fund be made available for middle-income housing mortgages exclusively within the state. In November 1978, Hartford, Connecticut, held a public hearing on social investment of its $80 million pension assets. Although a decision was not reached, questions were raised about investments in corporations that violate the National Labor Relations Act, thwart affirmative-action programs, and pollute the environment.

Other public systems are also weighing social criteria as part of their investment decision-making process. Although it has not been enacted to date, legislation has been introduced in Illinois which would have mandated the state's pension board to exercise its economic clout over corporations that are part of the system's portfolio; encourage consideration of social dividends as well as profitability; provide venture capital for family farms and small businesses; and construct quasi-public and senior-citizen housing. The Illinois pension board controls over $2.5 billion in pension assets. The California legislature recently considered a bill that attempts to establish "minimum social responsibility criteria" and to encourage trustees to vote proxies on social issues. Finally, the Wisconsin Center for Public Policy has been assessing investment alternatives for the state's $3 billion in pension money, without increasing risk or lowering yield.

Administration and Control of Trust Assets

The potential for advancing community and worker interests is even greater for state and local funds than for private sector systems. Most of the latter schemes are trusteed exclusively by employers, and only multi-employer and union trusts, representing a small percentage of total plan assets, provide for employee representatives on boards of trustees. State and local pension systems, on the other hand, often have both employee and consumer representatives who influence investment practices. Moreover, while nearly all private funds are turned over to financial institutions, usually with full investment authority and stock voting rights, about 50 percent of the nearly $37 billion in state and local equity portfolios are managed internally.

Most of the larger state and local plans place full control over trust assets in retirement or investment boards where employee members constitute a majority in 25 percent, and a near-majority in another 34 percent, of these systems. In nearly 75 percent of total state and local retirement schemes, there are at least some employee representatives who are elected, for the most part, through plan-member elections.[21] For example, the three major Wisconsin pension funds, representing $3.6 billion, are trusteed by a seven-member State Investment Board, with four members representing the public, and two representing the retirement systems. Although particular investment decisions are made by its professional staff, it does so within guidelines established by the trustees, and as with most other public-pension trusts, it is restricted by constitutional or legislative directives as well.

A strong case can be made for employee ownership and control over all pension assets in the public systems. First, 85 percent of state and local workers are required to contribute to their plans and thus a significant percentage of accumulated assets accrue directly through the workers themselves. Second, although public employers contribute to the systems, these monies are in lieu of wages, and this factor is taken into account in determining salary levels; thus, there would appear to be substantial justification for arguing that the funds should be under the exclusive control of the employees.

The high concentration of participants and assets in a few state-administered systems enhance possibilities for efficiently coalescing efforts aimed at attaining employee and community pension power. For example, the largest 7 percent of plans hold 95 percent of total accumulations. In fact, forty-three state and local retirement trusts, which are among the largest 100 pension systems in the United States, account for $117 billion. The California Public Employees Retirement System holds $15.4 billion, followed by New York State

Employees' ($10.5 billion), New York City and Teachers' ($10 billion), New York State Teachers' ($6.4 billion), New Jersey Division of Investment ($4.4 billion), Ohio State Teachers' ($4.1 billion), Ohio Public Employees' ($4 billion), Texas State Teachers' ($4 billion), and Pennsylvania School Employees' ($4 billion) retirement systems. These nine schemes alone hold $62.8 billion.

It is important to note, however, that banks and insurance companies serve as custodians and advisers for a substantial number of public pension systems, thus buttressing the power of financial institutions considerably. For example, 21 percent of total plans rely on the services of banks and 23.5 percent on insurance companies. While the power of these outside custodians and advisers varies widely, they often obtain full or partial control over the assets. Further, "in some cases one-half of the members of the investment committees [of state and local boards] represent financial institutions."[22]

Total pension-fund management in 1979, including private and public systems, is concentrated in 100 large-scale financial institutions that oversee investments of over 63 percent of the $500 billion tax-exempt assets, or approximately $314.3 billion. Significantly, 81 percent of these funds were fully discretionary.[23] The largest ten money managers held $113.5 billion in tax-exempt funds, which accounted for 50 percent of the total assets managed by these institutions. All ten had at least some state and local funds, with either full or partial discretion over investment decisions.[24]

Some observers have even suggested that there is a growing trend among public systems toward hiring outside equity managers and providing them with a high degree of investment discretion and stock-voting rights similar to powers gained through the private pension systems. For example, in the early 1970s, Oregon, Virginia, and Connecticut gave their respective equity managers nearly full authority over investment decisions.[25] In 1977, the $600 million Utah retirement system made similar changes.

Worker Unity: New Issues

With threats of higher employee pension burdens and lower retirement income, as well as rampant inflation and severe pressures to limit wage increases and lower available public services, the stake of state and local workers in the system is severely under-mined, thus providing incentives for the growth of militant public sector organizations and unions. Moreover, current private and public pension investment practices that adversely affect state and local economies and basic community and worker interests and needs provide an opportunity for developing a progressive con-sciousness among public and private sector employees, as well as for forging a coalition between them.

A 1979 nationwide Harris poll of employees, retirees, and major corporate leaders revealed that most workers are vitally interested in receiving information on the financial status of their plans, where funds are invested, and who is managing the trusts. Interestingly, when employees covered by private pension plans were asked, "Which do you think—that pension funds should not be invested in companies or countries with socially undesirable policies, or funds should be invested wherever they bring the largest return?", only 41 percent opted for the latter alternative. Fully 47 percent were opposed to investments in firms whose activities are counter to the public interest. A total of 84 percent continued to hold this view, even if social investing meant lower investment returns and thus lower pension benefits.[26]

Private sector workers share substantial concerns with public sector employees with regard to current and alternative uses of pension power. Increased capital available for social needs and economic growth in depressed areas enhance communities, all workers, and the poor. Funds targeted for union labor and to prevent runaway firms, pressures on corporations for social re-sponsibility, and community ownership and control of productive activities benefit the vast majority of citizens.

Private, state, and local funds together, accounting for $470 bil-lion at the end of 1978, and holding from 20 to 25 percent of total equities in the United States, potentially pose a formidable chal-lenge to monopoly capitalism and existing institutional arrange-ments. Ray Rogers of the Amalgamated Clothing and Textile Work-ers' Corporate Campaign cogently concludes in his assessment of pension systems that "once organized labor begins to use its own vast economic and political power and begins to understand how to pit one part of Corporate America against another part, the way it has pitted the workers against themselves and the poor—there is going to be a social, political and economic revolution in this country."[27]

There are a number of questions, however, that should be raised regarding the potential of pension power for promoting radical change in society. One particularly thorny issue is that of investing state and local retirement funds to attain maximum benefits for the community or even for the region from which the assets are accrued. It is this aspect of social investing that has sparked the interest of political leaders and unions and has become a major focus of discussion. However, community control over community-derived retirement assets within existing institutional arrangements would not automatically provide for a redistribution of resources to those areas and groups most in need.

For example, a board member of the Sacramento City Employees' Retirement Fund, with $96 million in assets, has recently proposed that the fund divest stocks in South Africa-related firms and redirect the assets toward single- and multifamily-insured residential mortgages and rehabilitation loans within the city of Sacramento. While an accompanying report shows that this would substantially increase both job opportunities and the public treasury of the relatively well-off Sacramento community, it would not, of course, redistribute resources to revenue-starved localities within California or the nation. As one observer points out, "in the absence of a thorough political transformation of local politics . . . poor areas [would] keep control of small underfunded pension funds, while rich areas [would] keep control of large funded pension funds."[28]

Second, while pension funds can be divested and redirected into firms and projects adhering to community-defined goals, or used to influence the direction of corporate activities through stock-voting rights, the retirement systems are, nevertheless, inextricably tied to the capitalist system of production and profits: a major goal of funding public pension systems and accumulating assets is to derive a "sufficient" return on investment so as ultimately to curtail the growth in the public employer's contribution rate, as well as to enhance pension benefits and provide new and liberalizing provisions such as investing and portability. Thus, pension funds are limited to achieving desired social and economic goals only within activities that provide "adequate" investment income.

Third, social investing may simply evolve into new alternative investment opportunities rather than worker control over the assets. Moreover, even if the latter were to occur, pension power would possibly only moderate undesirable corporate practices rather than challenge the basic capitalist relations of production and promote fundamental restructuring of society. Since pensions are dependent, in part, on the pursuit of profits, public employees and unions may very well become further integrated into the existing system, with radical change becoming an unlikely goal.

On the other hand, although pension funds could be made available for private development of desirable projects, they also present an opportunity to establish profitable, publicly owned enterprises directed toward responsible social programs. Not only would the latter option increase capital available for these needed projects, provide community control, and create additional jobs, it would also engender new and increased revenues for state and local budgets, which in turn could be used for needed programs that do not generate profits. Moreover, if public employees and private sector unions attempt to gain power over pension funds, it is most likely to activate the strong opposition of the financial and business community, a movement that is stirring already. It is possible that a progressive consciousness can develop among workers and the general public through a long and hard struggle over pension capital.

Further, as Andre Gorz argues, the struggle for and exercise of partial autonomous power by workers "prepares the way for a dialectical progression of the struggle to a higher and higher level . . . what must be done is . . . to make power tangible *now* by means of actions which demonstrate to the workers their positive strength, their ability to measure themselves against the power of capital and to impose their will on it."[29] If employees and communities succeed in wresting control over pension capital, despite some inevitable and fundamental systemic constraints, it can serve potentially as one step toward the ultimate transformation of society.

Notes

1. House Committee on Education and Labor, *Pension Task Force Report on Public Employee Retirement Systems,* 95th Cong., 2d Sess., March 15, 1978, p. 48.
2. Ibid., p. 165.
3. Tamsin Taylor, Lee Webb, and Richard Parker, "Public Employee Pension Funds: Their Potential for Neighborhood Development," in *Public Employee Pension Funds: New Strategies for Investment,* eds. Lee Webb and William Schweke (Washington, D.C.: Conference on Alternative State and Local Policies, 1979), p. 32.

4. House Committee on Education and Labor, op. cit., pp. 36–37.
5. Les Stern, "State, Local Funds Would Fail ERISA Test," *Pensions and Investments*, Sept. 10, 1979, p. 15.
6. House Committee on Education and Labor, op. cit., p. 148.
7. *Pensions and Investments*, Nov. 6, 1978, p. 35.
8. House Committee on Education and Labor, op. cit.
9. Lee Webb and William Schweke, "Overview: Issues and Problems," *Public Employee Pension Funds*, op. cit., p. 1.
10. Richard Parker and Tamsin Taylor, "Strategic Investment," in ibid., p. 9.
11. *Pension Investments: A Social Audit* (New York: Corporate Data Exchange, Inc., 1979).
12. Ibid., p. 16.
13. Jeremy Rifkin and Randy Barber, *The North Will Rise Again: Pensions, Politics and Power in the 1980's* (Boston: Beacon Press, 1978).
14. Jeremy Rifkin and Randy Barber, "Pension Power: Meet the New Masters of American Industry," *Public Employee Pension Funds*, op. cit., p. 24.
15. Jeremy Rifkin, cited in *Pensions and Investments*, Jan. 15, 1979, p. 10.
16. Cited in *Pensions and Investments*, Mar. 26, 1979, p. 2.
17. *Public Employee Pension Funds*, op. cit.
18. Ray Rogers, "Confront Power with Power," in ibid., p. 89.
19. Corporate Data Exchange, Inc., op. cit., p. 16.
20. *Pensions and Investments*, Nov. 16, 1978, p. 15.
21. House Committee on Education and Labor, op. cit., pp. 206–07.
22. John Harrington, "New Pension Funds Investments: An Evaluation of Potential Allies and Opposition," *Public Employee Pension Funds*, op. cit., p. 123.
23. *Pensions and Investments*, Apr. 23, 1979, p. 1.
24. See ibid., data calculated from information contained throughout the issue.
25. *Pensions and Investments*, Nov. 6, 1978, p. 31.
26. *1979 Study of American Attitudes Toward Pensions and Retirement* (New York: Louis Harris and Associates, Inc., 1979).
27. Ray Rogers, op. cit., p. 95.
28. Michael Kieschnick, "Issues of Social Costs, the Multiplier and Pension Fund Investments," in ibid., p. 58.
29. Andre Gorz, "Strategy for Labor," in *The Capitalist System*, eds. Richard C. Edwards, Michael Reich, and Thomas E. Weisskopf (Englewood Cliffs, N.J.: Prentice-Hall, 1978), p. 531.

8. The Financial Crisis in Cleveland

Andrew J. Winnick, Judith Gregory, and Jerry Mandina

On December 15, 1978, Cleveland, Ohio, became the first major American city since the Great Depression to go into default. Cleveland defaulted because the city was unable to persuade the banks—one bank in particular, Cleveland Trust—to refinance $14 million in short-term loans.

How is it that a city with a population of over 600,000, a city that serves as headquarters for the third-highest number of corporations in the country (including such giants as Republic Steel and twenty-two other Fortune 500 corporations) can reach such an impasse? As one examines the situation in Cleveland, a single theme recurs: the struggle between publicly elected city officials and the officials of major banks, industrial corporations, and legal firms for control over the public policies adopted by the city's government. One does not have to infer the existence of this struggle by reading between the lines; the people involved on both sides discussed it quite openly in a number of interviews.

Andrew Winnick is associate professor of political economy at Antioch College; Judith Gregory is director of research at Women Working, Cleveland; Jerry Mandina, formerly a reporter for WYSO-FM, is now manager of a community-owned radio station in Miami. This article is derived from a radio documentary, which was originally broadcast on WYSO-FM in the spring of 1979. A copy of the documentary can be obtained at cost from WYSO-FM, Antioch College, Yellow Springs, OH 45387. The authors wish to acknowledge other members of the WYSO Cleveland Research Group who put in many long hours doing interviews for planning, writing, and producing this documentary. In particular, we wish to thank Steve Pierce, and also Lauren Battaglia, Torgunn Blix, Gary Corvino, Jo Ann Kawell, Lydia Pilcher, and Mark Reynolds.

The National Significance of the Struggle in Cleveland

The conflict revealed so clearly in Cleveland can erupt in any American city. If elected officials reflect on their actions, as well as on their rhetoric, a basically anticorporate, propopulist posture, they must be prepared for confrontation. Cleveland can be viewed as a test of the popular support such elected officials can expect and a preview of the tactics corporate leadership may employ. As Jack Nicholl, Economic Development Commissioner in Mayor Dennis Kucinich's administration, put it:

> I think what you have [here in Cleveland] is a real encouragement for politicians, if you will, who are wondering whether or not their ideas have a base in their communities. What you have here is a proof positive that there is a base available in every city in this country to support radical politics. And I mean radical politics in the way we've talked about 'em through the sixties and seventies. You have a base of working people in the cities who are willing to support that. But what it requires is leadership. It requires political leadership that is willing to define the issues of whether or not corporations are going to be asked to pay their share of taxes, or whether or not we should cut government services to the poor. If you don't have that kind of phenomena occurring in city after city across this country, then I think things are pretty bleak. You cannot do much from the position of one city, and unless we can have a dramatic impact on national politics, these problems will continue indefinitely.

The corporate leadership seems to share this perception of the national importance of their struggle in Cleveland. James Davis is one of Cleveland's leading corporate lawyers, a recent president of the corporate-led Cleveland Growth Association, and a senior partner in a law firm that gets $1 to $2 million in fees from the privately owned Cleveland Electric Illuminating Company (CEI) each year—the same firm that wrote the state of Ohio's generous tax-abatement law, and that handles two-thirds or more of all the municipal-bond council work in the state. Davis has stated:

> Well, there are a couple of lessons that can be learned. One of them distresses me. I'm afraid that the Weissman-Kucinich temporary success will provide a lesson that demagogues in other communities will try to follow. And that we will have other communities subjected to the same kind of destructive attack and lack of cooperative policy, which so far has proven successful for Dennis in Cleveland.

Weissman is an ex-United Automobile Workers official who served as Dennis Kucinich's personnel director. The corporate leadership consider Weissman and the UAW to be the real power behind Kucinich.

Cleveland is also a test of the American people's willingness to face the very real conflict that may be necessary if control of government is to be wrested from the corporations. The conflict in Cleveland is verbal, legal, and financial—not physical—but the sense of turmoil and unrest is real. Dave Abbott, a past president of the Newspaper Reporters Guild in Cleveland, comments in this regard:

> People make fun of Cleveland because of all the turmoil here, all the conflict here. Well, conflict may be bad in a few ways, but on the other hand, what worries me is that people will run from the conflict. They'll look for the easy way out in order to escape from the issues that are being raised. If you're just concerned about easing the conflict and compromising, then I think you're turning your back on the average people in this country and people who don't have a lot of money; you're turning your back on the issues that need to be addressed.

And Jack Nicholl has remarked:

> One should wonder, if people feel uncomfortable with disharmony, with conflict, with abrasiveness . . . what's so bad about it? Under the facade of harmony, things were falling apart. Now we have a situation where, the fact is, all the cards are on the table. And you have conflict, *real conflict*, over major issues. Over different strategies of economic development, over different definitions of *who* government *should* serve. Now, it's in that kind of context that you can have *change*, you can have progress, you can have growth.

So let us look at the nature of the conflict in Cleveland. Dennis Kucinich was elected mayor in 1977. He ran independently as "the people's candidate" on a platform that attacked special favors for big business. He recently stated:

> There's a great issue that surfaced here in Cleveland, Ohio. An issue of national importance. An issue that deals with the clash between the public interest and the private interest. An issue which pits big money, big corporations, and monopolies on one side and the people—the poor and the working people—of a great American city on the other side.

The major crisis in this country today is the crisis of unelected corporate fatcats trying to usurp the duly elected government of the people. The people of Cleveland do not want a shadow government. They want a government they know they can call their own.

Typical of corporate comments is that by Brock Weir, the chairman of the board of directors of Cleveland Trust, Ohio's largest bank.

What we are being forced to live through these days in Cleveland is openly declared warfare by the administration. It is all justified by vague reverences to the rights of people. Understand where this viewpoint comes from; we have all heard it before. It's the old class-struggle theme, the haves against the have-nots, the little people against the big people, the oppressors against the oppressed.

Well, this line might sell behind the Iron Curtain—or in Iran; I don't think that the people of Cleveland are going to buy it.

But many people in Cleveland, including some trained and experienced analysts, did buy it. Norm Krumholtz, city planning director from 1969 to August 1979, commented:

The corporate economy has sought successfully, and has received, special interest favors. And that seems to me absolutely unfair. It's just not my general political philosophy to believe that banks and utility companies should run cities. And there's a population out there at large that is convinced that the corporations, and those who have power, have more influence over the course of government than they have. And I'm not sure they're not right.

Kucinich probably made the most colorful comment on this topic.

Now these corporate vampires have been around for ages. They spend most of their time in their darkened, well-appointed boardroom caves. And as we all know, they can only stay alive by sucking the blood out of our cities and states and us. Until recently not many people noticed the bite marks.

Kucinich made the same point somewhat less dramatically before a U.S. House of Representatives subcommittee.

I have accused Cleveland Trust of using its authority as the most powerful financial institution in the State of Ohio to overthrow a duly elected local government because we refused to come to political terms. I refused to pay the price that Cleveland Trust tried to extract. Cleveland did not reach default for financial reasons. Cleveland defaulted because the city's mightiest financial institution decided to use its economic clout to strongarm our administration into selling the Municipal Light System to the CEI. Every action of Cleveland Trust and its political operatives in City Hall the week of default reeks of political blackmail and corporate extortion.

And the newspaper reporter, Dave Abbott, confirmed this view.

Powerful members of the community are used to having things go their own way, and when they don't—they go crazy. And that's why Cleveland's in default.

Any doubts about the nature of the corporate response to this analysis are swept away by the now-famous statement by Cleveland Trust's Brock Weir, which appeared in the *Plain Dealer* shortly after the day of default.

We had been kicked in the teeth long enough. On December 15, we decided to kick back. We had been vilified, deprecated, and maligned, and we hadn't said one darn word. And we simply got tough as we had to get tough. We said no. Everybody's trying to make something of it and it's teeing me off.

Perhaps the clearest statement by a corporate leader was made by James Davis when he admitted in an interview that what is clearly at stake is "the elimination of Weissman and Kucinich from Cleveland City Hall."

How Does a City Get into Debt to Private Banks?

A city, like any other economic entity, must borrow when its revenues are insufficient to cover its expenditures. For Cleveland the problems begin in the 1950s, when business, jobs, and population begin to move to the suburbs. From 1950 to the present, Cleveland's population dropped from about 914,000 to about 600,000, going from the tenth largest city in the United States to the eighteenth.

This loss in population was compounded by an exodus of manufacturing firms, 640 of which left between 1958 and 1972, and of retail stores, more than 8000 of which left the city in the postwar period. From 1947 to 1972, Cleveland suffered a net loss of 122,000 jobs, 92,000 of which were in the manufacturing sector, where wages are higher than in the retail sales or service sectors. A recent

Library of Congress study of twenty comparable cities ranked Cleveland nineteenth in per capita income. Unemployment rates currently vary from 12 percent to 36 percent from ward to ward.

The exodus of jobs and people, and the resulting low income and high unemployment decimated the city's tax revenues. From 1961 to 1977 property-tax receipts dropped from $33.5 million to $24.6 million, or from 57 percent of the city government's revenue to only 15 percent. The city compensated for the loss in part by invoking an income tax. By 1977 it yielded $55.7 million, or 33 percent of the city government's revenue. But the income tax of only 1 percent, a low rate compared to that of many similar cities, still left Cleveland with what Joseph Tegreene, the former city director of finance and Kucinich's executive assistant, has called "a fundamental imbalance of revenues and expenses throughout the 1970s, which has been exacerbated by concurrent inflation and recession."

Thus, despite federal monies, which in 1961 contributed only $3.4 million or 6 percent to the city's revenues, and which rose by 1977 to $32.7 million or 32 percent according to one study, the city government increased its short-term debt from $29 million in 1971 to $126 million in 1977. Then, in the last days of the Perk administration, all but $39 million of this was converted to long-term bonds.

The amount and rapid increase of this debt, which before conversion had become comparable in size to a full year's operating income for the city, is all the more remarkable when one understands that during his administration of 1971–1977, Ralph Perk sold a number of the city's assets to private companies, using the receipts not for needed capital improvements but to help meet current operating expenses. This was the fate of the city-owned transit and sewage systems, as well as its port system, zoo, and hospital. When Kucinich came into office, an independent accounting firm found that the city's books were virtually unauditable. The accounting firm found that $52 million was missing, including $38 million in bond funds that had been earmarked for capital improvements but that had apparently been misspent for current operating expenses.

If we look at the history of expenditures in Cleveland (excluding those for public education, which are raised and administered by an independent board of education), we find that from 1961 to 1975, in the face of the population loss already cited and a rate of inflation of 80 percent, the direct total expenditures increased by $180 million. In real, corrected-for-inflation terms, this represented an increase of only 72 percent, or about 5 percent per year. Even more interesting is the increase in expenditures for interest payments, administration, fire, and police, which was 139 percent in real terms; for sewage and streets, which was 38 percent; while for health and public welfare, housing and urban renewal, and parks and recreation there was actually a decrease of 28 percent, again in real terms. Hence, the popular impression that it is the increased expenditures for these latter services that has driven a city such as Cleveland into default is simply not true.

During the eighteen months of the Kucinich administration a modern bookkeeping system was installed, much of the previously misspent capital improvement funds were restored, and the city's payroll was cut by about 1500 positions. The latter was accomplished without layoffs or a serious drop in services, by taking advantage of attrition in a work force that had become fat through patronage, and by transferring people to fill needed positions. In addition, in a recent special election the income-tax rate was increased to 1.5 percent. The resulting increase in revenues corrected the fundamental imbalance, enabling the city to operate on a cash basis. However, the outstanding debt still hangs over the city.

Until Kucinich became mayor, the city had no problem borrowing from the banks, despite the archaic and incompetent bookkeeping, the basic imbalance between current receipts and expenditures, and the misappropriation of capital funds. Non-Cleveland-based financial institutions and the public did not know about the fiscal mismanagement. Cleveland-based banks, however, with their intimate contacts inside City Hall, did know. Yet they too continued to loan the city money. Why? Because banks want cities to borrow from them. Such loans give banks powerful leverage over the policies enacted by a city's government. In addition, the Cleveland banks had an interest in shoring up the friendly Perk administration.

Consider the following: Perk was selling off the city's assets to private interests, assets whose public ownership dated back to the progressive era at the turn of the century, when Tom Johnson was elected mayor on a platform of municipal ownership of utilities and public control of business. Gaining control of these assets had been on the corporate agenda for a long time. Perhaps even more important to the banks were Perk's cooperative relations with big business generally. Big business's evaluation of Perk was stated in amazingly clear terms by corporate attorney James Davis.

> It took a long time to educate Perk, as a matter of fact. He came to office just like Dennis, he was a nationality demagogue. But you could at least talk to him and he finally could see. . . . Sure, he made mistakes, and he covered [up] a lot of this financial stuff; but . . . by the time he left office, he and George Forbes were sitting down daily. They didn't change their *public* posture, but—there was cooperation between the mayor's office and the council, cooperation between the Growth Association and them. I mean, I talked to both of 'em. And we could put things together.
>
> But the minute Dennis is there, he doesn't want to put 'em together. *Because his political life depends on not putting them together!*

It has been made quite clear that once Kucinich and his ilk are "eliminated from city hall," the bank's monies will flow easily again. Once again we hear from James Davis, this time speaking on the subject of the possible restoration of the city's bond rating.

> The bond rating of the city of Cleveland will be restored when there's honest, efficient, and competent management of the city's affairs in the City Hall. And when the people are together, and there is that kind of management in City Hall, it's my belief that it won't be too long before the city's bond rating will be restored. But without it I don't think the bond ratings will be restored. . . . The first step is to eliminate Mr. Weissman and his boy Kucinich from the City Hall.

Brock Weir, president of Cleveland Trust, made the point clearly when he recently stated in an interview:

> I'm convinced that with an attitudinal change on the part of our city government you would see an outpouring of commitment and initiative on the part of the private sector that will astound you.
>
> *Question:* But it's not possible to do that now?
>
> *Answer:* No!

The politically motivated fiscal pressure on Cleveland continues. In September 1979, the city defaulted on $3 million in short-term notes. The business-controlled, anti-Kucinich city council blocked the rollover of this loan and the banks refused to buy the notes. And within the following 60 days another $12 million in notes came due. These were also defaulted.

The Corporate Effort to Force the Sale
of the Municipal Light Company

To really understand the nature of the struggles between Cleveland's corporate oligarchy and the Kucinich administration, we need to look in detail at the case of Muny Light. The battle over Muny Light goes back many years. The basic facts are these. The city-owned Municipal Light Company provides about 20 percent of the city's electricity, including all street lighting. The privately owned Cleveland Electric Illuminating Company (CEI) services the rest of the city and virtually all of the suburbs. CEI is tightly interlocked with the city's big banks. Eight of the eleven-member board of directors of CEI in 1978 also sat on the boards of four of the city's banks—two of them at Brock Weir's Cleveland Trust. Since then, two more of Cleveland Trust's directors have joined the board of CEI. CEI does almost all of its banking with Cleveland Trust. Together, Cleveland Trust and National City Bank of Cleveland—Ohio's second largest bank—own 4.5 percent of the utility's stock, virtually a controlling share.

Over the years there have been numerous charges that CEI has engaged in illegal efforts to force the demise of Muny Light. These allegations finally resulted in the city's filing an antitrust suit against CEI in July 1975, claiming $330 million in damages. While this case was in the courts, the city also filed a complaint with the Nuclear Regulatory Commission, making the same charges against CEI in an effort to block the granting of a license to CEI to operate a nuclear power station.

On January 6, 1977, the NRC's Atomic Safety and Licensing Board upheld virtually every charge made by the city against CEI. The board held that CEI's actions "constituted a *per se* violation of the anti-trust laws," and "was an act of monopolization and also constituted [with other private utility firms] an [illegal] group boycott." The specific charges upheld by the licensing board were as follows:

1. CEI tried to force Muny into price-fixing.
2. CEI "caused" Muny blackouts by avoiding proper connections.
3. CEI purposely imposed "severe operating problems" upon Muny.
4. CEI forced the city to buy power it did not actually need.

Despite this ruling, the Perk administration stopped pursuing the antitrust suit and instead began negotiations to sell Muny Light to CEI, an act that would guarantee the immediate and permanent forfeiture of the city's $330-million suit. When Kucinich came into office on a pledge not to sell Muny Light, he immediately reactivated the suit against CEI.

The advantages to the city of retaining Muny Light have been enumerated in various studies. They include lower rates (7 to 8 percent lower, on average) to residential and commercial customers; lower electricity costs to the city for street lighting and public buildings; more jobs for city residents; and, finally, the possibility of a $330-million windfall if the city won the suit.

On the other hand, according to a study by the California Public Policy Center:

> CEI stands to gain at least four benefits from the purchase of Muny Light: (1) an additional 46,000 customers; (2) a handsome addition to its rate-base, which would allow it to raise rates (to an extent that would allow it to more than recoup its $158 million purchase price, Kucinich has charged); (3) elimination of its only competitor, allowing it to set prices without fear of competition for the foreseeable future; and (4) most importantly, dismissal of a $330-million anti-trust suit which it stands every chance of losing.

The city's desire to retain Muny Light was supported by a 1975 Federal Power Commission study of the more than 2100 municipally owned electric utilities, which showed that the average residential consumer of public power used 29 percent more electricity than the average residential customer served by a private power company and paid 14 percent less for it. The lower rates were in large part a result of the nonprofit nature of municipal utilities. They pay out no dividends, pay no federal income or profit tax, and can finance their capital needs with tax-exempt bonds, which can be marketed at low rates of interest.

The reinstitution of the suit and the ruling by the NRC set the stage for a showdown between the corporate leadership and the city administration. Cleveland Trust began to use its $5 million of the city's short-term notes, which were due on December 15, 1978 (another $9 million in similar notes being held by five other Cleveland-area banks), to blackmail the city into selling Muny Light. The terms were clearly stated: sell Muny Light, or we will refuse to refinance the notes and drive you into default. Kucinich refused to sell, and the threat was carried out—as much, by that point, to embarrass and get rid of Kucinich as to gain control of Muny Light.

If this outline of the events seems too conspiratorial, consider the following: at 6 P.M. on December 15, 1978, on Channel 3—on the very eve of the default—the people of Cleveland saw the following exchange:

Reporter: Basil is in council chambers right now, holding a live news conference. [Basil is Basil Russo, majority leader in the Cleveland City Council.] He has a major announcement concerning Cleveland Trust. Basil . . .

Basil Russo: Thank you. If the mayor would sign the resolution which was passed by Cleveland City Council this morning, the Chairman of the Cleveland Trust Bank has informed the council that his bank will purchase $50 million of city bonds. In effect, uh, what this means is that that will permanently end the city's financial crisis, it will save us millions of dollars in interest, and it will restore the city's credit rating. So, in effect, we now have a plan sitting on the mayor's desk that will absolutely end the city's financial problems, if he will only put his signature on it.

Reporter: That is, if he will only agree to sell Muny Light.

Russo: That is correct.

The scene then fades to another reporter back at the Channel 3 station who is about to interview Mayor Kucinich.

Reporter: Mayor, we appreciate your stopping by Action Three News and, as we just heard, the ball is squarely in your court. Mayor, if you will sign that resolution we have Cleveland Trust saying that we can have $50 million in city bonds, which will permanently end—according to Mr. Russo—the city's financial crisis. This is quite an offer from Cleveland Trust. Considering the hour, considering the day, what are you going to do?

Kucinich: And especially considering the fact that everyone says that Muny Light's not worth anything. Strange that they would want to cause the default of the city of Cleveland over a light system that's worth nothing, and all I have to do is sign my name to this paper and we have the whole city back again. Baloney. Cleveland Trust cannot blackmail the people of this city.

I'm saying that I am not going to sell Muny Light, that it is not a legitimate issue here. I have notified the U.S. Justice Department. I am going to ask them to investigate the action of Cleveland Trust and its connection to CEI, and I have every belief that the investigation, should it be brought about, will reveal things to the general public which will bring shame upon CEI, Cleveland Trust, and everyone connected with it.

Kucinich did indeed demand a Justice Department investigation, and also asked for and got a hearing before a congressional subcommittee. In the aftermath of all this, Brock Weir, chairman of Cleveland Trust, denied that he ever made Muny Light an issue.

> They keep bringing up the chimera of Muny Light and all the rest of this stuff. I could care less about Muny Light. You want my personal opinion, I think it's being subsidized by the taxpayers, but if the taxpayers of Cleveland want to do it, that's fine with me.

However, as Joseph Tegreene of the Kucinich administration pointed out:

> His contention that he could care less about Muny Light is at variance with the facts of December 15. The resolution of his board of directors on the morning of the fifteenth indicated that if the light system were sold, they would refinance the notes. His VP, Bruce Akers, made a statement to the press on the day of default that if the light system were sold, the bank would refinance the notes. The council president and the majority leader have stated that Cleveland Trust said that if we sold the light system his bank would refinance the notes. They never refuted that on the day of default.
>
> Muny Light is first and foremost the reason why Brock Weir would lend money to Perk and not lend money to Kucinich, in light of the fact that Perk wanted to sell Muny Light and Kucinich did not.

Finally, in the aftermath of the default, Kucinich went to the people of Cleveland with a referendum to allow them to decide directly whether or not to sell Muny Light. He pledged to be bound by the results of that vote. The corporations launched a major advertising campaign to convince the people that it was in their best interest to sell Muny Light. On February 27, the people voted 2 to 1 not to sell Muny Light.

Corporate Censorship of the News

Beyond the immediate battle between the corporate leadership and the city government over the issue of Muny Light, perhaps the most distressing aspect of this matter has been the overt effort by the corporations to censor the news, both television and newspaper. Two cases are well documented.

The Case of Channel 8

On November 15, 1978, one month before the default, veteran television newscaster Bob Franken gave the following report on station WJKW, Channel 8's 6 P.M. and 11 P.M. news:

> News Center 8 has learned that National City's board chairman, Claude Blair, has been saying in private that because of what he views as the Kucinich administration's antagonism toward the business community, he's considering not refinancing the notes held by his bank.
>
> This would probably mean the city would default. Sources quote Blair as saying that he is willing to accept the consequences for Cleveland as the price to pay to see Mayor Kucinich defeated in next year's election.
>
> My sources go on to quote Blair as saying that default, with all its problems, might be the best thing that could happen to Cleveland if it meant the defeat of Dennis Kucinich.
>
> What Blair proposed to do is to get all the banks to invest tremendous amounts of money to solve the financial problem. But only *after* a new Mayor takes office.

National City Bank of Cleveland, which is another of the financial institutions interlocked with the Cleveland Electric Illuminating Company, was quick to deny the charge. Its vice president, Theodore Jones, stated that "nothing could be further from the truth." Then on the following two days, during its newscasts, Channel 8's news director delivered a retraction of Franken's story. Convinced that his sources had been quite accurate, and that the retraction constituted a form of censorship, Franken resigned, charging that:

> The bank insisted that it dictate the retraction. The retraction that went on the air was dictated by the bank's lawyers. The [television station's] headquarters in Miami said that you will do whatever that bank says you will do, never mind whether the story is factual or not.

Franken's charge has been substantiated. The bank's vice president, Jones, has admitted that:

> A number of representatives of our bank had input with respect to the retraction. It was a joint effort between the bank's representatives and the representatives of the station.

But a U.S. House of Representatives subcommittee staff report concluded that the effort was not in fact merely "joint." The report states: "On November 16 and 17, a retraction *dictated by lawyers for National City was read, unchanged,* on the 6 and 11 o'clock news." And Franken testified to the subcommittee's staff, in the words of the report, that not only were his sources correct but that he had been approached since the story's airing by at least twenty additional people who confirmed the Blair statements.

The Case of the Cleveland Plain Dealer

Another well-documented case of censorship concerns the Cleveland *Plain Dealer*, the area's largest-circulation newspaper. Bob Holden, a staff reporter, had been covering the utilities and environmental beat. In December 1978 he wrote a story indicating that seven of CEI's eleven directors also served on the boards of four of the banks to whom the city owed money. The original article suggested a conflict of interest, since the sale of Muny Light was proposed as a way to avoid default. The published article made no reference to the possible significance of the board-director interlock. And a week later, Holden was pulled off the utilities beat and off the Muny Light story. The reporters and the Newspaper Guild became outraged. They had a by-line strike and accused the management of the *Plain Dealer* of succumbing to pressure from CEI. Dave Abbott, then president of the newspaper reporters guild, led this battle against management. Holden resigned, but the outcome was that Abbott and another reporter were permitted to complete the series on Muny Light and CEI without editorial interference. In a later interview Abbott stated:

> I firmly believed, having thoroughly researched the issue, that any thinking person *had* to come down on the side of keeping Muny Light, unless you were in the pocket of the utility companies and the business community that were motivated only by the selfishness of those groups and not by any real concern for the people of the community. There's just no way any thinking person could come down on the other side. . . . However, my newspaper endorsed the sale of Muny Light, as did an awful lot of other people.

And a paid advertisement carried in the *Plain Dealer* and other papers during the referendum on the sale of Muny Light stated: "The *Press* and *Plain Dealer* took a tough look at Muny Light and they say sell it."

The staff of the U.S. House of Representative's Subcommittee on Financial Institutions of the Committee on Banking looked into the charges of interlocking made by Holden and by the Kucinich administration. Their published, official staff report substantiates these charges.

> Faced with the clear and extensive CEI-bank links, it is reasonable to assume that the banks, particularly Cleveland Trust, did find their roles in conflict—on the one hand sharing directors, investing in stock, and providing credit to the corporate entity which sought to take over the Muny plant, while on the other hand serving as a source of credit and occasional financial advisor to a city administration vehemently opposed to the takeover.
>
> The interlocking relationship of Cleveland Trust Company and some of the other banks with much of the corporate community, and the deep animosities and political cross-currents in which some bank officers became involved suggest the strong possibility that factors other than pure hard-nosed credit judgments entered the picture.

The Issue of Tax Abatement and Other Public Subsidies of the Corporation

Another issue over which the corporate leadership and the Kucinich administration had been battling was direct financial assistance to the corporations in the form of *tax abatements* and other subsidies. In a tax abatement, the city exempts the corporation from part or all of its property taxes over some specified period of time, typically ten to twenty years. This represents a direct reduction in the business expenses borne by the firm and a commensurate loss of tax receipts to the city. A closely related device is for the firm to seek a *reduced assessment* of the taxable value of its property. This again reduces its taxes and hence the income available to the city. Another method is to seek to gain *the use of city-owned property for some nominal rent* and to then use that property in the firm's business in order to increase its earnings and profit. Yet another device is to seek *direct subsidies* by having the city build facilities for the exclusive use of the corporation or by having the city provide services to the firm free or below cost. A final form of assistance is the *indirect subsidy,* whereby the firm gains the use of services or facilities primarily, though not exclusively, designed for that firm—services or facilities that in other circumstances the firm would and could provide for itself.

The bottom line effect of all of these devices is the same. The corporations secure higher profits through a reduction in their business expenses, while the city suffers either a reduction in its revenues or an increase in its expenditures, thus worsening the city's financial position and placing a heavier burden on the taxpayers.

The irony and absurdity of this situation is that we have on one side the city of Cleveland which had to struggle to finance $267 million in current and capital expenditures in 1975, while in that same year the forty-one major corporations (that is, of the nation's top 1000) headquartered in Cleveland had total revenues of $23 billion. Thus, these forty-one corporations had eighty-six times more income at their disposal than did the city of Cleveland, and yet they had the audacity to ask that the city provide them with financial assistance. Here are the citizens of Cleveland, 20 percent of them living below the poverty level, unemployment raging at as much as 12 percent to 36 percent in many wards, with their homes, public buildings, sewage system, and streets all in desperate need of repair, being asked by the highly paid leadership of some of the richest corporations in the world to shoulder ever-higher taxes or do without urgently needed services so that the corporations can enjoy higher profits and their managers and owners more of the good life that is denied to so many.

The corporate leadership tries to defend this absurdity by focusing on the issue of jobs, claiming that if they do not get this financial assistance from the city they will be "forced" either to move from or, at the minimum, not expand their facilities in the city. But, in fact, study after study has demonstrated that this is largely a bluff. For example, economists Harrison and Kanter in a study entitled *The Great State Robbery* conclude that "state tax incentives for business have virtually no effect on job creation or economic development. But they do redistribute income—upward." And the Library of Congress, in a major study of the effect of state and local tax-subsidy and abatement programs across the country entitled *Patterns of Regional Change*, concluded that:

> No uncovered evidence suggests that these programs have had any significant impact on industrial location choice. In surveys of business executives, taxes are ranked low in the hierarchy of factors influencing location in the vast majority of cases. Nor is there any correlation

between state and local tax burdens and industrial development. In interviews with representatives of firms which have taken advantage of such programs, it was revealed that typically such firms made their locational choices first, and then discovered and applied for the program.

The Kucinich administration had made it clear that there would be no more tax abatements or other public subsidies to big business. And big business did not like it one bit. Kucinich stated:

My very strong opposition to the policies of the previous administration on the issue of tax abatement was tested as soon as I became mayor. Various people were interested in projects, and I issued statements saying that I would not support tax abatement under any circumstances. I didn't want to see any further burden of taxation shifted onto homeowners in the community, which is what tax abatement ultimately does. Every rip-off in the world is preceded by some magic words. For tax abatement the magic word is *jobs*. [The] National City Bank building in the heart of downtown Cleveland's business district was sold to the city council [who approved a $25 million tax abatement during the final year of the Perk administration] on the basis of jobs. But yet the people of Cleveland know that the minute that building is constructed, when they start lining up outside the employment office at NCB they're going to be told, "There's no jobs for you here. There's no jobs for unskilled, or for semi-skilled, or for blue-collar workers in a bank building."

Unfortunately, Kucinich's position has put him at odds with a substantial portion of the labor movement, which still believes that tax incentives are essential to the creation and maintaining of jobs. However, information such as that cited earlier has begun to have a real impact on the labor movement. For example, in Cleveland the United Auto Workers, which has 35,000 members in Cleveland and 15,000 more in the surrounding metropolitan area, has strongly supported Kucinich's position. Warren Davis, vice president of Region 2 of the UAW, put the matter rather forcefully.

Many corporations, when they plan an expansion, start the tax abatement wars within the communities to negotiate themselves a better deal. No city is safe from what is happening now. The corporations have literally raped our cities and now they want to rape some more. And obviously that just erodes the entire tax base of that area, and of course their tax burden at that point is shifted to working and poor people.
    Unfortunately, organized labor has been split in the city of Cleveland on that. Some union leaders see it in their interest to give tax

abatements to build, in many cases not understanding the big picture. What it's really going to mean, I think, is ultimately a worsening of our situation in the cities. Even the unions that have a short-term interest in these kind of cases are going to have to understand that the bullet is going to have to be bitten, and we're going to have to put the corporations on notice that they have to pay their share of the taxes just like our members, and other workers and poor people in the community.

What the UAW has recognized is that tax incentives to corporations mean poorer city services for everyone, less employment *by* the city, and higher taxes for home owners and workers; and that these negative effects far outweigh the marginal and often short-term gains that may occur in certain cases.

An important industrial example that should be mentioned is that during the campaign in July 1978 to recall Kucinich from office, Republic Steel "offered" to expand its ore-dock facilities on Cleveland's Lake Erie waterfront. What occurred is analyzed in a study entitled *War in Cleveland: The Untold Story*, by Fred Branfman, codirector of the California Public Policy Center.

> The request by Republic to expand their ore-dock in Cleveland was another fight between business and Kucinich that took on major symbolic importance. Pro-Republic business and labor union advocates argued that the ore-dock was just the kind of business facility Cleveland ought to go out of its way to attract. They argued that if Republic did not get the facility, it would cancel plans to expand in Cleveland, leading to a loss of thousands of jobs.
>
> Kucinich argued that granting port space to Republic for its dock would harm the port of Cleveland, lead to an overall drop in jobs, and not really affect Republic's decision to expand the rest of its operations. A study done by the city's law department concluded that the ore-dock would grant Republic a public subsidy of $3.2 million a year. The Mayor attacked the project as a "rip-off" and "sell-out."
>
> Kucinich argues that his position was vindicated on December 20. On that date Republic did announce its decision to move the ore-dock to Loraine. But Republic also announced on that day a $200 million expansion of its Cleveland facilities. The loss of the ore-dock did not stop Republic from its more important decision to expand in Cleveland.

Jack Nicholl, Kucinich's economic development commissioner, commented on the Republic Steel incident.

> Many people thought that this would be the sinking of Mayor Dennis Kucinich, because clearly if we didn't give in to Republic Steel, we must be crazy. We said at the time that Republic was pressuring us

to give them that deal, that Republic Steel has *no intention* of leaving Cleveland. They have literally hundreds of millions of dollars of investment here and they could build the ore-dock in Loraine or anywhere else in the near vicinity and they would still keep their facilities here and in fact expand them. The new president of Republic Steel said just the other day, "We had no intention of moving any of our facilities from Cleveland."

So here is a company that came forward with all their power and threats and said, if you don't give us what we want we're gonna abandon this city and we're gonna leave it. And we said, we're gonna call your bluff. You either give us a fair deal and abide by some common sense or you can stuff it. And we held firm, we didn't give in to Republic Steel; and we've been proven right in every dimension.

Why Was Kucinich Defeated for Reelection?

One final, rather unfortunate note must be added to this study of the financial crisis in Cleveland, without which it would be subject to some serious misinterpretation. Throughout this study, we have identified the extent to which the Kucinich administration consistently pursued a policy of placing the economic interests of the people of Cleveland over that of the Cleveland-based corporations and their leadership.

Why, then, was Kucinich's political base so limited that he was able to survive a recall election, mounted by the corporate elite against him, by only 236 votes? Why, in an overwhelmingly Democratic city, did he run a distant second to a Republican in the October 1979 open primary election and then lose decisively in the final election? Is the corporate and corporate-influenced media propaganda so persuasive? Are the divisions in the labor movement, which are fanned constantly by the corporate threat of job losses, so decisive? Are the people of Cleveland so concerned about the highly visible level of conflict between the city administration and corporate leadership? No, the answer lies elsewhere.

The Strategy of Race Politics

After Kucinich's dismal showing in the October 1979 primary, in which he received only 15 percent of the votes in the predominately

Black wards, it was obvious that he needed to reach out to the Black community in Cleveland. When questioned specifically about the racial issue, Kucinich responded by drawing a distinction between what he refers to as economic and social concerns.

I like to unify people around economic issues. We built a coalition in Cleveland, Black and white, working side by side on economic issues. We have differences of opinion on social issues. Even within the staff which I have there's differences of opinion on social issues. We have Blacks and whites who work side by side to push economic goals, but they do not agree as to how society's problems should be solved, particularly on racial issues.

While the achievements claimed by Kucinich are real and very important, there is little question that a Bartimole mid-October article commenting on Kucinich's final election campaign strategy was correct in concluding that Kucinich had adopted

a Race Strategy designed by Weissman [of the UAW] and based on taking advantage of the historic black/white divisions of Cleveland. . . . An alliance with CORK [Citizens Opposed to Rearranging Our Kids], the most vocal and active antibusing group in Cleveland is part of the Race Strategy. [Another part of this strategy is that w]hile Kucinich people were distributing racist material using blacks as scapegoats on the [white] West Side, they were distributing material on the [black] East Side, name-calling the exact white voters they lured with racist material.

In fact, after the final election, Weissman admitted in an interview with *In These Times*, November 14, 1979, the intentional strategy of what he called "race politics" as distinguished, in his terms, from "racist politics," and argued that the various leaflets were unavoidable "race politics." Weissman went on to argue:

The other side plays race politics. When you get hit with politics like that, you play for the backlash. Is that pandering to racism? It is, but it's our only way to keep some check on them. Race politics proceeds with a recognition of the widespread nature of racist feeling and at best brings people with racist feeling into support of your programs without contradicting basic principles.

In reaction to this cynical strategy, during the final weeks of the election campaign, Bartimole and some left organizations called upon progressives to withdraw their support from Kucinich. On the other hand, important liberal Black leaders, including former Mayor Carl Stokes and board of education candidate and probusing leader C. J. Prentiss came to Kucinich's aid, arguing, in Prentiss's words that, though Kucinich and his opponent had both committed "racist acts," Kucinich should be supported because of his "populist views." The net result in the Black wards was that Kucinich improved his position from 15 percent in the primary and 37 percent in the last general election, to 45 percent.

The Failure to Develop Strong Neighborhood-Based Organizations

Kucinich also had trouble working with some of Cleveland's well-organized and rather active neighborhood associations. For example, in the Buckeye area, the association publicly indicated their resentment at his heavy-handed attempts to use the association to build support for himself. In the St. Clair area he attempted, unsuccessfully, to build a new parallel organization when the existing one refused to support him.

Some progressives in Cleveland felt that Kucinich could have won reelection, even in the face of the business and media offensive and perhaps even the racial politics, according to John Judis of *In These Times*. He cites Paul Ryder of the Ohio Public Interest Campaign (OPIC), who argued that "if neighborhood organizations had flourished, people in the neighborhoods would have felt connected to City Hall." John Judis writes that

> a plan for building ward organizations [had been proposed to Kucinich] that would be both political and service-oriented, but in spite of official agreement, nothing was done to implement the plan. Instead, there was a growing feeling of distance from the administration, fomented partly by official arrogance and partly by Alinskyite community groups committed to perpetual confrontation.

The final result in the election was that Kucinich did far worse in almost every white and Black upper-middle-income ward than he had done two years earlier.

An Alternative Strategy

In order to gain some perspective on the recent events in Cleveland, it is important to compare them, for example, to what is occurring in Detroit. There, Ken Cockrel, a Black socialist lawyer, a former leader of the 1960s League of Revolutionary Black Workers, and currently a member of the executive board of DARE, the Detroit Alliance for a Rational Economy, was elected in 1977 to a four-year term on the city council in city-wide balloting. In the council, Cockrel has led the fight "to oppose tax giveaways to private developers," an effort parallel to that of Kucinich. However, in a recent *In These Times* article, Cockrel, unlike Kucinich, stressed the role of community organizations such as DARE, which he described as a "city-wide, multi-racial, community-based organization with socialist leadership," and argued that "the urban populism of the later 1970s can become the essential urban core of a popular left movement in the 1980s."

> The convenient banner of "anti-corporate economic democracy" has gathered impressive troops as the decade turns. All of us will soon be discovering if there is among us a common sense of direction which will make possible a long march through the 1980s. There is an answer to the problems posed by the unchecked power of the corporations, and that is collective control of investment decisions, or, by another name, socialism.

As we move into the 1980s, it will be instructive to follow the ongoing events in cities like Cleveland and Detroit and elsewhere, and the efforts of people like Kucinich and Cockrel. In so doing we can gain some important insights into just what it will take to transform American society into one in which the economic and social concerns of the people of this nation take precedence over that of the corporations and their leaders.

Part III

The Crisis in the Community

9. We Shall Not Be Moved: Urban Renewal in Philadelphia

Harold A. McDougall

Bankers, insurance and corporation executives, real estate interests, and major retailers are mobilizing to protect their investments in declining central cities. Their objective is to cut back municipal services to poor and working people, preserve the central business district, bring in upper- and middle-income persons, and drive out the poor and working class. They are pressuring local government to spend money in ways that support business and are using local government to attack the working class.

There are two aspects to this attack. First, the fiscal crisis has brought about a decline in employment, the elimination of quality municipal services, the disappearance of decent housing at an affordable rent, a rise in local taxes, and a rise in public utility rates. Second, big business's strategy for controlling the quality of urban life and the shape of the city's environment has been: (1) selective investment favoring the central business district over declining neighborhoods, with industrial development at the outskirts of town; (2) "gentrification," a term coined by London planners to describe redevelopment schemes designed to lure middle-income taxpayers and white-collar employees back into urban neighborhoods and displace working-class residents by jacking up the rents; and (3) repression, to silence the demands of working people for

Harold McDougall is an associate professor at Rutgers Law School in Newark. He is a member of URPE, the National Conference of Black Lawyers, and the National Lawyers Guild.

Special thanks to Kristin Dawkins, Eva Gladstein, David Gordon, and Jill Hamberg for their criticisms and comments.

more and better services and to destroy budding progressive power bases in working-class neighborhoods.

Basically, big business is using the state to make the class structure of our society more rigid and put us all back in our place; declining cities are one of the most important locations where this policy is being carried out. Working people are well aware that their living conditions are in grave jeopardy: the increasing hostility of local government has put them on notice. Small and scattered community groups are organizing around the basic problems and needs of people in their communities. Community organizations and neighborhood movements can, in fact, help determine the direction our cities—and our society—take during the present crisis of capitalism in the 1980s.

Community organizations often include middle-class and poor people as well as members of the working class. It is usually the working-class people who provide militant and well-organized leadership. As working people in community organizations protest the attack on their living standards, they come more and more directly into conflict with the local corporate, industrial, and financial interests which have mounted that attack. By opposing the state's execution of the big-business urban agenda, they clash with big business itself. Thus the struggle over living space in declining cities is a conflict between the two fundamental classes and therefore one of the "axes of social change."[1]

It is very important that neighborhood organizers make this point. At the work place, the lines are fairly clear, but in community struggles, it takes some thinking and some research to discover that working people's old and fundamental enemy is at the other end of the tug-of-war line. It is the task of organizers to make these key connections between deteriorating life-styles away from the work place and the class conflicts that appear in their most naked form at the work place itself.

It must be borne in mind, however, that community struggles can result in fundamental change only when coordinated on successively higher levels: first, through citywide alliances with other community groups and with progressive unions, and second, in the context of a national working and community people's party. Only such a party can coordinate struggles in the work-place and non-work-place contexts so that a fundamental reordering of class relations and a redrawing of the lines of state power can be brought about. The point of discussing non–work-place struggles is that they are an important interim step in building such a party.

The Philadelphia Example

Philadelphia deteriorated rapidly after World War II, and its downtown areas became depressed. The city lost 140,000 jobs from 1968 to 1978.[2] In the 1950s, the Greater Philadelphia Movement, a "progrowth" coalition of bankers, real estate agents, and corporate and insurance executives, worked with the Clark and Dilworth administrations to revitalize the city's economy through major downtown redevelopment and urban renewal.[3]

Refurbishing the Central Business District

The conversion of a four-block area at the heart of the city's business, financial, and administrative district to high-rise structures and the development of the Gallery Shopping Mall are part of a master plan developed in 1961 by the Greater Philadelphia Movement.

The 1961 plan called for clusters of "banks and insurance buildings around City Hall; department stores in the east; offices to the west; tourism cutting across the city; industry on the outskirts; townhouses everywhere else; and all tied together by a magnificent modern subway system."[4] In many respects, this plan has been carried out. The Gallery Shopping Mall, for example, a symbol of major revitalization in the central business district (CBD) was constructed at a cost of $100 million. Two out of Philadelphia's four major retailers were persuaded to stay in the city, rather than move to the suburbs, and anchored the mall. Already a Gallery II is planned, which will cost $150 million (much of it public money). Ironically, though the Gallery draws twice the shopping volume of a suburban mall, its clientele seems to come not from the suburbs but from all over the city—at the expense of small retailers.

Centralizing urban universities and downtown shopping, commercial and financial districts are part and parcel of the revitalization of the CBD. The University of Pennsylvania anchors the development of the entire western portion of Philadelphia, including 52nd Street, a major Black shopping area that was gobbled up by rapidly expanding university and support functions. A similar pattern, much further advanced, can be observed in North Philadelphia. In the 1960s, major battles were fought over the expansion of Temple University into this area. The university attempted to clean out the neighborhoods to house students, speculation rose to very high levels, and soon the entire area was devastated and abandoned.

Rapid transit for commuters into the CBD is also an important part of revitalizing the district. The Commuter Rail Tunnel now under construction will link two commuter rail lines that largely serve the suburbs in order to make it easier for white-collar commuters to enter the city. Meanwhile, the transit system that serves residents of Philadelphia itself has equipment older than that found in any other city in the United States.

Economic Development

The heir-apparent to the Greater Philadelphia Movement is the Greater Philadelphia Partnership, the key big-business coalition on urban policy. These "managers and leaders" are stepping forward to "fill a vacuum in civic leadership that has existed over the last 10 years" in Philadelphia—roughly the reign of Frank Rizzo. Their economic development strategies are designed to stimulate the local economy in ways that encourage new investment and new jobs.

The Greater Philadelphia Partnership, in consultation with the University of Pennsylvania's Wharton School of Business, has made plans for the future economic development of the city that go far beyond the earlier vision of the Greater Philadelphia Movement. Their principal objective is to transform Philadelphia into an international trade and financial center and world port, on the model of Rotterdam—playing a close second fiddle to New York. In pursuit of this objective, they are working to revise state banking laws to allow branches of foreign banks to locate in Philadelphia; establish industrial development commissions in other developed countries in order to woo new plants and corporate headquarters; construct a world trade center around the Port of Philadelphia; and develop the city's garment industry to compete in the international fashion market.

A key feature of Philadelphia's economic development strategy is the Philadelphia Industrial Development Corporation (PIDC), a quasi-public agency charged with keeping existing manufacturing and service establishments within the city. PIDC arranges low-cost land purchases from the city, tax breaks, and local and federal subsidies for businesses interested in relocating to or staying in Philadelphia. Over half the federal monies that the city receives through the Community Development Block Grant program—$4 million a year—goes straight to PIDC. PIDC's current assets are over $0.3 billion.

Members of the partnership are not pipe dreamers; these are some of the city's most prominent financiers and corporate executives. The partnership estimates that a consortium of Philadelphia banks could put together a $100-million package to induce a major overseas manufacturer to establish a plant in Philadelphia, as well as provide personal and mortgage credit to house the personnel the plant would bring along. Immediately on the partnership's agenda are plans to lobby for changes in state banking regulations, for tax concessions, and for local zoning variances to demonstrate that Philadelphia is a city "ready to service international firms."

Economic development schemes have certain drawbacks: luring business to an area often means giving tax breaks and other financial concessions that ultimately undermine the objective of putting the city back on a sound financial footing. Gulf Oil, for example, enjoys $1 billion worth of tax exemptions in Philadelphia. Arco has a similar arrangement. Also, what kind of industry is actually being attracted is not clear: Are they the sweatshops of the competitive sector, requiring a low-wage, suppressed, unskilled labor force?

Gentrification

In its *Year 2000 Report* the Delaware Valley Regional Planning Commission, an advisory body that plans for the Delaware Valley, including Philadelphia and its suburbs, described a number of possible futures for the region. One of these was "Future D": No Growth with Revitalization:

> Population growth would be held at zero—with substantial outmigration of people to elsewhere—though employment would grow 9.2%. Many suburban communities would return to urban centers;

housing needs would increase and fewer people would live in each household. Extensive rehabilitation and new construction would be recommended on vacant renewal sites. Existing services would be improved with greater reliance on public transportation.

The code word for this future is gentrification. As a result of the postwar exodus of industry and the white middle class to the suburbs, the inner-city area (which housed corporate headquarters) was allowed to deteriorate, and social control over subordinate classes was weakened. As the economy contracted in the mid-1970s, the energy crisis accentuated, the ecological repercussions of suburban sprawl accumulated, the urban tax base deteriorated, and city services took on social and fiscal crisis proportions. The viability of downtown corporate headquarters was threatened. With corporate hegemony in the central cities being threatened, and the living costs of middle- and upper-level technocrats and managers rising in the suburbs, gentrification and downtown corporate-renewal movement was initiated. Of course, for inner-city minority, poor, and working people, this means no future at all: neighborhoods slated for gentrification must first be emptied of their minority and working-class residents.

After extensive renovation and redevelopment of the downtown area in the 1950s, as well as the expansion of the University of Pennsylvania into West Philadelphia and of Temple University into North Philadelphia, the progrowth coalitions turned their attention to Society Hill, an interracial neighborhood where Blacks had lived since the 1700s. This deteriorating neighborhood was turned into a valuable residential and shopping area and tourist attraction, and Blacks were driven to the south of the city. Between 1960 and 1970, Society Hill's Black population decreased by 64.2 percent, while the white population increased by 32.7 percent. The 1976 interim census showed the upper-income white population had increased a further 13 percent.[5] The high-rise projects of South Philadelphia (Southwark and Tasker Homes), built to absorb the refugees from Society Hill, have become squalid slums.

Since the 1950s, gentrification has spread out from Society Hill, first moving south, then just north of Philadelphia's central city, where the Spring Garden Art Museum became the anchor for a renewal effort that continues to this day.

Today, all the older parts of the city are being gentrified (especially near the CBD), but activity is presently most intense around the University of Pennsylvania. Student demand for facilities at any price, regardless of quality, is exploited to drive rents beyond those that local residents can afford; students are thus used as blockbusters in reverse to clear out neighborhoods for occupation by middle- and upper-middle-income groups. The pattern is always the same—rents go up, people are driven out, and a lot of housing is abandoned. Soon after that, recycling is in full swing. In some of these neighborhoods, house shells go for $60,000, and one-bedroom apartments rent for $350 per month. Real estate speculators have coined brand names for the residential areas that have been packaged for redevelopment and resale since the 1950s. "Recycling," the term used by Philadelphia's neighborhood activists to describe this process, has become a fighting word throughout the city. The only neighborhoods presently immune are the northeast and the southwest near the airport, both largely white, working-class, and new.

The poor are being shoved from these central city neighborhoods out to inner-ring, declining suburbs like Darby and Upper Darby, full of tacky row houses constructed immediately after World War II and dilapidated after only thirty years. The aging white occupants of these communities were middle-class and middle-aged when they moved in at the end of the war. Now they are old and near death, and their communities are being steadily depopulated. Some of the survivors will be relocated to newly constructed housing for the elderly in the central city.

Triage and Planned Shrinkage

The term "triage" originated during World War II, when army field hospitals short on supplies divided their facilities into three wards: one for the patients who would get well with few if any medical supplies, one for the patients who would not get well despite medical help, and a third ward of patients who needed the medicine to get better and would recover if they got it. The triage policy cut off all medical supplies except to the patients in the third ward. In urban-renewal schemes, some neighborhoods are classified as "terminally ill," and services are, to all intents and purposes, cut off. This is what triage means in the inner city.

However, it is important to remember that neighborhood deterioration has been going on for a long time. A neighborhood deteriorates partly because municipal services—street repairs, garbage collection, police and fire protection—are provided in a spotty fashion. Working-class and poor neighborhoods have always received less than their fair share of municipal services. It is these declining neighborhoods that are designated terminal; under urban triage policies, the cities claim there are no longer sufficient resources to provide poor and working-class neighborhoods with even the most meager services. The rationale advanced is that these neighborhoods have somehow deteriorated beyond the point at which they can be saved!

Philadelphia community people understand triage very clearly. They correctly perceive it as another aspect of the recycling campaign of the city's ruling class. North Philadelphia, west of Broad Street, for example, is a neighborhood placed in the terminal ward. At the same time, central city public-housing high-rises are being emptied out, while the city refuses to build or maintain public, subsidized, or rental-assistance housing in poor, Black, and Latin communities.

In some instances, the application of triage techniques has gone beyond the mere refusal to save declining neighborhoods and commercial districts. Rather, a policy of planned shrinkage is put into effect, and services are drastically reduced or cut off completely, in an attempt to accelerate the deterioration of an area and clean out its population. Once the area is cleared, it can be recycled, and gentrification can begin. The term "planned shrinkage" was coined by Roger Starr, then chief executive of the New York City Housing and Development Administration. In the hospital paradigm, it is the functional equivalent of euthanasia—though some would call it murder.

Repression

The rapid deterioration of cities in the North—the crisis in services, particularly in housing, schools, and health—and the increasing determination of local big-business coalitions to manage the crisis to their own advantage, is leading to a class-charged standoff in the cities. In fact, the police repression and Ku Klux Klan activity that increasingly accompany racial standoffs in gentrifying neighborhoods could well be said to be laying the mass basis for fascism.

The repression that existed in Philadelphia under the regime of Frank Rizzo is known throughout the country and has been the target of a federal investigation and lawsuit. Rizzo refused to acknowledge any case of police brutality, even though by the time of the lawsuit, Philadelphia had paid more than $2 million in verdicts and settlements ordered by the courts to police-brutality victims. Rizzo also used federal law enforcement grants—provided in the 1970s to put police officers on horseback (taking them out of squad cars and placing them "closer to the people")—to create a mounted army that controlled Philadelphia with a reign of terror. Rizzo's civil disobedience squad allegedly learned the names of every political organizer and left-wing person in the city through coverage of demonstrations and general snooping. While current negotiations are on regarding another police pay raise, political activists are pressuring the new mayor for promises that a new police commissioner will be appointed.

Because the costly, desperate riots of the 1960s gave way to movements with a longer-range perspective, repressive strategies today are often focused on infiltration and on discrediting leadership. Rose Wiley, for example, a public-housing activist, came under heavy attack from Mayor Rizzo, who prosecuted her for embezzlement. Her organization, the Resident Advisory Board (RAB), a local public-housing umbrella organization, was nearly smashed in the struggle. It was only with great effort that the RAB was able to maintain its status as a tenant bargaining unit recognized by the Philadelphia Housing Authority.

The Results of Big Business's Strategy

Big business's urban policy is supposed to revitalize the city by polishing up the central business district, but this strategy seems only to accelerate the deterioration of other parts of the city. Philadelphia continues to decline economically, although its center gleams with renovation.

Finance capital continues to flow out of Philadelphia: from 1972 to 1977, the ratio of average foreign loans to average total loans increased steadily from 14 percent to 24 percent. Earnings on foreign loans are 40 percent of total earnings of Philadelphia banks. Philadelphia-area capital is international capital and is invested all over the world, while local small businesses starve. Manufacturing firms have closed, neighborhood shopping districts have deteriorated for lack of commercial credit, and houses lie abandoned for lack of mortgages and repair loans. The money flows out of the city, corrupting the very backyards of the banks making the loans. Yet even the bankers in the Greater Philadelphia Partnership, ostensibly organized to save the city, would hardly dream of altering the lending policies of their own banks. Rather, the strategy of the

Philadelphia coalition of insurance, real estate, corporate, and banking interests (which really is the "permanent government" of the city) is to ensure that the costs of their own system and their own decisions will be borne by Philadelphia's minorities and working class.

The Philadelphia Progressive Movement

Progressive forces all over the country are hampered by racial and other divisions existing among the people, particularly working people. This makes it difficult to organize around real issues: unemployment, social-service cutbacks, and destruction of the living standards of working people.

Philadelphia is a very racially tense city. It's a miracle that there is as much interracial cooperation as there is (or maybe it's not a miracle at all—just lots of good people working hard). Rizzo crystallized the racist attitudes widely held in the city's white community, especially among the working class. Whites who follow hockey—called "hockey whites" by Black people there—still celebrate a Philadelphia Flyers victory by beating any Black person they encounter on the streets. South Philadelphia, Rizzo's home neighborhood, is a type of Black no-man's land. Yet the very extremity of the racial tensions Rizzo unleashed and capitalized on touched off a strong resistance.

A citywide alliance of the most progressive community groups in the city, including the Black United Front, La Alianza (an Hispanic group), and the Stop Rizzo Coalition (a formation of the white left) finally defeated Rizzo: a charter change that the mayor sponsored, which would have permitted him a third term, was defeated by the voters in November 1978. The Black community (40 percent of the population) was the strongest and most united anti-Rizzo force.

The Housing Movement in Philadelphia

Housing for working-class and minority people in declining cities is overcrowded, below standard, rapidly deteriorating, and overpriced. At the same time, people's real wages are declining, and fewer can afford even substandard housing; in fact, the very existence of "people's" housing is in jeopardy because of the gentrification and clearance strategies of big business.

Organizing at the Base

Today's progressive community organization is typically a survivor of the 1960s led by people who grew to leadership during that period. Since then, most people—certainly most organizers—have come to understand American class conflict, having experienced Watergate, the Vietnam war, and various minority and women's struggles in a profound way. In line with this development, some community organizers and leaders, and in a few cases community groups themselves, have taken explicitly socialist positions on major issues. This is important, because socialism provides an ideology and an analysis that can connect the deterioration of city life, the failings of capitalism, and the promise of a better future. Organizers at this level who identify themselves as socialists can build ideological bridges within and among community groups through study groups, daily practice, and struggle. Knowledgeable organizers can help people understand the contradictions and class conflicts that both shape living space and determine the direction of the national political economy.

The typical community organization dealing with housing issues in Philadelphia, as in many other declining cities, is a civic association or block group. However, in Philadelphia these groups tend to be composed primarily of home owners, with a highly developed sense of neighborhood and a great awareness of how their area fits into the city's overall plan. The Philadelphia neighborhood movement is extremely strong.

The first stage in organizing around housing issues is direct action, where the threat to people's living standards posed by the urban policies of big business is most acute. People aided by short-term victories and developed by the process of struggle itself can be asked to reciprocate, even in a small way, to make the point that organizations that can help people are those in which the people participate and which they support. From this initial contact, information and guidance can be provided so people can develop their understanding of progressive action, what it involves, and where it can lead.[6]

A spectacular squatting operation—moving into and taking over abandoned houses repossessed by the U.S. Department of Housing and Urban Development (HUD)—was mounted by the North Phil-

adelphia Block Development Corporation (NPBDC) in the spring
of 1977. NPBDC undertook major repairs such as plumbing, roof-
ing, and heating; the squatters then performed what minor repairs
were necessary to make the premises safe and habitable. According
to written agreements between NPBDC and the squatters, the
latter committed themselves to maintain the property, pay the
utility bills and property taxes, and secure insurance. NPBDC also
agreed to represent the squatters in the event of legal proceedings
against them. The program, called "Walk-In Homesteading," was
given front-page coverage in the *New York Times*, particularly after
ten families were evicted and some were arrested, along with
NPBDC staff. NPBDC dealt with the possibly demoralizing effects
of arrests and evictions by quickly resettling evicted families in
other abandoned housing. Eventually, the charges were dropped,
and the approach of the opposition became one of attempted co-
optation rather than repression. At one point, HUD proposed to
State Representative Milton Street, NPBDC's founder, that he
keep the houses his constituents had already occupied, provided
the program was shut down, an offer he rejected.

In North Philadelphia, home owners seem to feel that the squatters are helping to stabilize the neighborhood in the face of rapid
and accelerating abandonment; some 275 families have homesteaded thus far. Even the owners have begun to cooperate. As
North Philadelphia gentrification has not taken off yet, property
owners have in the main decided it's better to settle than to engage
in extensive litigation to evict the families, especially when the
economic value of the property to the owners is presently very
little. At times, NPBDC people have occupied abandoned houses
that HUD or some local community-development groups planned
to rehabilitate and sell, and this has sparked some conflict. The
conflict is secondary, however, and could be easily resolved by a
careful check on the status of abandoned homes before they are
homesteaded. Philadelphia real estate interests are most threatened
by NPBDC tactics because of the possibility that privately owned
housing being held for speculation may be occupied and taken
over.

Building Alliances: Citywide Coalitions

The racial and neighborhood conflicts that divide poor and working
people in Philadelphia are being straddled somewhat by alliances

that oppose the big-business urban agenda. Thus, ties among working people and community groups in all parts of the city are being strengthened by the formation of united fronts.

Three important organizations in Philadelphia, which are standing coalitions of base-level groups and thus operate on the alliance level, are the Philadelphia Council of Neighborhood Organizations (PCNO), a citywide coalition of civic associations and block groups in 250 neighborhoods, organized in 1975; the Ad Hoc Committee for Housing and Community Development (organized by Milton Street), which claims a citywide membership and overlaps with PCNO, focusing on gentrification, displacement, and the allocation of federal block grant money; and the Tenant's Action Group (TAG), an umbrella organization of Philadelphia tenant unions, which overlaps somewhat with the Ad Hoc Committee. PCNO's program is basically reformist, with citizen control over block grants under the Housing and Community Development Act as its primary objective. To an extent, its more moderate strategy is dictated by the diversity of its membership, including middle-class homeowners and some whites. The Ad Hoc Committee, on the other hand, is more militant and pressure-oriented than the PCNO, reflecting to a large extent the charisma and dynamism of Representative Street, as well as the class background of the membership, which is somewhat different from that of the PCNO; more tenants than home owners, representing poorer neighborhoods, and so forth. TAG is probably the most clearly left-wing, with a substantial number of left-wing organizers and staff. A number of tenant unions represented in TAG are from elderly housing projects where many "old left" and former union organizers now live. TAG concentrates on issues of rent control, landlord-tenant struggles, public housing, gentrification, and triage.

The allocation of federal Community Development Block Grant (CDBG) funds has become the focal point of the housing struggle in Philadelphia and is the issue around which the most important alliances are being formed.

CDBG regulations require that up to 75 percent of all activities must benefit low- and moderate-income people, although this percentage may be waived. More than $240 million in community-development funds has been allocated for housing in Philadelphia, but administration of the community-development program has been so poor that HUD demanded the return of $6 million in 1977. Also, HUD recently audited city spending of federal money, re-

vealing racially discriminatory administration of the funds. HUD
has threatened to cut off all federal funds to Philadelphia if the
practices are not corrected but has taken no concrete action thus
far. Urban Development Action Grants (UDAG)—a related issue—
are competitive grants from a HUD discretionary fund, awarded
on the basis of a city's past record in equal opportunity housing.
Philadelphia's only application for UDAG funds was denied on
September 29, 1978, because of the city's poor compliance record.

In Philadelphia, forty-four neighborhoods are slated for community-development money. Much of the money goes for staffing,
which enhances neighborhood organizations' feelings of prestige
but engenders a false sense of progress when in reality very little
community-controlled redevelopment is actually going on. Yet the
illusion of progress hinders residents of these neighborhoods from
uniting with the more militant and politically developed people of
the north and central neighborhoods of the city. Rizzo's strategy
of divide-and-conquer was based on neighborhood rivalry and selective distribution of patronage—a promise here, a little planning
money there—a strategy particularly suited to Philadelphia's turf-
conscious, individualistic neighborhoods.

Alliances along the lines of common class interests are crucial
for transcending this kind of secondary division. It is important,
however, for alliances not only to resist the big-business urban
agenda, but also to develop people's alternatives. If the alliance
only seeks reform within the system, it will not last long: either
the real demands of the group will not be won, or they will be
won in illusory fashion, or some organizations within the alliance
will win their objective at the expense of others.[7]

State Representative Street has spearheaded a citywide drive to
oppose displacement, gentrification, selective development, and
triage. Neighborhood people are very conscious of big-business
strategy (the Society Hill renovation was an unmistakable decla-
ration of what big business planned for "bad neighborhoods").
Street's slogan is "Save the Land." In addition, Representative
Street has disrupted city council meetings in protest over the uti-
lization of CDBG funds to redevelop downtown areas rather than
revitalize inner-city neighborhoods. The excitement of these protests heightened the impact of the Stop Rizzo campaign.

There has been a signal lack of cooperation between the PCNO
and Milton Street's Ad Hoc Committee. This reflects the differences between the "reformist" and "progressive" forces, as well

as turf disputes which are rampant in Philadelphia. However, these disputes may be overcome if working people in Philadelphia can be shown that no isolated neighborhood, school, ethnic group, or category of workers is the sole victim of anti–working-class policies in the city, but rather the target is the working class as a whole. In this way, fragmented struggles can be transformed into a united, class-conscious movement.

Building a Party

Once experience at the alliance level has produced a more developed mass base, the stage is set for the development of a local working people's party, without which diverse community organizations and unions can never alter political and economic relations in urban areas. Such a worker's party would be a principal vehicle for linking the struggles of working people at the job and at home.

With such a party, working people's concerns about housing, the family, and education can be dealt with by working people as a whole, and a mass community response can develop to the urban strategy of big business. With a mass base, such a party could connect progressive urban politics to the national political process. It would be vertically integrated from the municipal, through the state, to the national level.

Until that national party is formed, community issues will remain secondary to work-place struggles and larger political conflicts, such as civil rights. In the meantime, alliance-level organizing and local party building can help working people gain a sense of their own ability to remake society by providing experience, development, and a model for the future.

This has been the case in Philadelphia, where a Consumer Party and a Coalition to Elect for a Human Rights Agenda, formed by alliances of the Black United Front, La Alianza, the Stop Rizzo Coalition, and other progressive and left-wing groups, grew out of the anti-Rizzo struggles and ran candidates for a number of municipal offices.

Lucian Blackwell, a progressive Black member of the city council and president of the International Longshoreman's Association Local 1432, ran for mayor on the Consumer Party ticket. He supported the human-rights agenda of the Black United Front. Despite divisions in the Black community, Blackwell won a sizable portion of the popular vote (19 percent). Whoever runs for mayor in 1983 will have to deal with Lucian Blackwell, John and Milton Street, Dave Richardson, and other progressive Black politicians and will have to answer some hard questions. In other words, the local independent political movement is in high gear.

Further, a Black congressman represents a Philadelphia congressional district, and state legislators like Milton Street may be seen more and more—Representative Dave Richardson is an example. Philadelphia, then, is a city where a multilevel political directorate could materialize to oppose the big-business agenda for the city and set an example for the struggles of working and community people in declining cities all over the country. This is an important first step toward a national working and community people's party.

Notes

1. M. Castells, "The Wild City," *Kapitalstate*, 4, No. 5(1976):2–30.
2. *Neighborhoods*, 4, No. 5(1978):1. Newsletter of the Philadelphia Institute for the Study of Civic Values.
3. J. Mollenkopf, "The Postwar Politics of Urban Development," in *Marxism and the Metropolis*, eds. W. Tabb and L. Sawyers (New York: Sadlier, 1978), pp. 117–53.
4. *Neighborhoods*, 5, No. 1(1979):24.
5. "How Whites Are Taking Back Black Neighborhoods," *Ebony*, Sept. 1978.
6. K. MacAfee, "City Life," *Radical America*, 13, No. 1(1978):39–59.
7. Ibid.

10. The Politics of Revitalization: Organizing in Newark

Terri Suess and Bob Cartwright

"Reviving" a city like Newark, New Jersey, is not an easy task, but with a clear understanding of the policies that cause urban decline and its counterpart, urban revival, the potential exists for organizing a people's movement intent on controlling work places and neighborhoods.

Although the highly acclaimed "rebirth" of Newark has worked to benefit downtown businesses, industrial interests, and Mayor Kenneth Gibson's national image, it has spelled disaster for many of Newark's residents. While some people have benefited by jobs at city hall that most likely would not have been available without the election of a Black mayor, most people have seen downtown and industrial development policies drain money away from needed human services.

Federal programs, local tax abatement and exemptions, and local budget cuts and administrative decisions have assured that gen-

Terri Suess is a researcher, writer, and organizer, formerly employed by the Newark Coalition for Neighborhoods. Currently she is a member of the Ironbound Group and Committee for Better Housing in Newark and serves on the steering committee of Organization for Community Change. Bob Cartwright has been active in Newark for over ten years and publishes a trilingual newspaper, *The Ironbound Voices*. He has been researching the economic and political structures of Newark and their effects on working-class and poor people. The authors would like to thank the following people, whose political insight, commitment, and organizing efforts made this article possible: Nancy Zak, Madelyn Hoffman, Jeanne Fortin, and members of the Ironbound Group; Mary Jo Hetzel of the Public Sector Crisis Collective; and Arlene Gieger, Jude Lamare, and Margaret and Everett Suess.

erous subsidies have gone for land acquisition, new development, and construction to build a new city for a new gentry. In fact, federal and local tax policies and budget cuts have siphoned money from public services, social services, health care, housing, employment, and transportation needs of most of the residents of the city in an attempt to reduce the size of the poor and working-class population in Newark and pave the way for an "economic revival," the return of middle and upper-middle classes.

Newark is a predominantly working-class city. The statistics show that almost 20 percent of all families in Newark fall below the poverty level and that 55 percent of all families are in low-status occupations. Out of a total of 91,140 families in the city, over 49 percent are headed by single parents, mostly women.[1] According to the 1980 census, Newark is 58 percent Black, 38 percent white, and 12 percent Hispanic. Newark lost 14 percent of its population during the last ten years, leaving it with a population of 330,104 today.

Because the needs of low- and moderate-income people in Newark have not been met by Mayor Gibson's administration, people have begun to organize in their neighborhoods, in their work places, and around specific issues—access to subsidized housing, removal of toxic wastes, property-tax issues. One organization formed to press for better conditions throughout the city was a multiracial coalition, the Newark Coalition for Neighborhoods (NCN).

People are beginning to see that subsidized economic development for business and industry, coupled with budget cuts in public programs, hurt all working-class people—Black, Hispanic, white, employed and unemployed, working women, and welfare mothers. Substantial changes must be made to move beyond piecemeal programs that throw scraps to certain groups while continuing to channel the bulk of our wealth to those who already hold the lion's share.

In Newark the struggle for decent living and working conditions is beginning to move beyond the question of race onto the question of class. With NCN as a resource and a vehicle, some organizers worked to understand where the economic and social problems in neighborhoods originate, and to develop local people's abilities, in order to call for new, comprehensive solutions that move all of us into a better situation.

As organizers and residents gain experience working together as individuals and groups, across age, race, sex, and employment differences, we are also trying to reach across neighborhood boundaries and link up with progressive organizations throughout the city, the region, and the country. We want to win more power to determine directly how we work, live, are educated, and play. To have that power, we need full access to information, and we must create collective organizations of people who can take full part in deciding how the technology and resources of this society are used. Although NCN was not the people's organization envisaged by some, it was an important step in helping to draw together more progressive groups and individuals in Newark.

Aspects of Revival

According to the Newark Economic Development Corporation, the city's revival is being funded by over $43 million in public and private investments through the federal Urban Development Action Grant program (UDAG).[2] These UDAG projects have been targeted for the downtown and industrial areas of the city, where developers put up as little as 10 per cent of their own money for new office, factory, or warehouse rehabilitation.

Government-subsidized loans provide another 10 to 20 percent of the project, and private lending institutions provide the rest at favorable terms and low interest rates. Usually, tax abatement accompanies the project plans, removing the property from the public tax rolls. A study by community researchers and students working with Tax Alternatives for Working People (TAWP) in Newark has found that over 10 percent of the total property value in Newark today is tax exempt because of Fox-Lance tax abatements granted since 1961.[3]

The loan subsidies and tax abatements generating so much investment in Newark work first to ensure developers' profits. These projects provide no guarantee of jobs for Newark people, or of jobs that are other than low-skilled, poorly paid, and dead end. Seven UDAG projects in Newark promised that over 1600 jobs would be provided by developers who received special loans and grants during the past four years. But a review of the projects showed after one year that no records were being kept of the actual number of new jobs provided and to whom. No monitoring was being done by the city planners, Newark Economic Development Corporation (NEDC), or the Department of Housing and Urban Development (HUD). In two projects where figures were kept, only 140 of 497 jobs projected actually materialized. It is questionable, however, whether these were new jobs that had any impact on Newark's high unemployment rate. There was no indication of who actually obtained the jobs, whether they were Newark residents, low-income, Black, white, Hispanic, or what percentage were women.[4] Redevelopment in the heart of the city is a blatant continuation of the 1960s urban renewal policies that drew so much criticism from Newark residents before the riots in 1967.

In the late 1960s and early 1970s, over 100 acres of land was cleared in the Central Ward to make way for establishment of the New Jersey College of Medicine and Dentistry and the expansion of Rutgers University and the New Jersey Institute of Technology. (The original plans for the medical school *alone* called for clearance of over 150 acres, but the plans were reduced because of community opposition.)[5] Other property surrounding the educational facilities was eventually burned, abandoned, cleared, and packaged for the construction of new housing and support facilities for doctors, professors, staff, and students of the newly refurbished regional education center.

Two historic districts near the colleges and the central business district—the James Street Commons and the Lincoln Park area—have been the focus for showcase rehabilitation by Newark's Housing Development and Rehabilitation Corporation, the Landmarks Preservation Commission, and the Mayor's Policy and Development Office. Black, Hispanic, and white low- and moderate-income people in the historic districts have been moved out of their homes with no guarantees of returning to the newly remodeled units.

Establishment of neighborhood strategy areas (NSAs) through the federal Community Development Block Grant program (CDBG) and the Section 8 housing program also work to enforce a policy of triage on the city's less desirable neighborhoods. In the name of targeting funds, NSA boundaries have been drawn around neighborhoods along major transportation routes close to downtown that will be convenient for professionals who hold jobs in the city—after the areas are rehabilitated and rebuilt. Other NSAs have been drawn around certain blocks with an eye toward commercial sector anchors.[6]

Who Benefits and Who Loses?

The pressing questions in Newark today are, For whom is the city being revived? For whom will city infrastructures and housing be redeveloped? For whom is industry being attracted? For whom will city budget cuts be restored and services improved?

Revival is clearly a struggle between the business, corporate, and financial community and the resident-workers of Newark. Either Newark's neighborhoods and downtown area will be redeveloped for the high-income and middle classes who can pay their own way or the present residents will find ways to fight back, reorganize the conditions that determine our lives, and stay.

Right now the scales in Newark, as in cities across the country, are tipped toward the return of the upper classes. Big business has control over local government, financial institutions, laws, and media. Newark residents, whose hope ten years ago rested with the election of a Black mayor, today have seen their best leaders co-opted.

One of the key elements in a typical U.S. urban-revival program is the forced decline of those areas slated for future renewal. It flushes things out for the next round of investment and profiteering; it is, in and of itself, a form of profiteering. And it is a horrifying process to live through.

A city's decline doesn't happen in a void. It is not caused by uncontrollable forces or by accident, as we are often led to believe. Newark's decline has happened systematically over the past twenty years. It started explosively in the Central Ward with urban renewal and spread out over the city in concentric circles. The decline was hastened by a myriad of federal, state, and local real estate policies and spending programs, followed by budget cutbacks. While residents today are experiencing a reduction of social services, private developers are receiving increased public subsidies as "investment incentives."

In the Central Ward, the Westside, the Lincoln Park area, Lower Broadway, and now in parts of the South Ward and Lower Vailsburg, we can document the effects of the same conscious policies over the past twenty years: disinvestment by businesses; redlining by banks and insurance companies; and withdrawal of city services—infrequent garbage collections, lack of street repairs, cuts in school budgets, mental health and recreation programs, and in library services and health care.

In this environment, housing is bought up cheap by absentee landlords who are allowed—through lack of code enforcement—to drain it for all it's worth. Often, buildings are torched for insurance money or abandoned to the city. What's left are large parcels of cleared land or block after block of abandoned and dilapidated housing waiting to be "packaged" and sold to investors for redevelopment.

It is an oversimplification to say that the decline of Newark, and central cities throughout the country, was caused by some vague "flight of the middle classes" to the suburbs in the postwar era. Slums and blight are the result of a wholesale economic evacuation of the city's neighborhoods, tied closely to the well-known economic incentives for people to move out if they could afford to: newly constructed highways, cheap gasoline, favorable home-mortgage interest rates, and new suburban housing stock, schools, and community facilities.

When the upper and middle classes leave an area and are replaced by lower-income working people, neighborhoods are allowed to decline, since maintaining property—commercial and residential—no longer pays. Lack of maintenance must then be countered by the persistent presence of organized people with the power to demand that their needs and wants be met.

Trading Power for Representation: Newark Today

Even though the citizens of Newark worked together to elect a Black mayor in 1970, and reelected him in 1974 and 1978, they themselves did not gain power. And conditions in most people's lives did not improve substantially. One elderly Black activist voiced the opinion of many: "I voted for Gibson three times, but if he were to run tomorrow, I wouldn't vote for him again. He brought a lot of money into Newark, but the way he handled it— it went right through his hands to big business."

Today Newark remains a city where 18 percent of the housing

stock is classified as deteriorating or dilapidated, while only 40 percent is classified as good.[7] These conditions are made worse by a .96-percent vacancy rate.[8] Almost two-thirds (64.3 percent) of students entering high school in Newark are unable to meet state standards for reading and math.[9] And while the real unemployment rate exceeds 35 percent, New Jersey State Department of Labor claims an ever-shrinking work force, so that it can project an unemployment rate continually declining from 13 percent.[10]

Not only does high unemployment persist in this city of 330,104 primarily Black and Hispanic residents, but young people are increasingly left to their own devices, with a shortage of supervised recreation facilities and programs. Since 1976 the city's recreation budget has been cut in half. These conditions, coupled with a police cutback-slowdown syndrome, have meant the response time to emergency calls often ranges from two hours to two days. In some sections of the city, people consider themselves lucky if a police officer *ever* responds to their calls for help.

The result is that many senior citizens and families are living in fear of their lives, while many young people and unemployed adults have little hope and few visions for a better future. And to make matters worse, figures show that a person convicted of a crime who is Black in New Jersey, is at least twice as likely to go to prison as a white person, and less likely to be enrolled in prison job-training programs.[11]

The average income in Newark remains 60 percent of the surrounding suburban communities, and it has been estimated that almost one-third of the city's population depends on some form of public assistance.[12]

Yet the people of Newark are paying one of the highest property-tax rates anywhere in the country—$10 per $100 of property valuation. And people occupying 22 percent of Newark's land area are carrying 98 percent of the local tax burden. During Mayor Gibson's tenure, the number of buildings subject to property tax dropped by 2646 (from 51,218 in 1968 to 48,572 in 1976), while the number of tax-exempt properties almost tripled, from 2714 (5.3 percent of the total) to 8014 (16.5 percent of the total).[13]

Not only has the City of Newark granted more tax abatements to corporations than any other city in New Jersey, TAWP researchers also found that almost 18 percent of Newark's property taxes go uncollected annually. Delinquent tax payments are held by large property owners and corporations for two years and paid at the last minute before the city begins foreclosure proceedings. On the other hand, foreclosure usually proceeds on small businesses and home owners who fall behind in their tax payments. TAWP also found in 1979 alone, over $23 million was deducted from the total value of taxable property in Newark through the tax-appeals process, resulting in a tax loss to the city of over $2 million annually. Major banks, Prudential Insurance Company, Mutual Benefit Life Insurance Company, Public Service Gas and Electric, Westinghouse, General Electric, and three major oil companies received 25 percent of all tax-appeal reductions granted in 1979.[14]

Meanwhile, the Port Authority of New York and New Jersey, which owns 21 percent of Newark's land area, pays $1 million per year in lieu of taxes on its total property valued at $1 billion.[15] If it paid a tax rate equal to Newark residents, it would contribute $43,200,000 annually to the city treasury. That would almost double Newark's local budget and go a long way toward closing the gap between human service needs and available money.

While major businesses and industries receive a variety of tax breaks, home owners and renters are left to bear the burden of city service costs. These tax breaks are clear give-aways to big business at the expense of working people when one considers that local taxes are one of the least important factors that corporate planners consider when making plant and office location decisions.

The Newark Coalition for Neighborhoods

In 1978 the NCN received two small grants, which allowed the organization to hire a staff person and set up an office in the spare room of one of the member organizations. The staff person was hired to monitor the city's Community Development Block Grant program and to help build a framework for continued research and organizing in Newark. A key task was to work with citizen-staff committees that researched citywide issues important in neighborhoods. The committees were intent on taking their findings into the community and mobilizing for action.

By building a track record in the press, on television, with posters, and leaflets, and by word of mouth through citywide actions and activities, NCN and member groups began to be seen as places where Newark people could come together to work on issues of pressing concern.

The city administration began to take the member groups of the coalition a little more seriously, and by 1980 private foundations were committed to funding ongoing work as a way to support the "neighborhood movement."

NCN has worked against arson for profit; displacement of people as a prelude to gentrification; the exacerbation of crime by police cutbacks and slowdowns; lack of employment; and lack of recreational facilities. By monitoring the Community Development Block Grant program and Urban Development Action Grants, we were able to study economic development schemes that work against the interests of most Newark residents and for the benefit of big business; we also looked at the shortage of day-care services and tried to bring together underpaid, overworked, day-care workers.

We held many committee meetings; worked with a school drama class to produce street theater about arson for profit; held a citywide speak-out against arson; and presented recommendations to the city council for policies and actions to stop the burning of neighborhoods. We held a citywide rally against crime and for recreation and jobs and followed that up with a march on City Hall.

We also brought Mass Transit Street Theater from New York City to present a play about runaway shops entitled "You've Got Nothing to Lose But Your Job." Mass Transit played to 135 people at St. Columba Neighborhood Club's Cafe Theater.

We now have a mailing list of over 1000 people and contact with ten additional block clubs, senior citizen groups, and human service organizations. We have brought issues into the local paper on more than two dozen occasions; had news stories aired on ten evening newscasts locally and twice on two New York metropolitan stations; and by the fall of 1980 NCN had been the focus of several articles in the *New York Times*.

But we have not confined ourselves to the established media. Four member groups have developed their own neighborhood newspapers, and two others have started newsletters. These have provided needed information to residents and workers in the neighborhoods, helped build neighborhood organizations capable of mobilizing people, and communicated stories of organizing successes.

As part of a strategy, organizers wrote proposals totaling $95,000 for funding various aspects of research, resource development, and organizing. This money was granted to NCN by five different foundations to meet the costs of renting an office for community meetings, workshops, films, and a print center. NCN research and outreach and ability to help people press demands became even more effective.

In addition, three locally recruited VISTA volunteers, hired through the National Association of Neighborhood's displacement project, have worked in two different neighborhoods to research and organize around displacement issues. And the Law Students Civil Rights Research Council in Atlanta, Georgia, agreed to fund up to eight work-study students from Rutgers and Seton Hall Law Schools to work with NCN and member groups.

Some of the more positive organizing efforts of NCN member groups were carried out by the St. Columba Neighborhood Club and the Ironbound Information Center. In the St. Columba neighborhood, organizers informed people of their rights under the Uniform Relocation Assistance Act. When a large developer started to rehabilitate over 200 units of housing and tried to push low-income people out of the neighborhood, residents were able to win first options on renting refurbished apartments. The struggle for decent housing continued after that, as residents had to fight to force the developer to make necessary repairs because of shoddy work and to pay money toward a long overdue electricity bill to assure service would not be terminated. Neighborhood residents also fought, unsuccessfully in this case, to prevent the closing of a neighborhood day-care center. St. Columba organizers also helped residents fight "computer mix-ups" in the emergency heating and food stamp programs that prevented people from receiving assistance. It is important to note, however, that organizing efforts at St. Columba effectively stopped once a sweat-equity program for small-scale rehabilitation was taken on as an organizational goal.

The Ironbound Information Center is one of the few coalition member groups that has consistently focused on organizing around the politics of health care, urban environmental conditions, city-service cutbacks, educational cutbacks, and industrial development. Community health activists and residents are working to force the Port Authority of New York and New Jersey to reroute low-flying planes from places where people live to industrial land and waterways. A block association and neighborhood school forced the city to have a private developer board up an abandoned 400-unit apartment complex in the neighborhood before rehabilitation proposals were granted. Now people who had been forced to leave the building several years ago are fighting for the right to move back into apartments when they are rehabilitated. They have also forced the developer to increase the number of large-family units in the project. Another block association is fighting attempts by industrialists and the housing authority to change the zoning in their area and take their homes.

In more than one NCN member group, work on concrete issues stopped when public and private funding for staff was cut and when private foundations funded groups to hire agency directors to write grants for small-scale neighborhood housing rehabilitation projects and light services. These groups then brought a few similar service-provider and sweat-equity oriented organizations into NCN as new members, changing the character of the board. This had far-reaching effects for NCN and helped set the stage for dismantling it as a community resource center capable of supporting serious organizing efforts.

Limits and Future Possibilities

There were clear splits within NCN from the beginning. On one side there were organizers, community residents, and progressive staff members who wanted to use NCN as a vehicle for people to put forth class-conscious demands relating to economic issues in Newark—city budget cuts, federal spending, tax policies, arson-for-profit, poor housing conditions, and dead-end jobs at low pay. On the other side were the service providers who were intent on organizational maintenance. Their main interests were in obtaining the next grant so they could continue to provide a very low level of service to the community while employing a few residents or rehabilitating a handful of housing units as showpieces.

Initially, the service providers were behaving in contradictory ways, thus enabling NCN to form and provide resources to activists, grass-roots groups, and rank-and-file trade unionists. On the one hand they were trying to protect their piece of the pie and continue to receive some funding for community-service programs, and on the other hand they agreed to a more progressive and activist organizing program.

When research done by NCN staff began to be used by community and working people, however, it was made clear that governmental bodies, corporate executives, and foundation directors were willing to support social-service and community housing developers' efforts to provide services at a very low level, but opposed attempts to implement a more comprehensive political strategy.

As detailed above, this strategy included both putting forth an overall economic and political analysis of Newark and organizing large numbers of people around political issues that related to residents' everyday lives: arson-for-profit, cuts in recreation and other city services, zoning changes, tax policies, federal and city spending that gave large subsidies to big corporations while taking away programs that benefited working people, and so forth.

The response of the elite convinced NCN board members that they could not both work with the politicians and executives and with the poor and working class of Newark. Most chose the former. This meant that a majority of the board took steps in the winter of 1980 to dismantle the NCN office and staff. Community groups and rank-and-file trade union people were barred from using printing equipment, typewriters, supplies, phone, and meeting space that were initially available to them at NCN. The Anti-Arson Project was frozen. Research documenting arson schemes has been prevented from being disseminated. Core staff people were either forced out or quit in frustration.

These steps to dismantle NCN were taken by a majority of the board as a direct response to foundation sources who indicated there would be no more money for NCN until "it agrees to compromise with the business community." Funds from that source and others were withheld pending removal of staff and the hiring of an executive director.

In the future, the NCN board plans to reopen the office as a local center for technical assistance for so-called community leaders' projects in the field of housing. The main emphasis is to be on sweat equity and other irrelevant small-scale housing projects.

This sequence of events has unfolded at the same time as the announcement of "Renaissance Newark"—a plan by the corporate, financial, and governmental elite to profitably make use of the land in and around downtown which was taken from those who lived there. We have described this process and called it displacement. Perhaps we should have termed it "The Great Newark Land Grab."

In the last six months, Mutual Benefit has announced that it will apply for tax abatement on a new $30-million office building in downtown Newark; Prudential has purchased an option on land near Newark's Penn Station (one of two railroads stations in Newark which have recently been awarded millions of dollars for rehabilitation), and it has also submitted a UDAG application for a parking garage for Gateway III, a proposed office complex on the site. A consortium of major corporations has purchased land at the other end of downtown, near the Erie Lackawana Railroad Station (also slated for rehabilitation) for a proposed 18-story office building. They have received a tax abatement and a UDAG grant for this project. A number of other similar projects are on the drawing boards of major corporations, who are now rebuilding the city they helped destroy. Only this time they will have more control over how it is built and more power to determine who will live and work here.

One of the most grandiose plans being discussed is one that includes Prudential and others as purchasers of a large part of Newark's Central Ward including two major housing projects. In addition, statements have been made by managers of other public housing projects that private developers are considering purchasing the buildings, rehabilitating them with public subsidies, and selling them as condominiums or cooperatives. Public housing could very well be turned over to private housing now because mortgages on the projects are being paid off.

We find it ironic that NCN was effectively dismantled as a community resource which helped residents and workers raise serious economic and political questions and voice their demands, while at the same time the corporate elite was solidifying its own plans for redeveloping Newark.

The staff of an organization in Washington, D.C., however, that funded the original salaried staff position at NCN for monitoring the Community Development Block Grant program was furious that the NCN board reneged on its commitment to actually use the results of the monitoring and carry out the terms of its contract.

The CDBG research which had been used by a variety of workplace and grass-roots community activists served as a focal point, then for a new alliance. The Washington funding source refused to re-fund NCN and instead gave a $10,000 contract to a new group called Organization for Community Change (OCC). The new group is comprised of organizers, community residents, and workers who came together while using NCN resources, staff, and meeting space—Black Workers, Committee for Better Housing, and the Ironbound Group. Through OCC the grant will allow for the purchase of essential machines, meeting space, telephone, and supplies to enable each organization to continue with its work of creating grass-roots and worker-controlled organizations capable of changing the conditions under which we live.

From our experiences with NCN it has become clear that if we are to make decisions for ourselves as workers and community residents and to frame our own demands, many people must have the skills, the time, and the right to acquire information, to understand its implications, to share information with others, and to make decisions based on that information. We must prevent "experts," "professionals," and "leaders" who have gone through a process of acquiring a title from intimidating others. Rather, we must find ways for many people with special insights and experiences to offer their ideas and skills.

During the course of our organizing, if we are really to change social relationships, we must develop the capability of as many people as possible to be critical, constructive, and confident thinkers—people who are able to create short- and long-term strategies for action. As people work on issues, consciousness is raised about conditions in our lives and about our rights. And most importantly, we help each other understand that we are not alone as we face problems and begin to develop a class analysis of how and why events occur.

As we work to build a larger movement, it is essential that we take direct action wherever possible. Organized people are powerful and cause change. Individuals and agency directors negotiating for those who are not informed, involved, or committed do not win lasting victories, nor do they build our collective power.

From our recent past experiences in Newark it is clear that if a collective process and development of a political consciousness is totally sacrificed to efficiency, cost-effectiveness, and short-sighted strategies of winning ever-shrinking portions of the economic pie, nothing in people's lives will really change. In fact, conditions of oppression will become worse. People working in Newark have been able to move some of these ideas forward in the past years with some small successes. The process, however, is one of long-term commitment to education, action, and the evolution of organizations.

Notes

1. *Annual Implementation Plan 1980*, Regional Health Planning Council of Essex, Morris, Union, Warren, and Sussex Counties, New Jersey, p. B-6, Table 2.

2. Newark received $11 million in federal Urban Development Action Grants that "leveraged" $32 million additional investments in 1979. UDAG money to Newark projects represents 12 percent of all federal money available under the program in 1979. See Thomas Bach and Joel Fraiser, "The Urban Development Action Grant Program: Despite Much Criticism, It's Been An Effective Tool," *The Daily Bond Buyer*, Special Conference Supplement No. 1, June 4, 1979.
3. Under New Jersey's Fox-Lance tax abatement program, one of the first of such programs legislated in the country, corporations building new plants or office buildings must pay either 15 percent of gross revenues or 2 percent of the project cost plus annual land taxes. They are relieved from paying taxes on assessed value of newly constructed properties.
4. Camilla Baker, "Does Economic Development through CDBG/UDAG Mean Jobs for Newark People?" (Paper prepared in August 1980 by a legal intern with NCN through a grant from the Law Students Civil Rights Research Council, Atlanta, Georgia.)
5. Ron Porambo, *No Cause for Indictment: an Autopsy of Newark* (New York: Holt, Rinehart & Winston, 1971). See also *Report of National Advisory Commission on Civil Disorders* (New York: Bantam Books, 1968), chap. 4.
6. *Newark Community Development Block Grant Application, 1979*, Mayor's Policy and Development Office (MPDO), 2 Cedar Street, Newark, N.J.
7. *Newark Master Plan, 1977*, MPDO.
8. *Newark Community Development Block Grant Application, 1979*, op. cit.
9. Paul L. Tractenberg, "Pupil Performance in Basic Skills in the Newark School System Since 1967." (Paper presented at a conference at New Jersey Institute of Technology "Newark: Ten Years After," October 1977.)
10. Based on figures from Newark's *Overall Economic Development Plan, 1978*, MPDO. Estimated labor force, 219,509; estimated employed, 142,150; unemployed, 77,359.
11. *New Jersey State Department of Corrections Annual Report, 1978*. In New Jersey, Black men make up 65 percent of the male prison population; Black women make up 77 percent of the female prison population. Prison training school enrollment dropped from 68 to 61 percent for incarcerated Black people from 1970 to 1975.
12. *Overall Economic Development Plan, 1978*, op. cit.
13. Stanley B. Winters, "Turbulent Decade: Newark Since the Riots." (Paper presented at a conference at New Jersey Institute of Technology "Newark Ten Years After," October 1977.)
14. "Taxes Fact Sheet," prepared by Madelyn Hoffman of Tax Alternatives for Working People, November 1980. Available through Ironbound Information Center, 95 Fleming Ave., Newark, N.J. 07105.

15. A study done by Associated Survey Company of Wayne, New Jersey, for the City of Elizabeth in 1976 said that the Port Authority of New York and New Jersey properties in Elizabeth were worth $400 million and that Port Authority properties in Newark were worth 2.5 times that amount—or $1 billion.

11. Welfare Rights: Organizing in Massachusetts

Beryl Minkle

The Coalition for Basic Human Needs

The mass welfare-rights movement that emerged and flourished during the 1960s was a casualty of the increasing antagonisms and co-optation characteristic of the mid 1970s. However, in the face of Nixon-era repression, the absorption of militant leadership into service programs, massive cutbacks under Governor Dukakis's administration, and attacks on the rights of women and minorities, welfare-rights organizing managed to continue on a local basis throughout the state. The 1970s witnessed an erosion of benefits and rights fought for in the previous decade and was a time for protecting hard-won entitlements; of necessity, the 1980s must see a resurgence of mass welfare-rights organizing, linked to broadly based coalition building. To counter the social-austerity solutions of the New Right, welfare recipients, low-income working people, and their advocates must continue the struggle for benefits and build a mass movement that would go beyond the issue-oriented efforts of the 1960s to challenge the capitalist class-based policies of the federal government.

As cutbacks in the welfare budget occur more frequently in the wake of economic recession, rising unemployment, and the energy

Beryl Minkle is a social worker at Children's Community Corner, Chelsea, which is affiliated with Associated Day Care Services of Metropolitan Boston. She is a member of UAW-District 65 and a contract negotiator and steward for the center. Special thanks to John Brouder, Frank Brusinski, Janet Diamond, Joanne Gates, and Paula Georges for their information and assistance in preparing this article.

crisis, and so-called tax-relief plans are proposed as solutions on federal and state levels, the poor and minorities are stepping up activities to protect their diminishing rights. The formation of the Coalition for Basic Human Needs (CBHN) marks a resurgence of a nonpartisan, grass-roots effort to build a movement that can represent recipients and low-income working people in Massachusetts. CBHN chapters are located in twenty-three cities throughout the state: Boston, Quincy, North Shore, Framingham, Haverhill, Gloucester, Medford, Gardner, Greenfield, Pittsfield, North Adams, Northampton, Lynn, Cambridge, Somerville, Cape Cod/ South Shore, Fall River/New Bedford, Brockton, Lawrence/Lowell, Leominster, Worcester, Dorchester, Attleboro, and Springfield. There are also three CBHN college chapters located in the Boston area, at the University of Massachusetts Harbor and Park Square campuses, Bunker Hill Community College, and Roxbury Community College. Each chapter elects a representative to attend monthly CBHN policy board meetings.

Welfare Cutbacks

The CBHN takes its name from the Springfield Coalition for Basic Human Needs, a neighborhood-based welfare-rights organization affiliated with the local Community Action Program (CAP) agency in that area. The CBHN first appeared as a group in February 1979 at the state hearing of the Human Services Coalition. After the hearing, the newly formed coalition made a number of unsuccessful attempts to discuss with Governor King the emergency-assistance cutbacks and the proposed cut in the 6-percent cost-of-living welfare increase. Finally, in March 1979 the tragic deaths of six members of the Ramon family in Dorchester catalyzed a protest march to the State House and a sit-in at the governor's office. The Ramon family's fuel deliveries had been cut off when they could no longer afford to pay and their emergency assistance allotment had been used up. Their apartment caught fire when the toaster and space heater they were using for heat blew a fuse.

The march and sit-in united Black, Hispanic, and white recipients and activists in common struggle and demands for welfare entitlements and reform. During a later confrontation with CBHN members outside Lieutenant Governor Thomas O'Neill's office, Mrs.

Lillie Landrum, a leader of Massachusetts Welfare Recipients for Welfare Reform (MWRWR) and a spokeswoman for the CBHN, explained what the current welfare stipend meant to recipients.

> Let me tell you what we get . . . we get $90 for rent, but the average rent is $140. We get an allowance of $25 a month for heat, enough to buy about 50 gallons of oil. We get $16 for gas and light, but that costs $33. A family of four gets $125 for food and clothing. When we buy food, we can't afford clothes. If we don't buy food or clothes, maybe we can buy oil.

Lieutenant Governor O'Neill publicly stated his dissatisfaction with the governor's welfare policies, and his remarks were quoted in the *Boston Globe* the next day.

The CBHN also pursued meetings with administration officials, including Human Services Secretary Charles Mahoney and House Ways and Means Committee Chairman John Finnegan. The meetings with Mahoney and Finnegan finally took place after lengthy negotiations about location, time, and the number of coalition members who could attend the meeting. The coalition refused to send a delegation and instead decided that the entire CBHN should observe while a small group of representative speakers discussed the issues with the officials. The officials accepted this format and the meetings were well organized and orderly. The CBHN eventually met with state government resistance in April 1979, when members of the coalition were not allowed admittance into the House Gallery to observe testimony on the welfare budget and were actually thrown on the ground by guards.

Under the pretense of providing for only the "truly needy," the King administration engineered budget cuts that pitted low-income working people against welfare recipients and further reduced actual benefits to recipients. The cost-of-living increment passed by the legislature included a 2 percent increase retroactive to January 1979 and a 4 percent increase retroactive to July 1979, both to be paid in January 1980. This increase would have amounted to $34 million to welfare recipients. It was vetoed by Governor King.

In addition to blocking the cost-of-living increase, King proposed nearly scrapping the emergency-assistance payments program. His plan would have reduced the number of eligible recipients from 122,000 to 65,000 and reinforced Department of Public Welfare restrictions, making it impossible for recipients to purchase needed fuel, food, or clothing. To justify these cutbacks, King launched an antifraud campaign, in an attempt to confirm widely held myths about the thousands of "welfare cheaters" who are exploiting the subsidy system.

On June 9, 1979, the CBHN and seventy other state organizations co-sponsored a Boston march and rally as the "Coalition to Oppose King's Budget Priorities." The thrust of this event, which drew approximately 500 people to the Boston Common, was to challenge the administration's spending priorities, which had nearly eliminated funding and services to poor and working people in Massachusetts. The rally drew together welfare recipients, students, day-care workers, women's rights activists, state workers, antinuclear activists, the elderly, Third World groups, and members of religious organizations throughout the state. The four demands at the rally were:

1. Support for all human services
2. No layoffs of state and city employees
3. A moratorium on nuclear power plant construction and licensing
4. Support for affirmative action

The overall theme of the rally was the need for cooperation and coalition-building to effectively fight the oppressive economic plans and programs promulgated by government and big business.

As a result of active organizing to fight the cuts, the CBHN was able to claim a victory in gaining the 6 percent cost-of-living increase and assurances of a reinstatement of the more adequate July 1978 emergency-assistance program. Although the *Boston Globe* tried to explain the victories as signs of the governor's liberalism, credit must be given to the welfare-rights groups within the CBHN which fought to win the entitlements.

With the intensification of the fiscal crisis, recipients and workers are now waging a more defensive struggle to retain present benefit levels rather than pressuring for increases. The CBHN and over thirty co-sponsoring organizations met again on the Boston Common on May 9, 1981, to protest the devastating cuts to human services and increases in the defense budget proposed by President Reagan. This rally, planned by the ad hoc Massachusetts Coalition for a Fair Budget (in conjunction with the national Anti-Hunger Coalition, which sponsored similar rallies on the same day across the United States), also drew 500 people, including recipients, union members, religious groups, Third World and women's organizations, students, the elderly, mental-health workers, welfare advocates, and others.

For the past two years the CBHN has fought threatened cuts in the food-stamp program. On July 11, 1979, over 300 people from throughout New England attended a CBHN-sponsored rally at the regional office of the U.S. Department of Agriculture in Burlington, Vermont. Recipients were opposed to new regulations which did not take into account the higher energy and food costs faced by New England residents. Under the new regulations, applicants would no longer be able to deduct actual shelter expenses from their income. People with higher shelter costs, including low-income working people and recipients, would be ineligible or have their food-stamp benefits reduced. Since this rally, the CBHN won some of its demands. The cap on shelter and medical deductions has been lifted for the elderly and disabled.

Problems around food stamps increased in May 1980 when federal funds were short because of a sharp rise in unemployment and inflation. Over 1100 recipients across the state turned out for demonstrations. The CBHN joined other groups across the country to demonstrate against "Foodless June." In Boston, 300 recipients, mostly women and children, demonstrated at the JFK Federal Building; 400 people, many from the Hispanic community, marched through Springfield, demanding "Jobs or Food Stamps." Other smaller protests were held in New Bedford, Leominster, Fitchburg, Pittsfield, North Adams, Northhampton, and Greenfield. The results of these mass demonstrations were guarantees of full benefits until the end of the fiscal year.

In the wake of Proposition 2 1/2, CBHN organized the only statewide voter-registration campaign of welfare recipients and other low-income citizens in recent years. Although the tax-cut proposal passed, the drive forged new alliances with the Legal Services Corporation and other advocacy groups and succeeded in reaching many recipients and low-income people who were previously unaware of the coalition.

The coalition has learned that victories and gains in welfare rights are often short-lived and results ephemeral because of lack of legislative commitment to progressive welfare reform. Entitlements that were fought for and won disappear too easily at the whim of the political administration, necessitating ongoing organizing and struggle.

In June 1979, it seemed certain that the CBHN's struggles had paid off in getting the legislature to remove the restrictive recipient-status rule (which made AFDC recipients ineligible for rent and utility arrearage payments) and to mandate the Department of Public Welfare to implement a more adequate emergency-assistance (EA) program. However, in October 1979, the DPW issued new EA regulations that did not embody the actual recipient-status rule but did contain new regulations that were discriminatory and restrictive to welfare recipients. As in the past, coalition members appealed through all channels available to legislators to reinstate the EA regulations of July 1978. They met with representatives to draft legislation, held press conferences, arranged meetings with administrators and testified at public hearings. At the close of the year's legislative session, it became clear that no EA program was forthcoming. Ironically, legislators had voted themselves $20,000 in pay raises. When Secretary Mahoney then refused to meet with coalition members, seventeen women, most of them welfare mothers, decided to stay outside his office at the State House and be arrested, rather than return home to the same conditions under which they and their children had been living for the past year.

The women were later tried and found guilty of trespassing. A disorderly conduct charge was dismissed, and the judge ordered the cases filed for thirty days and then sealed. None of the women had ever been arrested before, and in the words of Susan Moir, one of the seventeen women:

> Any action, including getting arrested, is worth it to make the fact known that this state government is making decisions that will lead to severe hardship for thousands of women, children, and disabled people this winter.

Amy Tillem, another of the women, had this to say:

> I know of children who get real sick because of inadequate heat. I know many women who have been told there is no EA program at all. We have to take our fate into our own hands. And if that means coming to the State House to challenge the cold-hearted and bourgeois policies of cold-hearted and bourgeois legislators to the point of being arrested, so be it. If waiting to confront the men who are playing with the lives of thousands of people for political and economic gain is trespassing, then we are guilty. But it's not and we are not.

Subsequent to this action, on November 8, 1979, the Department of Public Welfare reinstated a severely limited arrearage program, and on the following day the DPW held a public hearing on these revised regulations. The CBHN delivered testimony on the need for reinstatement of the July 1978 emergency-assistance program and then walked out of the hearing, criticizing it as a sham.

Constituency of the CBHN

The CBHN is attempting to solidify links with other welfare-rights groups in Massachusetts, including Massachusetts Welfare Recipients for Welfare Reform, the Massachusetts Welfare Rights Organization, Massachusetts Coalition Against Workfare, North Shore Welfare Rights, as well as various grass-roots tenants and welfare-rights groups, and Third World and women's groups.

This current welfare-rights movement is developing in a decade whose conditions differ from those of the 1960s. While the 1960s were a period of economic boom, the 1970s and 1980s have witnessed an economic crisis. Civil-rights movements are less active than they were in the 1960s, and the rise of the Ku Klux Klan and right-wing movements threatens more divisiveness and factionalization within neighborhoods and communities. The same numbers of people, active militancy, and media attention are not present. The movement, which is building itself upon the foundations of the past, must adapt its strategies and tactics to present conditions. While actual organizing work has been ongoing at the local level, the CBHN had relied upon advocacy organizations for material resources and paid staff. With the recent defunding of the latest parent organization (March 1981), Massachusetts Community Action (MCA), by the Federal Community Services Administration, the coalition has maintained itself independently, relying on private grants (primarily from the Campaign for Human Development) and supportive assistance from the Legal Services Corporation, the Policy Training Center, and the Boston Women's Commission in Exile. MCA was instrumental in writing the present grant. The change in funding instigated a change in organizational structure so that all members and staff of CBHN are, or recently were, welfare recipients.

The usual strategy for organizing a CBHN chapter involves contacting veterans of previous welfare-rights movements and going door-to-door, campaigning in housing projects, day-care centers, legal-service agencies, community centers, and welfare offices informing people of their welfare benefits and the nature of the most recent cutbacks. The CBHN has focused on winning access to tangible benefits by organizing mass benefit campaigns around special grants. Emergency-assistance cutbacks were taken up by the CBHN as an issue to initiate a statewide campaign, given the importance and impact of fuel-assistance payments. It was seen as an issue that would draw out great numbers of people thus giving the campaign some chance to effect change.

Since the members of CBHN are white and Third World women, there is a keen awareness of the ways that institutional sexism and racism forces women onto welfare, and of the social and cultural conditioning that keeps women down. To counter this oppression, the CBHN incorporates self-help and nonhierarchical processes in statewide decision-making and planning. Local groups remain autonomous in building their own chapters and concentrating their energies on their own immediate issues while continuing to coordinate with the larger coalition.

The CBHN aims to become an effective voice in defending and improving the living conditions of people in Massachusetts and sees its purpose as:

1. Working toward greater democratic control including affirmative action in all of the institutions that affect people's basic human needs;
2. Planning campaigns which (a) win change; (b) involve large numbers of people in the resolution of an issue; (c) develop and support community leadership and local organizations;
3. Pressuring national, state, and local officials on legislation or administrative change affecting basic human needs through grass-roots organizing efforts;
4. Uniting with other groups that suffer under the regressive policies of state and federal administrations, so as not to allow one group to be pitted against another;
5. Publicizing and distributing fact sheets and alerts to our membership and supporters; serving as an information center to avoid duplication of effort;
6. Educating the public on the real situation and needs of low-income people and welfare recipients;
7. Working toward a guarantee of jobs or income: (a) jobs for all who are willing and able to work, coupled with a massive

training program at full pay, union scales; (b) guaranteed annual income with protection for the individual rights and dignity for the recipients. Opposing all forms of "workfare," which forces the poor to slave and scab for an income;

8. Protecting poor women's right to choice and defending against abusive sterilization.

Goals of the CBHN

On a concrete level, a long-term goal of the organization is an examination of the welfare system and its programs to discover which benefits actually do exist, and which are difficult to take advantage of because of eligibility restrictions. Another goal is to make people aware of how organizing can pay off.

While the coalition is building itself upon the foundations of past efforts, it is also forging new alliances with individuals and groups and developing a common analysis of the nature of state and federal government budget priorities. A long-term goal of the CBHN is to expose the fundamental weaknesses of the economic system and to examine the ways in which the system brings crises in the public and private sector upon itself, that is, capitalism's need for cycles of unemployment and marginal employment. The antiworkfare drive of the early 1970s (against Governor Dukakis's plan to force welfare fathers into temporary, unskilled jobs offering no career advancement, job security, workers' rights, or wage benefits other than a welfare check) sought to clarify these links. The CBHN also points out the way in which King's tax-relief programs simply pit low- and middle-income groups against the poor, by cutting back on human services that benefit both the poor and the working classes. A main issue here is cutting out "welfare" for the corporations and eliminating tax loopholes for the rich, instead of focusing on "fraud" among welfare recipients. Such analyses demonstrate how the welfare system demoralizes recipients and tries to keep them in their place. It examines how the meager welfare handouts have historically been offered as appeasements to angry recipients, and how CETA and WIN job-training programs are deliberately designed to be stop-gap and short-term measures, promising jobs at the end but not being able to deliver because of the system's dependence upon a marginal labor force. This line of analysis could serve as a basis for further linking the welfare movement to other working-class struggles.

Obstacles and Allies

The CBHN has run up against some of the same conflicts that traditionally arise in welfare-rights organizing campaigns. While some politicians are allies to the drive, there is often a struggle with liberal politicians who are uncomfortable with confrontation strategies and will work more easily with the coalition when its groups lobby for support on an issue.

There has been a lack of cooperation in general with the trade unions, which are largely isolated from women's and minority-group issues. Most unions do not take stands on issues that are not supported by their membership, and medicaid funding for abortions or busing, for example, are not popular issues in most trade unions. It is the rare trade union that sees itself as organizing the unorganized, since the prime concern of most unions is job protection, which often stands in the way of giving all-out support for CETA employees, even those who have joined unions. Some unions resent the work-eligible welfare recipients, who they see as benefiting from both welfare and a job. Oftentimes, workers who are the most antiwelfare fear that they too may be laid off and forced onto welfare to survive.

In the face of this, it was a hopeful sign to find allies among some of the more progressive trade unions. Among those endorsing the CBHN-sponsored rallies were Locals 8744 and 2431 of the United Steelworkers of America, the Greater Boston Legal Services Attorneys Union, the American Federation of Government Employees, the Service Employees International Union (SEIU), AFSCME hospital workers from Local 470, and District 65 of the UAW. District 65 is committed to organizing day-care workers, women workers, and minorities and fighting for work-place control and job-security issues concerning public sector employees.

In addition to the traditional antagonisms between welfare recipients and low-income workers, there is also conflict between caseworkers and welfare recipients, both of whom exist at the bottom of the wage ladder. Often caseworkers are untrained, earning little more than the recipients, without the support systems within the department to help them deal with the pressures of the job. Workers with overwhelming case loads who are trying to do a good job but are frustrated by the lack of resources they can offer clients often either "burn out" and quit or become angry and bitter about their work and take it out on their clients. A few manage to create opportunities for positive client contact, and some, with the support of sensitive, trained supervisors, may become strong advocates for recipients. Radical social-service workers who are fed up with attempting to do casework on an individual basis advocate for their clients as a class through community organizing and by fighting oppressive welfare policies and governmental intrusion into recipients' personal data and private lives. Although the opportunities for organizing do not exist as much as they did during the 1960s, progressive social workers are working as activists alongside recipients, supporting each other at meetings, rallies, and public hearings.

Groups such as the Boston Jobs Coalition (BJC) are currently organizing unemployed people. While their first goal is to establish a stable organization, a staff person discussed the long-range possibility of bringing low-income workers and welfare recipients together into a movement to fight workfare and other union-busting tactics. However, there are presently not enough resources to do more than support welfare-rights activity from the sidelines.

It is still very difficult to overcome some of the obstacles which are endemic to organizing welfare recipients, and the CBHN struggles with them, as have other movements in the past. Some of these obstacles are as follows:

1. For very poor people, survival is the first priority, and there is usually not much energy left for fighting a more abstract struggle once tangible benefits have been won.
2. There are usually frequent crises in poor people's lives because of the lack of necessary resources, such as quality emergency housing in the event of a fire, flood, domestic violence, lack of money for fuel bills and emergencies, job instability, etc.
3. People feel stigmatized by being on welfare and don't want to be identified as such. Also, they may not want to get involved because they may be working a job "under the table" to make ends meet and don't want to be singled out or labeled a "fraud."

4. Most welfare recipients are single mothers coping with their children's needs and problems, leaving little time and energy for other commitments.
5. A number of welfare recipients are members of immigrant groups who may hesitate to join a welfare-rights movement because of language or cultural barriers, as well as fears of being publicly identified as a recipient or a radical.
6. An individual may be afraid of joining a movement or going to a rally because of lack of previous experience and peer support.

The problems left-liberal groups have in dealing with racism makes coalition-building more difficult unless racism is addressed as a first priority. By not supporting affirmative action for minorities, welfare rights as a feminist issue, or desegregation for fear of alienating their white home-owner constituencies, organizers alienate themselves from the welfare-rights network and potential support that could be gained through collaborative actions.

Anyone who has worked with coalitions is aware of the inherent difficulties, as well as the rewards, of this type of work. The CBHN, like any other such organization, must grapple with conflicts of strategy; issues of group autonomy versus collective decision making; class, educational, language, cultural, and racial differences that shape attitudes and behaviors; constituency and "turf"; and so forth. Dealing with one or the other of these issues is an ongoing and necessary process.

Conclusion

The CBHN may signal the resurgence of an organized, mass welfare-rights movement beginning to take shape in Massachusetts. Its organizers admit that there is a lot to learn from past efforts and a need to struggle with a coalition approach, which requires compromise and cooperation among various points of view.

With the recession and fewer economic concessions from the government, short-term and long-term strategies for winning benefits must include ways of building morale and avoiding burn-out. The use of small support groups and the emphasis on self-help and a nonhierarchical structure within the coalition will probably further this process.

Many recipients have learned the value of organizing and fighting for their rights from the efforts of past groups, and as people continue to get hit with more and more cutbacks, they will use their organizations and the coalition to fight back. Having experienced some victories as a result of their struggles, people will continue to assert themselves to gain rights and have some belief in their capacity to alter the situation around them. In the 1980s it is likely that activism among women and Blacks will increase, as they were the hardest-hit groups during the 1970s. There is now more public awareness of the pressures on single mothers, and organizing is geared toward obtaining more day care for children. A great number of the issues raised as recipients' rights are also those taken up by feminists, providing support from the larger women's community on behalf of welfare recipients. Blacks across the country are reconsolidating their efforts to fight the racist attacks from the right. The issues raised by the Mel King mayoral campaign—community empowerment, public housing, decentralization of city administration, desegregation, and decent employment— will not just go away. Blacks, the unemployed, the working poor, and welfare recipients are beginning to recognize their mutual self-interests and join in coalitions to fight common issues together as a class. There is a great need, and a great potential for a group such as the Coalition for Basic Human Needs to join with other related struggles and to grow in numbers and strength. This process has just begun.

12. Repressive Welfare

Downtown Welfare Advocacy Center

Long ago Mr. Buckle, who was a great philosopher and historian, collected facts, and he showed that the number of people who are arrested increased just as the price of food increased. When they put up the price of gas ten cents a thousand, I do not know who will go to jail, but I know that a certain number of people will go. When the meat combine raises the price of beef, I do not know who is going to jail, but I know that a large number of people are bound to go. Whenever Standard Oil Company raises the price of oil, I know that a certain number of girls who are seamstresses, and who work [night] after night long hours for somebody else, will be compelled to go out on the streets and ply another trade, and I know that Mr. Rockefeller and his associates are responsible and not the poor girls in jail.

First and last, people are sent to jail because they are poor.

—Clarence Darrow, 1902[1]

Downtown Welfare Advocacy Center was started in 1974 by New York City welfare mothers; it is a nonprofit organization dedicated to protecting and expanding the rights of welfare recipients and other low-income people. DWAC sponsors the Redistribute America Movement (RAM), New York's statewide welfare-rights group with 5000 members, predominantly welfare mothers. Our goals are: (1) to contribute to the development of a broad-based movement concerned with the issues of people's needs and right to survive, including the right to an adequate income; and (2) to inform and counsel poor people on all the organizations, services, and entitlements available to them; to train recipients in methods of self-advocacy; and to advocate for them when necessary. DWAC is located at 853 Broadway, Room 1105, New York, N.Y. 10003.

As in:

- Joel Dolkart, a lawyer and a director of Gulf and Western, who stole $2.5 million from two law firms. He got a suspended sentence.
- Yankee president and executive George Steinbrenner, who was indicted on fourteen felony counts, including coercing his own employees to lie to the FBI. He ended up pleading guilty to two counts and paying a $15,000 fine.
- Vice-President Spiro Agnew, who pleaded "no contest" to an indictment for accepting cash bribes in the White House. He never saw the inside of a jail for even one minute.
- In 1976 the Allied Chemical Corporation, which pleaded "no contest" to civil charges that it dumped large amounts of the toxic chemical Kepone into the James River in Virginia. Hundreds, possibly thousands, of citizens were made sick, but no one from the corporation was prosecuted. It is estimated that it will cost $8 billion to clean up the contamination.[2]
- A woman in Austin, Texas, was sentenced to life in prison for $925 worth of "welfare fraud." (The *annual* welfare payment, including rent, to a family of four in Texas is approximately $1600.)

We, the poor, continue to be mugged and slandered every step of the way. We can't afford meat, so we've turned to pet food. We have been mugged by the utility monsters, who gobble our last dollars even as they are cutting off our electricity. We have been mugged by the slumlords, who rent us rat-infested, heatless shelters with lead-poisoned paint, and who kick us out to renovate for higher-paying customers. We have been locked into welfare prison from which there are few escape hatches other than physical jail cells. We have been mugged by the "land of opportunity," which gives us two chances: *none* and *slim*.

We have been slandered by the "free press,"—the press that is free to publish articles on our laziness, our lack of responsibility, our predilection to welfare fraud, and our stupidity, the same free press that ignores our outcries for justice and jobs, mercy and mobility. We have been slandered out of existence by our government, which doesn't even include us in its unemployment statistics. We age faster and die younger than our wealthier counterparts, and when our children freeze or starve to death, the real causes are hidden behind the label "failure to thrive."

We are slandered by our social workers, who want to teach us how to budget our money even as they complain that their own salaries are too little to live on. We are mugged and slandered by self-proclaimed progressives who flock by the tens of thousands to protest nuclear energy and ask why the poor "don't get involved." Yet where are they when we demonstrate to keep from freezing to death in the winter? (Yes, people still do freeze to death.) We are mugged by the women's movement which pulls out the troops to defend our right to medicaid abortion and disappears when we organize to feed the children we've already got. ERA for whom? We are last on every employer's list until there's a war, when we shift quickly into first place—first to kill or be killed.

The English poor laws of the 1600s shaped the system of relief in Western society. They were specifically developed as a response to uprisings by hoards of beggars who had become landless and homeless as a result of prevailing economic power plays and war. Even then, the poor were primarily women, often widowed, and their children. The attitudes that dominate American welfare policy are essentially the same, namely:

1. Poverty is really a commentary on the personal inadequacy of the poor. Poverty as a function of the social system itself is not really considered, and therefore not really acted upon.
2. There are two categories of poor: the "deserving" poor, such as the aged or disabled, and the "undeserving" poor, such as the "ablebodied."
3. Even though grants to the deserving poor came with less stigma, both categories must be kept low enough to encourage people to leave the welfare system and discourage others from entering that system.
4. "Employable" people must be forced to work, no matter what the conditions of work or the value of such work.
5. To avoid work, people will move in droves to different localities to get something for nothing.
6. The poor are always immorally "conning" the system and shouldn't be assisted too easily—hence the increasingly complex eligibility and recertification requirements.
7. Most importantly, support for human needs and basic justice to the poor are never the real motivation for relief. Relief is

measured not by individual needs but by how much (or little) is necessary to maintain social order.

This poor-law philosophy fit in well with the American notion of laissez faire. Until the depression, the hands-off-the-poor policy of the federal government assumed that if you leave people alone, the best will go to the top and the unfit will fall to the bottom. Before the 1930s, some states had welfare pensions for the aged, blind, and widowed. However, in fourteen of the states that did have welfare, recipients were clearly identified as second-class citizens and were denied the right to vote.

The depression, of course, delivered new hoards of "beggars" to the bottom; former middle- and working-class people suddenly found themselves unemployed, needy, and without an adequate assistance program to accommodate their needs. Massive poor-people's organizations developed and with them the notion that the system had failed, not the individual. Demonstrations and riots delivered a new fear to the oligarchy, and lickety-split, in less than a decade, the present welfare state emerged in the form of the Social Security Act of 1935. The actual provisions of it were minimal and still left millions without coverage, reflecting the *least* that could be done (so as to avoid arousing too much opposition from the remaining "taxpayers"). World War II delivered economic prosperity to many. Time and a fair amount of propaganda brought back the concept of the undeserving poor in the form of the lazy, good-for-nothing, welfare cheat.

The civil rights movement in the 1960s helped spawn the National Welfare Rights Organization (NWRO), which for a time put the blame back on the system. Some concessions trickled down, and many thousands (if not millions) of poor people began to get at least some of the rights to which they were entitled from a system that was still blatantly failing minorities and women.

By the early 1970s, the professional organizers who had assisted in the development of NWRO essentially packed up and left, for the most part moving on to the organizing of the "overtaxed" middle class, focusing on an anticorporate agenda, the very nature of which, for all practical purposes, excluded the very poor. The financial backing of poor-people's organizations (other than those of the poverty pimps) has been essentially eliminated—few foundations are willing to take more than a very small chance on the poor alone, unassisted by "professionals" in the field. Most of the money that does go to poor-people's organizations is primarily for economic development in one form or another and acts essentially as a muzzle on organizing. (While your tenants' association is busy reconstructing and then maintaining your own building, you can hardly move on to organizing the building next door, much less your block or your neighborhood.) In addition, this reconstruction acts as a signal to the new urban gentry that the time is ripe to move in, displacing the poor and lower-income residents.

In the absence of any substantial movement of poor people, the 1970s have produced heightened repression and extreme human suffering. Antipoor and racist attitudes have been carefully nurtured to allow conditions for poor people to worsen significantly. While the real dollar value of welfare benefits has decreased over the past ten years, institutional control over poor people has risen dramatically.

Many people not involved in current welfare struggles believe that the infamous night raids (where social workers stormed into the homes of welfare mothers to try and catch a man in the house) are a thing of the past. Yet these raids continue through more sophisticated means. In New York, the welfare department has contracted with private bounty hunters, who are paid for each man they allegedly locate in a welfare mother's home. These "locates," as they are called, are ostensibly established through phone calls to the mother's neighbors and landlord. When the bounty hunter determines that a man resides in the house, the mother's case is closed. Most of the so-called evidence cannot legally sustain the termination of benefits. In one case that came to our attention, the father who had supposedly been located had in fact been dead for three years. Nevertheless, a significant net savings from the temporary termination of the mother's benefits leads the city to willingly pay these bounty hunters. Other schemes to reduce the rolls involve complex computer-match systems which often incorrectly locate a man in the house and then automatically terminate the case.

Institutional control over poor people has reverted to other practices, which many thought had been foreclosed by the reforms won with the Social Security Act. Prior to 1935, the system of relief relied primarily on poorhouses and a voucher system. In New York City, Mayor Fiorello La Guardia commissioned a study, which produced overwhelming evidence that the services purchased by this method delivered shoddy goods and extremely poor housing to families in need. La Guardia's commission along with former

Governor Lehman recommended that people be given direct control over the purchase of goods and services through direct cash payments. The cash-payment principle prevailed in the Social Security Act of 1935, and vouchers were eliminated.

By 1940, New York's landlords were clamoring to bring back vendor payments and started forcing recipients to "voluntarily" accept vendor payments in order to get any housing at all. The federal government has intermittently chastised New York (and other states) for such practices and forbidden voluntary vendor payments altogether. At the same time, federal law established a 10 percent ceiling on the number of recipients who could be issued restricted payments, requiring evidence that the recipient had used her money contrary to the best interests of her children. Over the years, landlords have lobbied for an increase in restricted payments in the form of two-party rent checks, which guarantee rent to the landlord regardless of the landlord's failure to deliver services and maintain the building in a habitable condition. The landlords' persistence has paid off. In 1978, the federal limit on restricted payments was raised to 20 percent, despite findings that the greater the number of restricted checks in a building, the greater the increase in housing-code violations over time, and the buildings with the largest percentage of tenants on two-party rent checks are also the buildings with the highest rate of tax delinquency.

However, as a result of organizing community opposition to two-party rent check programs, and negotiations between HEW and DWAC (with the aid of the Center on Social Welfare Policy and Law), HEW promulgated new regulations making it more difficult to place recipients on two-party rent checks. New York City has now been ordered in court to remove all AFDC recipients from two-party rent checks until they can follow the new regulations as written. Unfortunately, this victory may be short-lived, as our new president would like to see a return to the days of direct payments to landlords, turning back the clock to before 1935.

In New York, a state which is often incorrectly identified as providing the highest welfare benefits in the country, each member of a four-person family currently receives a maximum of $2.08 per day for nonshelter needs, including some medical expenses, most food expenses, all transportation, utilities, clothing, furniture, and education expenses, items needed for personal care, and all other necessary expenses. Because shelter grants have been frozen since 1975, 50 percent of the welfare recipients in New York are forced to use a portion of their $2.08 for rent, thus leaving them with even less income to provide for nonshelter needs. Prior to 1969, the welfare grant was based on individualized needs, and a multitude of special grants were at least potentially available for such things as winter coats, refrigerators, and home repairs. In 1969, the legislature took over the responsibility for determining welfare-grant levels from the welfare administrators. At that time, special grants were replaced by a flat grant, which varied only by family size, and the welfare agency's twenty-year practice of automatically increasing grant levels to conform to price increases was promptly eliminated.

The flat grant that was created was inadequate from its inception. It provided no allotment for reading materials, gifts, or recreation, and severely underbudgeted allotments for all other needs, especially food and utilities. As a result, the grant amounted to approximately one-half of the federal government's designated lower living standard, the budget New York had claimed was the benchmark for its welfare grant.

Clearly, inflation has affected people living on fixed incomes most severely. Not surprisingly, welfare mothers have fared the worst. While those who have always been deemed the deserving poor—the elderly and disabled—have been granted automatic, albeit inadequate, semi-annual cost-of-living increases in social security and supplemental security income benefits, welfare recipients enjoy no such relief from the ravages of rampant inflation.

In New York over the past ten years, the costs of basic essentials have more than doubled, and in many cases have tripled, while grants have been increased by only 11.86 percent. The last increase was in *1974*, when the flat grant was "raised" to reflect the *January 1972* cost of essential items of need. Thus, ten years after the state legislature assumed direct control over benefit levels, welfare grants have literally been reduced by one-half.

An analysis of grant levels reveals only one aspect of the worsened conditions faced by poor people throughout the country. Increased harassment at welfare centers, slave-labor workfare programs, complete disregard for the privacy of welfare applicants and recipients, as well as numerous measures designed to convince Congress, the Department of Health and Human Services, and the public that welfare fraud is being reduced have all ensured that fewer eligible people get on the rolls, and that fewer benefits are delivered to those found to be eligible. In New York, unemployment rates in some communities have risen to 80 percent, but welfare rolls have steadily decreased and fewer and fewer people are able to secure the full benefits to which they are entitled even under existing law.

For the most part, these kinds of overtly repressive institutional controls are well hidden from the general public, as are even more blatant forms of repression, such as the physical brutality experienced by welfare mothers at the hands of welfare-center security guards, hired to maintain order. To the extent that the government requires public support for its repressive tactics, it has engaged in remarkably effective campaigns to reassure the public that poverty is a function of individual failure. Thus, workfare programs are established to reeducate the poor with the prevailing work ethic, and expensive antifraud campaigns have gained widespread public endorsement.

The social-work community, generally accepting of the antipoor myths, has rallied around a call for an increase in the services provided to the "disadvantaged" family. While ignoring the reality that a mother simply cannot survive and care for her children on $2.08 per person per day, reformers seek budget counselors to help with money management. Similarly, programs for child-protective services have increased, and foster care has been greatly expanded over the past decade as a panacea for the mother who can't cope. While states pay on the average $10,000 a year to support a child in foster care, only about $700 a year is provided in welfare benefits to support that same child in his or her own home (that's the New York figure—other states provide even less per child). Services of real value to poor women, but less profitable, like day care and education and training programs, are virtually nonexistent and are rarely even suggested by proponents of the services solution.

But social workers, trained by the system to uphold that system, are not the only ones who fail to ask the right questions about welfare—questions about the billions of dollars pouring directly into corporate coffers, the lack of taxation of securities and other kinds of capital, and the tax loopholes for the very rich that end up shifting money from the poor to the wealthy; questions about the immense sums of money being spent on the administrative costs of the welfare system, costs that continue to rise despite the decreasing number of people actually on welfare.

Many self-proclaimed progressive or populist organizers and groups seem to have gotten so caught up in directing their efforts at the middle class that they have subtly (or in some cases blatantly) given in to feeding the antipoor mythology. Such supposed good guys as Tom Hayden, who has access to significant national press, oppose welfare-grant increases on the basis of cost containment. Faced with the tax question, most liberals do little to combat the distinctly destructive "it's coming right out of my pocket" syndrome. Instead of educating the middle and lower-middle class as to their common interests with the poor, they have abdicated any responsibility for the poor, serving as isolationists and keeping these relatively powerless groups separated. Among other things, they have not even hinted at the ways in which the presently constituted welfare state operates to keep not only the direct receivers of its benevolence poor, but also to keep wages down by playing the unemployed and waiting against the employed.

Middle-income people need not feel ripped off by measures to assist the poor. For instance, the money put into the hands of welfare recipients is immediately recirculated back into the economy—through landlords, grocers, utility companies, and so forth. It should be easy to see that the average $10,000-cost of keeping a child in foster care is not economical if the reason for foster care is chiefly the poverty of the mother (which is the case with most of the half-million children currently in foster care). Good emotional and physical health and a decent education rarely go hand in hand with abject poverty. Yet many of the 11 million children living below the poverty line in this country will go without these essentials for a substantial part of their childhood, frequently becoming adults with increased institutionalized needs as a result of not having been properly educated, clothed, fed, or sheltered. Welfare is neither cost-effective nor humanly effective. Poor children denied even nominal access to the American dream often exhibit antisocial tendencies, which can land them in jail to the tune of many thousands more in tax dollars per year per individual. As Mother Jones succinctly stated in the early 1900s, "I asked a woman in prison once how she got there, and she said she had stolen a pair of shoes. I told her if she had stolen a railroad, she would be a U.S. senator."[3]

Middle-income people should also stop accepting the myth that welfare recipients and other poor people are the only beneficiaries of federal benefits. If we take a closer look at the larger picture, we find, for example, that "federal housing policies, by stimulating private homeownership, have had a regressive effect on the distribution of income. The federal income tax deductions for homeownership produce a substantial net redistribution from renters to owners, which amounts to a transfer of wealth from lower to middle income Americans."[4] If we look even deeper, we find that the poorest 20 percent of the U.S. population receives only 6 percent of the national income.

We might also alter the dynamics of public understanding if we considered that *prices,* over which no welfare recipient presently has any control, are related not only to the profit bogeymen, but also to the welfare of the workers in general. Welfare recipient A purchases *x* quantity of utilities from a company whose prices are set to deliver wages to workers and profit to the company, in addition to covering the taxes of all involved with the single exception of the purchaser. When you are on a fixed income, like welfare recipient A, *you* pay for everyone else's welfare from minimum-wage worker to the chairman of the board in everything you buy.

This whole debilitating system works so long as welfare recipients acquiesce by not disrupting it. Their natural "allies," such as social-welfare agencies, community-action programs, and legal services, are certainly not going to disrupt it, since they are always in too compromised a position vis-à-vis their funding sources to agitate successfully, no matter how cognizant they are of the real problems. In exchange for passivity, welfare recipients are allowed to stay (barely) alive and totally disparaged. Any services rendered by them are never recognized as work or even as beneficial to the society at large, unless the mother fails at this enormous task and a foster mother takes her place at a great expense to all concerned.

It is imperative that *all* progressive individuals and groups ally themselves with the struggles of poor people, by identifying with those poor people organizing for change, lending resources and active support to actions, and rallying around the concrete demands of poor people. The myth that it is not possible to organize poor people must be obliterated because it is just that—a myth.

In 1979, DWAC and a very young RAM organized one of the largest rallies in ten years in Albany. Taking our issue, "Welfare Budgets Are Killing Our Children," to the legislature, we demanded a welfare-grant increase to meet 100 percent of recipients' needs. Almost 3000 welfare recipients and supporters participated in a mock funeral and moved thirty-five legislators to support a grant increase that only two had supported before the demonstration.

We organized support from unions, churches, and politicians, and in 1980 we went to Albany with as many demonstrators and many more supporters of a grant increase. The grant increase passed in the Assembly, but died in the Senate. It was clear to us that we had moved all the liberals; now we had to move the conservatives, especially the upstate ones who claimed their constituents weren't in favor of a grant increase. So we devised the clothing campaign, a new way to look at the grant-increase issue.

We used the welfare law authorizing replacement grants for clothes in cases of catastrophe. We declared inflation catastrophic, as do most Americans, and began our campaign and membership drive to fight for more money and build RAM so we could continue that fight.

On September 15, 1980, RAM demonstrations were held in thirteen cities at welfare centers, and New York City had demonstrations at seventeen centers. In New York City, seventeen recipients and prominent supporters were arrested in an emergency welfare center take-over while demanding clothing grants. Governor Cary was hit in eight of his town meetings throughout the state by RAM members demanding to know when there would be a welfare-grant increase. We organized a community picket against tax abatements for a luxury hotel, which resulted in the owner's next planned tax abatement being denied and helped to answer the question, "Where could a grant increase come from?"

And we finally won—a 15 percent increase that we were told would never happen! Our victory is not just the winning of an increase but the way in which it was won. First, people who are traditionally terrified of authority struck fear into the hearts of government officials who hold the reins of power over them. Second, supposedly unorganizable welfare recipients planned the campaigns and carried them out, from leafleting in poor neighborhoods and welfare centers to selling raffle tickets and hitting up local churches and social agencies for money to talking with the media and pointing out the truth about life on welfare. And finally, we showed that the days of direct action aren't dead; that the place to be *is* in the streets.

Clearly it is critical that welfare recipients organize and that allies assist in this task. Throughout history poor people have gained concessions only when they have organized to disturb the status quo, to create a disruption that cannot be ignored. In this process links need to be made with all who don't have an adequate income to make the demand for a universal system that guarantees a decent life to all—regardless of job status. Only with a guaranteed adequate income can people make real choices about what work they will engage in. By no other mechanism can we truly alter the circumstances of the poor or the job market itself, which presently employs most people in meaningless work with few quantifiable benefits.

- A seven-months pregnant woman is knocked down the stairs by a guard at her welfare center.
- Five pregnant teenagers are denied benefits illegally at the same Manhattan welfare center in one day.
- A rape victim is denied welfare in Queens, New York, for failure to provide information on the whereabouts of the "absent father."
- One mother who sold everything she owned before applying for assistance found herself rejected *because she and her child were homeless!* Finally, she was helped by a third party to locate an apartment and establish eligibility. Because she had no furniture and her grant was insufficient to buy any, she and the child slept on the floor. The Bureau of Child Welfare stepped in to take the child away. The mother was arrested for child neglect.
- One woman on welfare who found a night job applied for child-care expenses from welfare. She was told she couldn't be covered for "day care" because she worked at night, and "day care" meant daytime. Because she had to pay so much for child care out of her earnings, she ended up back on welfare within four months.
- After six documented visits by housing inspectors who listed dozens of rent-impairing violations but produced no results, one mother used her rent check to make essential building repairs. As punishment, she was placed on a two-party rent check. Soon after, her heat and hot water went off, and one of her children was hospitalized with pneumonia. When the baby was well, the doctor wouldn't release her, because there was no heat. Yet the hospital cost was $300 a day—more than the cost of moving the family to a better apartment.
- A family in Brooklyn was on a two-party rent check, and was being "recouped" (their welfare allotment was being reduced to cover an old utility bill). The mother put all three children in bed with her the night before, hoping to keep them warm despite no heat, hot water, or utilities. Her other two children woke up the following morning next to a dead baby.
- Richard M. Nixon, who narrowly escaped impeachment and criminal prosecution, receives hundreds of thousands of dollars annually in cash payments and services from *our* pockets, despite

having only narrowly escaped impeachment and possibly even criminal prosecution. His friend, Gerald Ford, who pardoned Mr. Nixon completely, also lives on the government dole and will continue to do so for the rest of his life.

Notes

1. Clarence Darrow, *Crime and Criminals: Address to the Prisoners in the Cook County Jail* (Chicago: Charles H. Kerr, 1975).
2. Jack Newfeld, *Village Voice*, Oct. 29, 1979.
3. Kathryn N. Burkhart, *Women in Prison* (New York: Doubleday, 1973).
4. Paul Starr and Gosta Esping-Anderson, "Passive Intervention," *Working Papers for a New Society*, 7, No. 2(1979):19.

13. Why Talk about Socialism?

City Life/Vida Urbana

City Life/Vida Urbana is a community-based socialist organization in Boston. Formed in 1973 as the Tenants Action Group, it has evolved into a multi-issue organization with more than eighty members and active associates. Our goal is to build a multiracial working-class socialist movement in the Boston area by organizing around housing and displacement, public education, work-place struggles, racism, sexism, and violence against women. We publish a newspaper called *CommUnity News/Noticias de la ComUnidad,* and we sponsor socialist study groups for the people we are working with. This selection explains some of the reasons why we believe that it is important to talk clearly and openly about why we are socialists.

Our organizing work has deepened our conviction that a class-conscious movement has to have socialism as its explicit goal. The question of socialism cannot be put off until some later stage because we have reached the stage at which only a socialist program can point the way out of the trap the cities are in. Short of eliminating profit as the basis of the housing industry, there is no way to break the cycles of disinvestment and decay, and of inflated housing costs, gentrification, and displacement. Likewise, only the socialization of investment will be able to reverse the loss of jobs

This selection is excerpted from an article which was originally published in *Radical America,* 13, No. 1. Copies of the full text, which includes a more detailed description of our work and our views on socialism, feminism, and Leninism, are still available at City Life, 670 Centre Street, Jamaica Plain, MA 02130.

and end the fiscal crisis. And nothing less can provide the material basis for the elimination of racism.

Changed political and economic conditions make this more clear today than it was in the 1960s. Then, it was possible to struggle in the name of justice for civil rights, "participation," and gains in housing and welfare for the poorest sectors of the working class. The economy was still expanding at a rate that allowed the poor to be given a piece of the pie without much being taken off the plate of anyone else. What most of these poor-people's struggles, no matter how militant, boiled down to was a demand for the state to "give us more." But at that time, to an extent, they could succeed. Today this is no longer the case. The idea promoted by Frances Fox Piven and others that if we could only revive the mass disruptions and other tactics of the 1960s, we could stop the erosion of the gains made back then ignores economic reality. U.S. capitalism can no longer afford buttered guns.

In the 1960s—prior to global recession, the energy squeeze, and the balance of payments crisis—the growing rate of inflation, egged on by staggering public debt, could still be tolerated. But today inflation is becoming a threat to capitalist growth and, among other things, public spending has to be held down. An increasing proportion of the public funds that *are* spent must be spent to subsidize profitmaking, directly or indirectly. The alternative (within the limits of capitalism, of course) would mean reduced incentives to invest and economic contraction.

In other words, today there is much less flexibility in the system. Even when those in power might prefer, for political reasons, to grant concessions such as urban reconstruction, welfare programs, or environmental controls, they find it hard to do so without cutting into someone's profit and undermining the economy in one way or another. Thus when something is given with one hand, it is taken away with the other (wage gains are eaten away by inflation, tax cuts to home owners are compensated for by other, equally regressive forms of tax exploitation or by service cutbacks, and so on). Now that the American empire has passed its peak, there will be few ways that working-class people in this country will be able to win *more,* in material terms, except at the expense of other sectors of the working class. Under these circumstances, there is little chance of reform movements that remain within a capitalist frame of reference winning any substantial improvements in working-class living standards.

This is one reason why our strategy differs from that of the current populist reform groups. It is our view that these groups will be able to win few, if any, economic gains, and that such gains as may be won will either be illusory or, at worst, will actually increase the gap between the more advantaged sectors of the working class (whites, longer-term residents, home owners) and the lower-income, less established sectors.

In every area of our organizing we are confronted with the ways in which working-class people are in conflict with each other. The deepest divisions are along lines of race, but there are other ways that groups are pitted against each other: tenants versus home owners; one neighborhood versus another; the steadily employed versus the marginally employed and welfare recipients; citizens versus undocumented residents; public school parents versus taxpayers with no kids in the school system; city versus suburban residents; and of course women versus men and homosexuals versus heterosexuals. If a movement broad enough to have real power is to be built, many more of these people will have to be persuaded of the common class interests that transcend these particular divisions. The context for building this class consciousness is struggles that unite people around interests that they do have in common.

However, a movement that is limited to struggling for individual economic gains, and whose goals are defined solely in terms of "economic justice" will not be able to develop this class consciousness and class unity. For while there may be some reforms that, if won, could benefit most working-class people, there are many ways in which the short-range material needs of different sectors of the working class are objectively in conflict. There can be no economic reform program—within the framework of capitalism—that addresses the needs of all of us. A movement based primarily on the promise of direct material benefits without a change in the system will either set its followers up for cynicism when the demands cannot be won, or will be dashed on the rocks of racism and interest-group politics when it becomes clear that some people's needs must be sacrificed for the benefit of others.

Does this mean we should stop fighting for economic reforms? Definitely not. But it does mean that our goal in waging these struggles must be to challenge the basic assumptions of capitalism, the constraints that stand in the way of *all* of us having fulfilling and materially secure lives. One side of this challenge involves exposing the fundamental irrationality and exploitativeness—not just the "corruption" and "injustice"—of the present system. The other aspect of it involves the development of an alternative: a socialist program that must be conveyed to people in convincingly concrete terms.

A socialist program for the United States isn't something we can develop simply by sitting down and writing it. Although we could sketch some of the broad outlines now, to a great extent such a program will only begin to appear plausible, winnable, or even desirable to people as the struggle develops and as people are changed in the process. For one thing, a workable socialism will require the redefinition of many of our needs away from individualized consumption and in the direction of more collective forms. Under socialism, less alienating and individualized forms of housing, transportation, and recreation could provide the basis for some of the nonmaterial benefits—like security, increased social contact, a feeling of community—that even now people perceive as missing from their lives. But no speech or pamphlet alone will convince people that the missing dimension, a sense of community and collective purpose, can be regained and is worth fighting for. But the actual experience of collective struggle *can* convince and transform people, just as it did many of us in the 1960s.

Another essential ingredient for socialism that can only be developed through mass struggles is working-class leadership and the confidence among working people that we can take over and run things better. To us in City Life, socialism means that the working class is in power at all levels of society. But the power to govern is not something we can just "take"; it has to be created through struggle, mass participation, and over a long period of time. This is why we say the means of struggle are as important as the ends. In any particular battle, the extent to which people are mobilized, take collective risks, break through old patterns of individualism, sexism, and racism, gain a sense of their potential power, and strengthen the skills and accountability of leadership is as important as whether the particular demand is won or lost.

This is a point on which we disagree with both the populists and with the traditionalist "ML" (Marxist-Leninist) groups, and where we think the two approaches have a lot in common. Both the populist and the current party-building groups, from what we have seen, tend to rely on hierarchical forms of organization and on methods of struggle that do little to increase the confidence, decision-making ability, and leadership potential of rank-and-file members.

City Life does not claim to have all the answers. While we have a lot of confidence in the politics that have been laid out here, there is clearly a lot more that we need to learn. We hope that other people and organizations will respond with descriptions of their own organizing experience and their conclusions from that experience, whether they tend to support or call into question the lessons we have drawn.

Part IV

The Crisis and Public Sector Unions

14. Public Sector Unionism

Paul Johnston

Crisis in the Public Labor Movement

The past decade has seen an explosion of organization and militancy in the public sector unmatched by anything since the CIO drive of the 1930s. Organized labor would have declined instead of growing in absolute numbers if it were not for the growth of the public unions in that period. Since the mid-1970s public workers are more unionized than private workers. At the same time, these new unions are facing crises on at least three levels.

First, there is the external political-economic attack: pay freezes, speedups, layoffs, contracting out, and so on, because of the general U.S. economic crisis, the fiscal crisis of the state, and the New Right mobilization underway to cut those sections of the state that are supposed to provide human services; and union-busting, scapegoating public workers with the image of the "$17,000 street sweeper," making public workers the victims of the taxpayers' rebellion, taking the heat off those who dominate the arrogant and wasteful state bureaucracy itself.

Paul Johnston is a union organizer and human-rights activist in the San Francisco Bay Area. For the last three years he has worked in Local 400 of the Service Employees International Union. An earlier version of this paper, "Democracy, Public Work and Labor Strategy," appeared in *Kapitalistate*, 8(1980):27–42. The paper is the product of dialogue with the editors of *Kapitalistate*, members of the URPE collective, and various trade unionists in the San Francisco area.

Public labor's inability to confront these crises leads to crisis number two, the crisis of the labor strategy. Even teachers', building trades', and other craft unions, which with their own me-first political strategy, which had often succeeded in the past, are losing today. Exclusive focus upon the wage demand and exclusive reliance upon the strike tactic limit the unions' power and help management consolidate its base to prevent any meaningful gains. Consequently public workers on strike are often isolated, politically disarmed, and defeated.

In a typical public sector strike situation, newly unionized workers face their first great battles with the government. The bargaining begins, patterned on the private sector and laws copied from the private sector. Labor starts with unrealistically high wage demands, to leave room for the "negotiations game." This process works its way toward the withdrawal, or threat of withdrawal, of labor in a strike. The union threatens to let the grass grow, the children go unschooled, or the poor and ill suffer until management comes around.

Management has its own ready-made counter strategy. The union serves as a convenient political scapegoat for public officials caught between relatively declining tax revenues, spiraling demands for public services, and the taxpayers' rebellion. The union as villain takes the heat off management for its bureaucratic corruption and ineptitude, its criminal priorities, corporate profiteering, and so on. Management and politicians, in league with chambers of commerce and the press, seize the time to crush the upstart workers and their new unions. In what could be called the $17,000 street sweeper formula, they move to build a reactionary base in defense of the public treasury against the greedy unions. The union loses. After the strike the membership is confused, demoralized, and bitterly divided, and the stage is set for further attack.

Not all public strikes end in such disaster. But examination of strikes that *do* succeed shows that they owe their success not to the direct destruction of capital investment, as in the private sector, but to the generation of political power. Without the recognition that labor's power is political in the public sector, public unionists do not do the things necessary to win and use that power. And they lose.

Third, the public sector unions face an internal crisis. Though 59 percent of the work force supports unionism *in principle,* only

19 percent support the present U.S. labor bureaucracy. Overpaid managerial staff leadership faces a deeply distrustful rank and file. The power of the bureaucracy depends little on organized worker participation and largely on management and its controls of the union machinery. Such a bureaucracy is wonderfully vulnerable to organizing from below; but public workers are unaccustomed to democracy and participation, and even left-wing activists find it difficult to rise beyond an oppositional role to responsible leadership. This proves to be a key problem in the public sector, for public labor strategy requires a stronger rank-and-file infrastructure than in traditional economic unionism. In the open-shop conditions of the public work place, actual union membership rarely reaches beyond 70 percent, though the union is required to equally represent nonmembers and members. *Without* a strong infrastructure, the membership stays below 30 percent. This means too little money and too little organizational strength to meet the many demands on the union organization. Most public unions are more open to rank-and-file participation than many private sector unions; but even the more democratic unions are saddled with the reputations, the roles, and the expectations earned over the years by labor unions in the private sector.

How can these three crises be confronted? How, specifically, can labor tap the real power of rank-and-file organization not only to repel painful attacks but also to progress toward some degree of liberation? How can we correctly define the issues we face, our organization, and our strategy? What is the potential for a political unionism in the public sector? We can find the answers to these questions in the story of a successful public sector strike.

The San Francisco Housing Authority Strike of 1979

In the San Francisco Bay Area there is a growing history of failures, partial failures, and, increasingly, successful efforts to apply a public service strategy to strikes and other campaigns. The housing authority strike of 1979 in San Francisco is a dramatic example of what can be done.

The housing authority had long been notoriously mismanaged. It had been looted over the years by the local Democratic political machine, craft unions, Jim Jones (of Jonestown infamy, ex-chairman of the commission), and others. The authority was the biggest slumlord in the city. Hundreds of apartments were vacant havens for crime; housing projects were filthy. People were (and still are) robbed and children raped in the projects as an ordinary occurrence. At the time of the strike, the authority was in a deep fiscal and political crisis.

The work force included about 120 Local 400 members[1] (clerks, police, and other tenant service workers), and about 150 craft workers, each represented by their own union. Local 400 members had conducted a strike two months earlier in August of 1979 against management's intention to implement contractual pay raises ten months late. The strike was settled in the workers' favor on the first day. The membership, mistrustful of management's good faith, decided to keep the strike structure intact. The structure included a tenant-relations committee, which in the August mobilization had launched a rent strike in support of the workers. So when the strike broke out in October, the workers were well prepared, with a strong internal organization for large-scale mobilizations and picketing, for tenant-community relations, food, fundraising, and so on.

In the months preceding the strike and during the strike itself, the mostly Black female clerks began for the first time to organize within the union. They consistently pushed the leadership and the rest of the membership to take a stronger, more vigorous stand. In response to this the leadership structure changed and was changed. Importantly, all the decisions concerning the strike and its conduct were made by the general membership of the section (at its own repeated insistence).

The strike began in late October when the twelve authority carpenters walked off the job demanding a raise. Then, although the craft union leadership had not bothered to seek strike sanction, the Local 400 workers decided not to cross the picket lines. They came out too, along with the rest of the craft unions, which were also seeking raises (plumbers, laborers, etc.). Though the Local 400 contract had a no-strike clause, Local 400 members decided to place their own demands on the table. They observed that, since management was violating the contract, they had the right to do the same. A week into the strike, Local 400 put up its own lines.

At the beginning of the week during which Local 400 stayed out behind craft lines, Local 400 members requested and received directly from all the craft strikers the commitment that they would honor Local 400 lines in return, if ever asked. Meanwhile, the housing authority police (who had very recently organized into Local 400) chose not to join the strike but to contribute part of their pay to the strike fund instead.

The issues were well defined. Local 400 had a set of ten demands, ranging from implementation of the earlier pay settlement, to a set of health and safety demands, to demands against specific acts of discrimination against CETA employees. On the first day of the strike the workers decided to define their central issue as mismanagement, and to demand that in order to resolve the strike not only must all issues be resolved but steps taken to end mismanagement of the authority. Many of the Local 400 strikers were tenants and ex-tenants of the authority. As a group they were fed up with being blamed for the failures of the authority and very resentful of the authoritarian administration.

During the first week of the strike the Public Housing Tenants' Association (PHTA) stood on the sidelines. Then, when Local 400 picket lines went up, they joined the strike. A call for a rent strike went out to 21,000 tenants. Many tenants came to the picket lines, brought food to the strikers, and, through the PHTA, placed their demands on the table.

At this, the housing police asked that their safety demand (two persons to a patrol instead of one) be added to the strike issues. They were invited to join the strike as a condition for making that a strike demand; on a close vote they decided to do so and joined the strike. At this point—for the first time in San Francisco labor history—craft, miscellaneous, and police employees were on strike in mutual solidarity.

The November mayoral elections were drawing near. The strikers made use of the elections by focusing upon the mayor's office, demanding that the mayor curb authority management (which is subject to their appointment powers). During the strike the workers did far more than picket their work locations. They took such actions as a march (by municipal transit bus) to invade HUD regional offices (Housing and Urban Development, the federal funding agency), coalition marches and demonstrations with craft workers and tenants (including a "garbage march," which deposited piles of the accumulating garbage from the housing projects on the steps of the mayor's office on the day before the election), a "Solidarity Disco" fund-raiser, and so on. Had they quietly stayed at their picket lines, the strike could have continued for months as management anticipated; instead they repeatedly grabbed the city and federal bureaucracy and shook it until they got the action they wanted.

Craft strikes have repeatedly lost in the public sector over the last decade. But craft unions rarely receive support from other workers and from the public. They were pleased and amazed to receive it now. The craft unions negotiated settlements on Friday of the second week. A Local 400 settlement was negotiated on the following Sunday on all issues. But no settlement was reached with PHTA. Local 400 had been conducting "coalition bargaining" (sometimes conducted by allied unions) with the tenants' association. City management, rushing for a settlement prior to elections on the coming Tuesday, stood by in amazement when Local 400 members voted Monday morning not to consider or vote upon their settlement until the tenants had an agreement. Craft union leaders were amazed too as their membership honored Local 400 picket lines for three more days until final settlement with the tenants was reached.

In addition to fully satisfactory settlements on all strike issues, the Local 400 strike settlement included affirmations by management that employees had valuable insight into how the management and operations of the agency should be improved, and that the existing mismanagement was a legitimate source of employee outrage. Management agreed to improve specific parts of its operation (including demotion of the personnel officer), and further agreed to a year-long process, called a "work improvement project," to give employees and tenants participation in improvement of management operations at both work unit and authority-wide levels.

Worker problems in the housing authority are by no means over. As of this writing, the authority appears to be moving toward another collision with the craft unions over pay. Regardless of what happens, however, the Local 400 section now knows how to strike and how to win in the public sector. They know how to unite the work-force, how to build a strong strike structure, how to target mismanagement while dramatizing their own desire to be of service to the tenants, how to build a tight coalition with tenant organizations, and in general how to gather and wield political power. Through the strike activity they have strengthened their own investment in better service and increased both worker and tenant participation in management.

The housing authority is a microcosm of the 31,000-member San Francisco City work force, where Local 400 represents the large "miscellaneous" group of workers. The success of this strike is certainly due, in part, to the small size of the work force; similar resolutions to the same contradictions in the city would be far more complex and difficult. However, because of its very simplicity, the housing authority strike provides clear lessons about the character of an effective political strike.

The Political Versus the Economic Strike

We can generalize from the experience of the housing authority strike to define the distinctive features of the political strike. The economic strike moves only in the realm of market relations. In what is traditionally called an "economic contest," workers put their determination and willingness to suffer immediate loss of work and pay against the company's ability to endure disruption of production and thus destruction of investment, in order to win a higher price for labor. A public strike based on this model may be successful if *and only if* by some means it delivers political power. Perhaps it threatens a function politically vital to the government, or it demonstrates or threatens to galvanize effective political support for the strikers' demands or against the officials opposing the union. It could also be politically effective if it has economic impact on business or public revenue. Whenever such a strike succeeds, and the circumstances surrounding its success are analyzed, it invariably proves the rule that labor's power is political in the public sector.

The political strike is not a sudden work stoppage called upon contract expiration, but a continuously developing political mobilization of union members and allies around demands carefully defined in a politically potent manner, basing itself upon the activation of rank-and-file organization, the testing and proof of solidarity in the work force, the mobilization of labor-community coalition resources, and creative actions to support negotiations and achieve a settlement.

The strike mobilization is the best possible opportunity to expand rank-and-file organization and leadership in the union. Suddenly the union has staff resources of creative, responsible people that may number in the hundreds or even in the thousands. Both the immediate impact of the strike and the long-range effect on the union's strength and internal life depend now on the ability of strike leadership to open up its structure, and the ability of the membership to become involved in a responsible way.

The strike organization unfolds from a strike preparations committee building each of the eventual strike committees, building a strike threat, consolidating and preparing the membership for strike duty, and carrying out pre-strike mobilizations and work actions, into the actual committees including negotiations, press, food, relief, transportation, internal communications, picket-field action, community relations, emergency services, and, finally, the strike leadership council itself, composed of chairpersons of each committee. The emergency services committee is a public sector innovation; it deals with the effect of the disruption of services upon consumers, potential allies of the strikers. Community relations is also such an innovation. It moves on a broader level to mobilize community resources, political allies of the union, and public opinion in general on the side of the workers. The picket committee is modified; its duties include mobilization of the strikers to take various forms of creative direct action.

The rule of the game is that there is no rule of the game for political action in a strike. Creative "guerilla" tactics are needed to respond to the unexpected circumstances, opportunities, and dangers that will develop during the course of the strike, upon which the outcome may ride. Should the union salvage sewage treatment plant operations before irreparable damage to the environment occurs? Is it possible to win over the police to the strikers' side? Should certain workers remain on the job, receiving pay and contributing to the strike fund while others strike, continuing, perhaps, certain vital services? What about a rotating strike? A one-day work stoppage as a political protest? A unilateral modification of work rules to improve services? Leaflets in the community? Disruption of billing and tax collection? Joint action and coalition bargaining with consumer interest organizations? Electoral action, including the circulation of voter initiatives?

The economic strike is a one-time mobilization; the political strike is part of a year-round political mobilization. The single focus upon contract expiration time disregards budget determination hearings, elections, passages of particular laws, and other government action that may require equally strong mobilization. The political strike as described above contains strategic principles that seem to be necessary for a year-round program of political unionism.

Public Service Unionism

The class relations and the struggles faced by public sector workers provide the basis for organizing democratic public service unions. Five main strategic principles emerge. First, because relations in the public sector are directly political, *union goals and strategies must be evaluated from a political standpoint*. Potential resources for political power, politically achievable goals, politically effective issues in coalition building and in isolating management when necessary must all be combined to promote politically effective tactics. The union's main political resources are (1) the organization, unity, and general political activity of its membership (in work place, electoral, and other community spheres); (2) the coalitions it can build with sections of the community, including other unions and even sections of public sector management; (3) the membership's knowledge and potential control of the work process; and (4) its ability to define the struggle in terms favorable to itself. Pay levels much higher than normal make terrible strike issues. Coalitions organized against layoffs and the service cuts they entail, around public sector mismanagement, around democratic demands, can all be politically potent.

Political power must counter public sector management's attempts to scapegoat and bust the union by blaming painful effects of strikes, high taxes, and other public problems on workers' greed. Strategies that wield economic clout in the private sector can play right into the hands of management's strategy. This doesn't mean abandoning the strike, however, but developing a more sophisticated political strike strategy.

Second, *issues should be broadened to include the potential for a democratically organized agency:* how the agency should be run. When labor begins to deal directly with "the merits, necessity, and organization of public work," excluded by labor law from collective bargaining, strong political impact can result. The mere impact of the concept of worker participation in and dialogue with public sector mismanagement can be explosive. The $17,000 street-sweeper strategy can be turned around by politically mobilizing a community base that supports union demands by exposing issues such as mismanagement and political favoritism for big business. As those most intimately informed of the inner workings of public agencies—and as those who do the work—public workers are in a unique position to criticize. This can be very helpful in making management move in wage negotiations; it can also help the unions dramatize to the community the difference between those who control and benefit and the workers at the bottom of the bureaucracies. In this way public workers are defined as public servants in a new sense: as responsible public servants, intent upon serving the needs of the community. The intention is to serve the community, and to participate in defining community needs and how they are to be served, *in opposition to* government and business forces that stand in the way and define those according to capital instead of to people; the utilization of vestigial democratic forms and the demand for their expansion to accomplish a restructuring of public agencies, giving priority and power to self-organized workers and a self-organized community. These demands for the realization of the myths of public service and democracy are not just good for morale and public image; they provide basic guidelines for public labor strategy that can help shape our struggles in a politically potent manner.

Third, *solidarity within the public work force should be organized*. Because the public work force is one of such diversity, the challenge is to bring all the distinct groups of nonmanagement workers into a single organization, a single union or close coalition of unions, providing mutual support and working in a unified manner. The common mistrust between different groups under the same employer, and management's manipulation of this mistrust into cycles of mutual scabbing are too familiar to public workers.

Union leadership and negotiating structures can be established to provide unity *and* autonomy, both essential for solidarity. Each unit can be guaranteed autonomy and support in return for its own commitment to the others.

Important is the relationship between the relatively privileged workers and the ever present second-class workers. The relatively privileged group is often quite comfortable with its status. But no alliance is solid unless the privileged workers are willing to recognize and reflect the second-class treatment of their co-workers.

This inequality usually falls between whites and nonwhites and between men and women, because structural inequality in the work place is part and parcel of patterns of national and sexual domination in the whole society. One error often made when dealing with such issues as affirmative action and racial or national tensions on the job is the tendency to separate and counterpose work issues and discrimination issues. To the extent that the union can define its struggle against discrimination as, simultaneously, a campaign on behalf of second-class workers, it can unite the democratic struggle against, for example, racial oppression with what is often the main issue in the work force.

"Temporary" workers in San Francisco, for example, are anything but temporary. They are an underclass, one-third of the work force, hired outside regular civil service channels, doing the same work as "permanents" but for less pay and no fringe benefits, not even social security. They often work for five, ten, fifteen years in this status, and they are mostly minorities, usually women. The permanent workers are mostly white, usually male. A union campaign against the abuse of temporary employment must combine labor and affirmative action issues, and to the extent that it is supported by permanent workers, it can build solidarity within the entire work force. It is not always possible to convince relatively privileged groups to support such a plan. Workers often must achieve a certain amount of personal growth or enlightenment in this and other areas before they can become good union members. But with a small, organized core of the more progressive among the privileged workers it is at least possible to neutralize chauvinist tendencies and work toward certain unity.

Fourth, public sector unions should *build new urban coalitions and establish a labor-community alliance*. Solidarity inside the work force connects directly with labor-community coalitions, for the diversity of the public work force reflects and intersects the diversity of the community. For example, if the progressive potential in today's public unions, even at present levels of organization, is allied with the progressive potential of minority communities, then the core of an explosively powerful and progressive urban coalition can emerge. For this to happen a break with the racist history of much of the white-dominated labor movement must occur. Public unions can become known as fighters for affirmative action. The large agencywide unions that emerged in the 1970s are naturally equipped to make this break, for they generally include major concentrations of minority workers and they *need* the labor-community alliance. The growth and progressive organization of Black,

Latino, Asian, and other minority communities in urban areas has occurred alongside the growth and progressive organization of the public work force. Alliances can take many forms in campaigns against discrimination, against service cuts and layoffs, in grassroots initiatives and election campaigns, in struggles over the management policies of schools, hospitals, and utilities.

Finally, public sector unionists should be able to *build a broad organization of participatory rank-and-file leadership*. Such an infrastructure is necessary in the public sector open shop just to sustain membership and dues. And effective political mobilization further requires it. Some public union bureaucrats must be replaced. But public union leadership is, by and large, more responsive to rank-and-file pressure because of the open-shop situation, and more likely to be relatively progressive because of the recent origins of the unions and the severe struggles most are encountering. No doubt it is difficult to break through a top-heavy bureaucracy. But the bureaucracy *includes* and *survives* only with passive, subordinate, and dependent attitudes of those at the base. Without this foundation it crumbles. When this foundation begins to organize itself, the union bureaucracy is enormously vulnerable. When this foundation is organized, it has radical new power in the union, and the union has radical new power to win political contests. Without its support, the union lacks its most basic political resource and can be defeated. Without the member's initiative and collective action, the best-intentioned union leadership can accomplish little; with them, no bureaucracy can stand in the way.

Unique Social Relations of Public Work

Too often, analyses of the state see it only as a political institution, or an executive, or a form of domination, or a distillation of class relations, or an agency for general social reproduction. Though each of these perspectives has its value, a multidimensional view is required. One dimension usually ignored is the state as work place. On the other hand, analyses of labor usually assume a work place engaged purely in capitalist production. Moreover, when labor in the state sector is examined, the focus is too often limited to those characteristics it shares with private sector labor, such as service production, white-collar and managerial work. There is a general failure to grasp public work as an essentially distinct productive mode. Public workers have unique relations to taxpayers, to the electorate, to consumers (or victims) of public work, and to state power itself. The position they occupy is qualitatively different from private sector workers in the "pure" capitalist work place. The meaning of work and unionism for public sector labor must be understood through exploration of these unique relations.

The private sector worker is a direct employee of capital. Labor power is sold to capital as part of the process of capital accumulation involving the production of commodities to be sold in the capitalist market. What is to be produced is defined by the demands of that market. The public worker, in contrast, works for government or state power. Labor power is sold to the government for the production, not of commodities, but of social use values, which are goods or services defined as useful to society at large by those who hold state power. What is to be produced is determined through political decisions, not simply through the economic laws of the market.

To be sure, there is no actual sharp line between public production of social use values and private production of commodities. Instead, there is a great mutual interpenetration of these two modes, with each mutually perverting the purity of the other in a broad range of combinations and mutual interventions. Relations are essentially political in both sectors, but even as state production expands in the service of commodity relations, overt political mediation of formerly commodified relations expands. These two ways of organizing work and defining, producing, and appropriating value, though not always or even usually existing in pure form, represent two distinct productive principles. Capitalist production, on the one hand, produces exchange as well as use values, and appropriates the surplus value generated in the wage-labor relation from the producing worker to the ruling capitalist. State production in the noncommodity sphere, on the other hand, is not "productive labor" in Marx's specifically capitalist sense; it is a distinct set of relations, productive on its own terms. Though the capitalist state serves finance capital in many ways, pure state production produces not exchange value but social use value, direct social production. Surplus value is not appropriated in its exchange-value form. The distribution of power and resources, the making of rules, formulation of policy, and the processes of domination and exploitation are more direct. The maintenance of the wage and tax systems, however, means that in state production the government functions as a collective capitalist. The use value produced by state workers is appropriated by those who hold state power. In exchange, they receive wages based on private sector standards and upon the political power (or lack of power) wielded by the workers themselves. The use value produced is defined as "useful" to the extent that it *reproduces*—continues, defends, supports, feeds, legitimizes, adjusts—the social formation.

Therefore demands raised by state workers must be raised against the state itself. Issues and battles, then, that in the private sector may be limited to economic terms become political (or political-economic) in the public. Questions, which for private workers exist only remotely—how taxes of all kinds are raised and distributed, how a public budget is composed, how elections are conducted, how the political community views the workers—are immediate work-place facets for public workers. On the terrain of labor struggle, a battlefield that has historically precluded political struggle in the United States, public workers are finding that every question (including the amount of a pay raise) is a political question, that power is political, that labor relations are political, and therefore that labor strategy must be political.

Thus the elimination, or partial elimination, of commodity relations in state production brings public workers closer to the meaning in their work; to the definition, satisfaction, and frustration of social needs, including their own. Who does what to whom is determined by political power, legitimized by explicitly justified views of social reality and social needs. The veil of commodity relations is partly lifted and public workers find themselves in practical working relationship to the collective needs of society. Whether they keep society's parks and buildings clean, fix society's potholes, clean society's water, teach society's children, or regulate society, questions concerning the meaning of the work begin to come clear as the object and the product of the labor is, visibly, society itself. For the public worker subject to the state as both citizen *and* employee historic divisions between private and public domains become blurred. Work relations, from patronage to merit system, are political. Battles over taxation, over the maintenance, expansion, or destruction of particular public programs, and all the social contradictions that cluster around the state connect directly with pay, working conditions, and union power. Public workers are brought face to face in their work with the problems of society, as reflections of their own lives. Working in housing projects inhabited by rats, roaches, and hopeless people, in schools degenerating into urban prisons for the increasingly uneducated children of the poor and working classes, in the depravity of a health-care system geared for profit, in a welfare system promoting the degradation and waste of human beings, in the horror of mental institutions, they are faced daily with the arrogance of those who hold power in the big public bureaucracies that supposedly serve the people. Trapped inside whole systems, the vast majority of public workers find themselves not only blamed for this cluster of failures, but, through pay cuts, layoffs, speedups, and contracting out, they are forced to pay for them as well.

This means that questions of worker control emerge in a different form than in the private sector, for the institution to be controlled is not a commodity-producing enterprise but rather an agency of social production supposedly accountable to and serving the community. So while the most immediate questions of control over work and working conditions, safety, and so on are contested as in the private sector, this is not within the context of a company dependent upon capital movement for its life. In order to achieve power to defend their interests, public workers have an interest in challenging basic questions of public policy, development, finance, and management of the agency. In rejecting inherited models of greedy, me-first unionism, public unions can turn the legitimizing ideologies of democracy and public service against the capitalist state by demanding that they be made real.

Labor relations in the public sector are strongly influenced also by the stratification, hierarchy, and incredible diversity of the work force. The local public agency, for example, employs a virtual cross section of the community, varying levels and kinds of blue-collar, clerical, technical, professional, administrative, and managerial positions, hierarchically organized and segregated by nationality, race, and sex. An agency will commonly include many different industries in one political and fiscal entity—such as transportation, education, or health. Just as the organization of the CIO required that workers overcome craft and skill-level distinctions to achieve necessary power, so public sector organizing requires a still broader unity, bringing together workers whose sole common denominator is supposedly serving the democratically determined needs of a single community. As with earlier private sector unions, this unity was less evident in the early organization of craft groups, such as teachers and social workers; later, especially since 1970, has come the emergence of the broader union of miscellaneous workers. Not surprisingly, the old craft unions are weaker and the new agency-wide unions are stronger since the present crises. This diversity and unification are also significant because the public labor force intersects such significant parts of the community: whites and different minorities, renters, taxpayers, health-care consumers (or victims), and so on. Alliances built here weave together a new and significant kind of labor-community alliance.

Also, the service character of some public work renders social relations more direct and visible. It is wrong, however, to see this as a distinction between public and private. Commodity production includes many services, and state production includes many functions outside a direct service relationship. But in the direct service relationship, the contradiction between the public sector legitimizing myths of democracy and public service and the realities they conceal cannot help but intensify the political, and human, personal impact of social needs falsely defined and inadequately served.

What is the relation between public and private sector work and labor strategy? Despite crucial differences mentioned above, the two sectors have certain things in common. Public workers are subjects of a state in the service of capital; private sector workers are employees of capital backed by the state. On overlapping battlefields they face the same enemy. Workers move from private jobs to public and back again. Most important, the expansion of the state as a work place had been accompanied by the general expansion of political intervention in formerly nonpolitical sectors, including the lives and jobs of private sector workers. The Chrysler bail-out, the nuclear power controversy, rent control measures, and wage guidelines are but a few examples. Much that was formerly private and economic is now socialized and politicized for private as well as public workers.

As a democratic-socialist movement grows in the United States, public workers will certainly be part of it. But debates about free enterprise versus state production have only a limited significance to the employees of the great public bureaucracies. Public workers must, if the movement is to make any sense for them, project a *different kind* of public work than hitherto seen in the United States: not blind subordination to a state bureaucracy but work motivated by the determination to serve the democratically defined needs of the community. For these workers, progressive organizing centered at the work place is also centered upon the state, and must deal directly with questions of state and democracy—the unanswered questions of socialism—in the visibly *political* economy of the public sector. This effort to exercise collective and personal mastery over both work and government in coalition with the larger community served provides an avenue toward that old communist dream of social liberation: the supercession of both the state and the employer as such. Then work becomes public service, and government follows democratic dialogue concerning human needs.

In summary, the socialization and politicization of labor in the public sector mean the socialization and politicization of formerly private and commodified issues and forms of struggle. The unique conditions of public work demand a new unionism. When public unions grasp this, they can fashion a strategy that will allow them to successfully confront the crises they face, a model of political unionism increasingly applicable in the private sector as well. Potentially democratic-socialist consciousness, organization, and effective struggle are implied and can be "surfaced" by effective organizing. Public workers can thus serve as a democratic counterforce, and contribute to far-reaching social transformation.

Notes

1. Local 400, Service Employees International Union, represents most of the lower-paid "miscellaneous" public workers in the city, and is the author's employer.

15. Public Sector Unions and the Labor Movement

Michael D. Yates

Since World War II, the economic activities of governments at all levels in the United States have grown rapidly. For example, public expenditures (federal, state, and local) on goods and services as a percentage of the gross national product rose from 10.9 percent in 1947 to 21.2 percent in 1976.[1] One consequence of this growth has been the striking increase in public employment, both absolutely and relative to private employment. The number of public sector workers has nearly tripled since 1947, while private manufacturing employment increased by only about 14 percent.[2] The ratio of public sector workers to all such workers rose from 12.5 percent in 1947 to 18.8 percent in 1976.[3]

What, then, are the implications of this expanded public sector work force for the labor movement and the class struggle in the United States? Can public employees revitalize and radicalize the labor movement and thereby bring about social change in the United States?

Revitalizing the Labor Movement

Labor in the 1970s: The 1920s Revisited

During the 1920s and the early 1930s membership in labor unions in the United States diminished to the point where contemporary

Michael Yates teaches economics at the University of Pittsburgh at Johnstown in Philadelphia. Special thanks to Tom Riddell and the other primary reviewers of the Public Sector Crisis Collective for their helpful comments and advice in preparing this article.

observers were seriously asking whether the labor movement would survive another decade.[4] In 1932 prominent labor economist George Barnett of Johns Hopkins University said, "I see no reason to believe that American trade unionism will so revolutionize itself within a short period as to become in the next decade a more potent social influence than it has been in the past."[5] The American Federation of Labor had for the first time failed to grow during a period of prosperity (the 1920s), seemingly succumbing to employer paternalism and the antipathy and hostility of the general public.[6]

Of course, in retrospect, there were other reasons for labor's decline during the 1920s. Although downplayed in the accounts of most labor historians, private and public attacks on labor organizations flourished during the decade.[7] From the savage repression during the steel strike in 1919 to the brutality of vigilantes during the textile strikes in 1929, most employers remained implacably hostile to trade unions and did not hesitate to use violent means to suppress them. Employers found willing allies for their anti-unionism in local, state, and federal officials and courts. A record number of injunctions were issued in labor disputes between 1920 and 1930,[8] and the U.S. Supreme Court had either outlawed, severely restricted, or questioned the legality of boycotts, picketing, and strikers.[9] Compounding these difficulties was the AFL's firm commitment to craft unionism at a time when machinery and the detailed division of labor were making it increasingly irrelevant.[10] It was not possible to organize mass-production industries on a craft basis, and it is little wonder that workers responded less than enthusiastically to efforts to do so.[11] Finally, the radical opposition both inside and outside of the AFL, which often forced the AFL to be more militant and which favored industrial unionism, was destroyed by a combination of internal dissension and government repression.[12]

Today the labor movement in the United States looks a lot like it did in the 1920s.[13] Union membership as a percentage of the labor force has declined steadily since the early 1950s, from a peak of nearly 26 percent in 1954 to approximately 20 percent in 1976.[14] Politically, organized labor has suffered a string of defeats. The AFL-CIO failed to get a situs picketing bill (a bill which would have allowed a single union to picket an entire construction site without committing an illegal boycott) passed in 1976, and in 1978 it could not secure passage of a relatively minor reform of the Taft-

Hartley Labor Act,[15] despite a strong lobbying effort. A combination of right-wing and employer organizations succeeded in preventing the reform bill from even coming to a vote in Congress.[16] At the state level, labor's enemies have also been on the offensive. A right-to-work law reached the ballot in Missouri in 1978, and only a mass mobilization of workers by rank-and-file labor and civil rights groups prevented its passage. California's Proposition 13, which has forced cutbacks in public services and employment, is in every respect, an antilabor law.[17]

In addition to troubles on the political front, unions face employers who are becoming increasingly hostile toward both union organizing and collective bargaining. From the open repression of J. P. Stevens to the more subtle tactics of General Motors, corporations are resisting unionization with a zeal reminiscent of the 1920s.[18] Where unions do manage to win representation rights, employers simply refuse to bargain in good faith. Where unions have been long established, employers are demanding the elimination of contract provisions that have existed for years and that are crucial to the welfare of union members and the survival of the unions themselves.[19]

The current stagnation of the labor movement is all the more serious when we consider the fact that, although an increasing proportion of the labor force is made up of wage laborers, public antipathy toward labor unions seems to be increasing. There is widespread belief that unions are corrupt and that they cause inflation. A recent Gallup poll indicated that only 59 percent of the public approved of unionization in principle, and 15 percent approved of union leadership.[20] The implication of these numbers is that a lot of workers do not favor unionization as a principle! Support for this can be shown in the decreasing proportions of representation elections that unions win each year.[21]

Public Employees: Another CIO?

Would it be reasonable to repeat today Professor Barnett's prediction of 1932? Is the labor movement dead, or is there the possibility of a rebirth? After all, not long after Barnett made his comment, the labor movement enjoyed its greatest expansion ever, brought about by the rapid organization of workers in the nation's giant industrial corporations. The cataclysm that struck the economy during the Great Depression created conditions that allowed the labor movement to regenerate itself and prove Barnett wrong.[22]

Workers, employed and unemployed, recovering from the initial shock of economic collapse, began to organize militantly—demonstrating, picketing, forming unions. Political and economic stability were so threatened by these actions that direct repression of labor seemed to be a dangerous strategy to important segments of the ruling class. In addition, much of the general public blamed business for the depression, and openly supported the workers. Ultimately President Roosevelt, hoping to prevent the radicalization of the working class and to form an electoral majority for the Democratic Party, was compelled to openly endorse the rights of workers to join unions and bargain collectively. At the same time, a core of farsighted labor leaders, led by John L. Lewis, were driven by the changed social climate to scrap the AFL's outworn craft unionism and seize the opportunity to organize millions of coal miners and steel, auto, and rubber workers into a new labor organization, the CIO. Within six years of the CIO's formation in 1935, it had organized and enrolled 5.2 million workers. This growth continued during World War II and, together with a tremendous expansion of the AFL (forced to meet the challenge of the new unions or die), caused union membership to increase from 4.2 million in 1936 to nearly 15 million in 1947.[23]

The CIO revitalized the labor movement, not simply by organizing industrial workers but by giving new hope (and often employment) to political progressives and radicals, long abandoned by the AFL. The new unions took progressive stands on race relations and women's rights.[24] They were in the forefront of those who wanted the government to guarantee full employment and economic security; they lobbied diligently to get Roosevelt's social security legislation implemented.[25] They were guaranteeing the extension of basic civil rights to the work place, and they were a potential check on the unrestrained use of monopoly power by big business. Some radicals even saw in the famous sit-down strikes and the militance of many unions the embryo of a radical labor movement that would begin to fight for workers' control within the factories and socialism in the larger society.[26] At the least, the very size and progressiveness of the CIO appeared to ensure a growing labor movement and a more liberal national government. A large and powerful labor party did not seem to be outside the realm of possibility.[27]

Is there today another CIO which will again revitalize the labor movement? One recent development, which has helped to prevent an absolute decline in union membership and which has once again

stirred the hopes of progressives and radicals, has been the remarkable growth of unions in the public sector.[28] Beginning in the
1960s, public employees began to organize on an unprecedented
scale. While as late as 1956 fewer than 1 million government workers were union members, by 1964 there were 1.5 million and by
1970, 4.5 million members. Inspired by the civil disobedience of
the social movements of the 1960s and frustrated by the continuous
decline in their relative wages and working conditions, public employees struck illegally, shut down critical public facilities, and
ultimately forced public employers (school boards, city councils,
state legislatures, etc.) to recognize their unions and negotiate with
them. Many states and the federal government were eventually
compelled to repeal repressive legislation and enact new laws,
giving public workers the right to organize, to bargain collectively,
and in a few cases to strike. And the AFL-CIO was forced to help
public employees unionize, if only to maintain its sagging
membership.

Quantitatively, the growth of public sector unionization is comparable to that experienced by the early CIO unions, and there
are qualitative comparisons as well: the aforementioned laws passed
to guarantee public employees the same rights enjoyed by private
workers since the Wagner Act of 1935; progressive attitudes on
race and sex;[29] fairly early opposition to the Vietnam War;[30] and
promotion of progressive social-welfare programs such as national
health insurance.[31] There was, in the 1960s, even some of the spirit
of hope, of a new beginning for the labor movement, felt by people
in the CIO. As John O'Neill, former director of organization for
the United Federation of Teachers, said in 1970:

> Especially significant in these earlier days [early 1960s] is the fact that
> the UFT was being watched and admired by all students of the trade
> union movement operating on the local and national scene. While
> making unprecedented gains for its members in bread-and-butter
> matters, it was also providing a different type of union leadership,
> a possible pattern for all public employee unions. The image of the
> UFT was that of a young, dynamic, honest, and militant trade union
> changing the life-style of the heretofore stereotyped school-marm
> teachers at the same time that it was deeply committed to, and
> involved in the civil rights struggle and was on the "right side" of
> virtually all social issues. In those days it was impossible to go to a
> gathering of union people without noticing the open admiration for
> the UFT. The word was out that this was where things were
> happening.[32]

A look at some of the contract demands made by American Federation of Teachers locals around the country during the 1960s confirms and amplifies O'Neill's statement. The union sought to incorporate progressive reforms of the classroom, the curriculum, and the school system into its contracts. It developed a "20-20" plan, whereby there would be no more than twenty instructional hours per week and twenty students per class for all teachers. The balance of the school week would be devoted to individual study and tutoring. The UFT sponsored a More Effective Schools (MES) program, which involved an intensified commitment to low-income, inner-city schools. It envisioned greatly reduced class sizes in such schools, special tutorial programs, and better school-community relationships. In 1969, delegates to the AFT national convention "urged that collective bargaining demands include the adoption of textbooks and materials providing an in-depth account of Black and other minority and ethnic group contributions, and the encouragement of affiliates to concentrate on eliminating racist doctrines that permeate the total curriculum, and that these measures be included in collective bargaining agreements."[33] Similar demands were made with respect to "sexist doctrines" and inadequate textbook coverage of the labor movement.

Other unions of public workers made demands aimed not only at improving their members' working conditions but also at providing more and better public services. For example, in 1967 the Social Service Employees Union of New York City made a series of contract demands that had as their purpose the liberalization of welfare benefits and the rights of welfare recipients. American Federation of State, County, and Municipal Employees (AFSCME) guards at Attica Prison successfully negotiated (after the Attica rebellion) increases in clothing and food allowances for prisoners.[34]

Insofar, then, as revitalizing the labor movement is concerned, it can plausibly be argued that public sector unions had, during the 1960s and early 1970s, an effect similar to that of the CIO during the 1930s. Millions of workers were organized, hundreds of bitter strikes were fought, laws were passed, and new and progressive demands were made upon employers and sometimes won. However, revitalizing the labor movement is not the same thing as radicalizing it, that is, moving it in a socialist direction. Recently, some leftists have argued that the special nature of public employment and the new and expanded role of the government in the U.S. economy make it possible for public employee unions to spearhead the radicalization of the labor movement.

Radicalizing the Labor Movement

The CIO Precedent

Socialists had hoped in the 1930s that the organization of the mass-production industries would move the labor movement in a radical direction. Radicals, including many communists, helped to organize the CIO unions and often held leadership positions in them; even the nonradical leaders like John L. Lewis were pressing hard for progressive programs for their members and for the nation as a whole.[35] At last it appeared that the U.S. labor movement would develop along the more radical lines of its European counterpart.

The hopes of the radicals, and the progressives as well, were short-lived. By 1947 the new Republican Congress, strongly pressured by business interests, had gutted the Wagner Act with the regressive Taft-Hartley amendments.[36] Government repression of unions and radicals picked up again during and after World War II, culminating in the Cold War hysteria of the McCarthy era.[37] Unfortunately, the CIO reacted to these attacks not with an aggressive mobilization of workers, but with an almost total capitulation. First, most CIO leaders refused to support Henry Wallace's efforts to continue the New Deal politics of Roosevelt. Then, they caved in to the right wing (and, of course, to big business) and purged some of the most progressive CIO unions (notably the ILWU, the UE, and Mine, Mill, and Smelter Workers) as well as hundreds of radicals in those unions that remained in the CIO. Finally, the CIO unions began to make "productivity deals" with the companies, abandoning efforts by the rank and file to control the speed of the assembly lines and gain some control over their work places.[38] By the mid-1950s the commitment of the CIO to organize the unorganized, fight for civil rights, democratize the work place, and promote progressive national politics had faded badly. By 1955 the CIO had become so conservative that it merged with the AFL under terms that placed George Meany in firm control of the labor movement.

The Record of the Public Employee Unions

In retrospect, it is probably true that the CIO unions did not have nearly the radical promise that they seemed to have in the 1930s. While it is true that government and corporate repression after the war was a very important factor in the decline of the CIO, it is also true that the founders of the CIO never had any intention of promoting radical unionism and socialism. And the industrial workers themselves, while capable of spontaneous rebellion and great courage and militance, were not inherently radical. Very few of them were socialists, and the radicals who helped to organize and sometimes led their unions did not do the things necessary to encourage them to develop a socialist class consciousness. Instead the radicals practiced syndicalism, which presumes that trade-union work and trade-union consciousness lead automatically to a radical consciousness and politics.[39] This is a false presumption, and the belief in its correctness must, in part, be held to blame for the CIO's demise as a progressive, potentially radical movement.

Does the mass organization of public employees contain the seeds of a possible radicalization of the labor movement? If so, how can these seeds be nurtured and brought to full growth? If we look only at the recent record of the public employee unions, the prospects do not seem encouraging. Some of the unions, AFSCME, for example, have maintained a progressive, democratic image and continued to fight for liberal political reforms, but they have not, with a very few exceptions at the local level,[40] shown signs of becoming radical. Others, like the AFT, have shifted dramatically from their earlier progressivism. In the late 1960s the UFT strongly opposed certain pilot projects in Black and Puerto Rican communities aimed at strengthening local popular control of the schools. Many minority union members and the communities themselves saw the UFT's opposition as racist; as a result of a confrontation between the UFT and the people in Ocean Hill–Brownsville over the transfer of some white teachers, quite a few minority teachers quit the union.[41] More recently, the AFT filed an *amicus curiae* brief on behalf of Allen Bakke's claim of reverse discrimination. Internally, the union's democratic structure has been replaced by President Albert Shanker's autocracy. Shanker's politics have moved so far to the right that they are virtually indistinguishable from those of his patron, George Meany, or Ronald Reagan for that matter. In 1978 a group of substitute teachers in Chicago argued persuasively that Shanker is collaborating with the CIA to suppress democratic unionism around the world.[42]

In general, public sector unions have behaved in much the same ways as have those in the private sector, ways which hardly portend the radicalization of the labor movement. They have struck for recognition and for higher wages; they have lobbied in state capitals; they have sometimes been militant and sometimes conciliatory. They are even making "productivity deals" with public employers.[43]

I am not personally aware of any pervasive red-baiting in the public sector unions, but it has occurred.[44]

New Possibilities for Public Employee Unions

Despite the unpromising evolution of public employee unions so far, there are some unique features of these unions, which if properly exploited could lead to a more radical unionism. One thing that has been a powerful deterrent to the radicalization of workers in the United States is their belief in the legitimacy of the government.[45] Despite government repression, and despite government support of business, workers have believed that it was possible for the government to be their advocate. Thus during the 1930s, UMW organizers told miners that the government wanted them to join the union, and they believed it and hung pictures of FDR on their mantels to show their gratitude.[46] Historically in the United States there has been a partly real and partly perceived dichotomy between economic dictatorship and political democracy. Workers have long known that their work places are not all democratic. Those who own the factories make the rules; those who work in them follow the rules.

Even if workers have often expressed hostility toward the government and skepticism about its democratic character, most of them believe that the government is basically democratic, or more democratic than other governments, or as democratic as it is ever likely to be. It has been very difficult for radicals to demonstrate the connection between political democracy and economic autocracy in such a way that workers would see the need to form a political party to gain control of the state and use this control to dismantle the economic dictatorship. Workers have been led to believe that work places *must* be structured undemocratically,[47] and also that they are equal to everyone else politically. The freedom of movement or autonomy of the government, its ability to make political concessions to workers without changing basic economic relationships, had reinforced this belief that the United States is a democracy.[48] Thus, workers have not been attracted to radical political parties, believing that they could actively participate in government through the traditional political parties. Some radicals, perhaps sensing this, have concentrated their energies upon building up labor organizations that would eventually seize the factories directly.[49] However, such workers' control movements have not had much success either, probably because workers have not felt it to be their right to seize other people's property,[50] and because the state's law enforcement agencies have systematically smashed any attempts by workers to do so.[51]

Today, however, the role of the government has changed dramatically from what it was before World War II. It has been forced, in order to prevent another Great Depression, to directly prop up the economy by buying billions of dollars of output from private firms, by establishing an elaborate social-welfare system, and by hiring millions of workers itself to produce the enormous volume of government services necessary for the smooth functioning of monopoly capitalism. All of this has required higher taxes and increased public debt,[52] the latter often financed by increasing the money supply and aggravating the inflationary pressures inherent in a monopolized economy. To curb inflation, the government takes actions directly harmful to public workers; it lays them off and compels them to work harder. It structures their work places exactly like those in the private sector, with rigid hierarchies and a sharp separation between those who conceptualize the work and those who do it. In other words, the government acts more and more like a private capitalist in its relationship to its own vastly expanded work force. This occurs precisely because the government's "autonomy" has been reduced; because it is tied too directly to the ability of the economy to expand (or to accumulate, in Marxist terminology) and therefore to survive, it cannot allow its own employees to do things (fight for higher wages, gain control of their work places) that will jeopardize its ability to tax and spend in whatever ways are necessary to maintain economic and political stability.[53]

The new and critical functions that the government now serves place public employees in an important position within the working class. The state may now find it more difficult to maintain its legitimacy, its right to govern, in the eyes of the people. Public workers, through their unions, may be able to create and intensify a "crisis of legitimacy," which will make it more difficult for the government to govern and more likely that workers will come into opposition to it in a radical manner. And they can do this by responding aggressively to the government's austerity programs, which have undermined their wages, hours, and working conditions.

Public workers see that the government does not treat them in a democratic manner; it treats them as workers, as people who take orders in return for a wage payment. However, public workers, because they carry out the orders of the government—of school boards, city councils, state legislatures and bureaucracies, federal departments—are also in an especially good position to see that the various levels of government treat most of the general public, especially the working class, undemocratically. For example, public school teachers can see daily that the public does not even minimally control the schools, and they could attest that there is little democracy between themselves and school administrators. Social-service workers of all types regularly observe the callousness and brutality with which the state treats the poor, the sick, and those in prison. Welfare workers can see that welfare functions to pacify the poor and to maintain an abundant supply of low-wage labor. All public employees are aware of the corruption that characterizes state agencies, and they know that government officials are but minimally concerned with or responsive to the public.

Public employees could become vital sources of information for the rest of the working class on what state, local, and federal governments are doing; they could encourage all workers to organize to force the state to act in the workers' interest. Further, public employees could themselves pressure the state into providing more and better public services by directly or indirectly incorporating demands for them into their contracts. By demanding that the state provide decent schools, hospitals, housing, prisons, welfare, and roads, public employees would be demanding that the state serve the people—in other words, behave as the "democratic myth" says it should. Teachers could demand smaller classes; nurses could demand smaller patient loads; fire fighters could demand better equipment.

What possible progressive and especially what radical outcomes might occur if public sector unions acted as public-worker advocates? First, this could help to unify the working class. The U.S. working class is very badly divided along ethnic, racial, and sexual lines, each segment within it too easily convinced that another group is responsible for its problems. Public employees themselves have been blamed by employers for the current fiscal crisis, and such scapegoating has not fallen upon unreceptive public (including workers) ears. In commenting upon what he believes is the futility of "economic" strikes by public workers, Paul Johnston traces the development of a typical public sector strike:

Labor starts with unrealistically high wage demands, to leave room for the "negotiations game." This process works its way toward the withdrawal, or threat of withdrawal, of labor in a strike. . . . Management has its own ready-made counterstrategy. The union serves as a convenient political scapegoat for public officials caught between relatively declining tax revenues, spiraling demands for public services, and the taxpayers' rebellion. The union as villain takes the heat off management for its . . . ineptitude, its criminal priorities, corporate profiteering, and so on. Management and politicians, in league with chambers of commerce and the press, seize the time to crush the upstart workers. . . . [They loudly denounce] the $17,000 street sweeper, [and] move to build a reactionary base in defense of the public treasury against the greedy unions.[54]

Although Johnston's argument is overstated, it does contain more than a grain of truth.[55] To combat this scapegoating and at the same time build alliances with other workers, public workers could begin to articulate demands that all or most workers can support and fight vigorously to win.[56] Through educational outreach (teach-ins, media advertising, public meetings) and contacts in central labor councils, public employees could convince private sector workers to fight with them for public services that workers have a right to demand. A union of teachers at a public college, for example, might use such tactics to press for a reduction in tuition so that more working-class children could attend.

If coalitions of public and private sector workers succeed in winning more public services, then both groups are better off and more likely to fight together in the future. However, public employers will strongly resist demands that they provide schools, hospitals, roads, and police and fire protection to meet the needs of workers. They will say that these things are too expensive, that they would require exorbitant taxes, that they are not really necessary. As this (inevitably) happens, public workers could demonstrate the fallaciousness of the public employers' arguments, while continuing to impress upon all workers their *right* to demand that the government meet their needs. Here, public employees could expose the bias of local, state, and federal budgets toward the interests of businesses and the well-to-do, showing that taxes overburden lower-income groups and expenditures promote higher profits for business, not better services for workers.[57] Public-employee unions could convene meetings throughout the country to develop alternative local, state, and federal budgets, budgets that shift the burden of taxation away from the working class onto those with higher incomes and the corporations that they control. These alternative budgets could detail more humane and rational expenditure schemes, geared toward public services and employment. As new budgets are developed, public unions could conduct and mobilize demonstrations, rallies, letter-writing campaigns, media blitzes, door-to-door canvassing, and referendum campaigns to make the workers' budget law.

By demanding public services for the working class and by showing clearly that government budgets can provide them, public sector unions would put public employers on the defensive and ultimately force them to reveal through their actions that democracy in the United States is indeed a myth, that the purpose of our government is to preserve privilege by preserving capitalism. In other words, as the state refuses to serve the public when it has been clearly demonstrated that it could do so with existing resources, then the state may lose its legitimacy. But instead of this leading to worker apathy, or worse yet fascism, it could lead to a feeling among workers that they could and should organize to win control of the state and change it so that it does serve them. Radical public sector unionism could become the basis for a workers' political party whose goal is to capture state power.

Will Public Workers Meet the Challenge?

How likely is it that this will actually happen? Is it mostly just wishful thinking? Socialist union activists like Paul Johnston believe that public sector unions must abandon the model of private sector unions, that is, so-called bread-and-butter or business unionism, and become political unions in the senses I have just described. They must stop relying upon economic strikes, which alienate them from other taxpaying workers, and upon the traditional lobbying tactics, which are based on the assumption that during a budget crisis all the unions need are some people in their hip pocket at the state capital to fight for their part of the budget. Instead Johnston recommends using political strikes (strikes to force the state to provide services to workers) and actions that benefit and educate all workers and lobbying based upon mass mobilizations of workers.

Failure to do these things will allow public employers to isolate and ultimately destroy public-worker unions.

Although I am not so certain that the public sector unions must take Johnston's advice if they are to survive, I do believe that they must follow it if they are to be catalysts for the radicalization of the labor movement. It must be recognized, however, that there are enormous obstacles to public unions fulfilling their radical promise. First, there must be changes in the internal structures of the unions. Most of these unions are structured along the lines of AFL-CIO unionism, with its bureaucratic, top-down organization and emphasis upon economic bargaining. The Industrial Union Department of the AFL-CIO, for example, funneled large sums of money into the UFT, helped to train its organizers, and intervened on behalf of the union during critical periods in its early history. Many other public unions are simply outgrowths of what were originally private sector unions. It is not surprising then that the new unions are controlled by rather conventional leaders and that they have usually behaved like private sector unions. It will be necessary to challenge these leaders and their actions, but this will be a formidable task. It is not even certain that rank-and-file unionists will immediately embrace a radical model for their unions. After all, they have been indoctrinated by the same forces as other workers. In addition, the initial economic successes of public sector unions must surely have strengthened the power of those within the unions who believed that bread-and-butter unionism was all unions could or should practice. Those rank-and-filers who were not already politically progressive had no evidence that their unions could and should be different than other unions and were therefore disposed to follow the lead of those leaders who "delivered the goods."

Public sector unions have the potential to unify the working class in opposition to the state, but there will be difficulties here as well. Both the private and the public sector work forces are divided into many, sometimes antagonistic, categories. What could public-employee unions do, for instance, to combat racism within the entire working class? On balance, the racial record of the public unions is somewhat better than that of private sector unions, and perhaps they could serve as models of what racially united unions can do. But racism is so deeply ingrained in whites that it will be a barrier to unity among workers for a long time to come, and is there anything about the uniqueness of public-worker unions that will give them a special role in ending it?

The heterogeneity of public and private workers creates other problems. Given the diversity of public employees, it will not be easy for them to cooperate with one another, let alone agree on specific strategies and programs. They may all face similar dilemmas, but they may not necessarily perceive them in the same way or draw the conclusion that solidarity with each other and with other workers is necessary. Relatively elite public employees such as police, fire fighters, and tenured teachers may try to protect their superior economic positions at the expense of other workers. The public sector labor movement might come to resemble that of the private sector: a small "aristocracy" of well-paid workers at the top and a mass of poorly paid, partly organized proletarians at the bottom. Needless to say, a public labor force split into hostile camps is not the ideal vehicle for the radicalization of the working class.

The specific demands made upon public employers around which worker unity is to be forged will not be easy to formulate either. Consider two examples: lower college tuitions and reform of the prison system. It might be thought that all workers would favor lower tuitions so that more working-class youth could attend. Yet, I know from personal experience that many teachers do not want tuitions reduced or more scholarships given to poor families. Can we even be sure that white workers and men would support more scholarships for racial minorities and women? Prison reform creates still more serious problems. To police officers, prison guards, and many other workers, this might mean harsher laws, stiffer sentences, and more capital punishment, none of which would deal with the real issues and none of which would unify the working class in a radical manner. Other examples could be examined (for example, welfare reform), but they would all make one thing clear: it will be very difficult to develop alternative packages of public expenditures that will appeal to a majority of workers and at the same time help to generate a radical consciousness among them.

The economic needs of public workers may also prevent them from leading a mass movement for public services. Large numbers of public employees remain unorganized and underpaid, and even those in unions are not keeping up with inflation.[58] Hence, standard trade union demands are going to be uppermost in the minds of a lot of public workers, who, if given a choice, might prefer higher wages to better roads, schools, mass transit, and hospitals. Of course, it is possible to combine demands for more pay with those for better services, and a politically conscious membership could perhaps do so and still win public support. Johnston suggests, for example, that public employees conduct economic strikes in ways conducive to gaining support and increasing political consciousness. Teachers on strike for higher wages could conduct alternative classes for their students and sponsor teach-ins to place their salary demands within a context of the alternative state budgets that would allow higher wages, lower tuitions, and more scholarships. Or, more generally:

> Public workers can use their strike mobilization to gather signatures for an initiative for upcoming elections, then return to work with no contract and spend the subsequent months campaigning. The initiative measure should be designed to educate the public and obtain support. It could implement key contract demands, cut management salary, reform election laws, budget determination and fiscal procedures, tax laws, and so forth.[59]

A final difficulty for radical public unionism is that it is not now legal for public employees to bargain over the nature of public services. Most of the collective bargaining statutes contain restrictive "management rights" clauses, which strictly limit the scope of bargaining to wages, hours, and terms and conditions of employment.[60] These clauses often allow public employers to legally refuse to bargain over class sizes for teachers or materials used by road-repair crews or rights of welfare recipients. If public employees strike over such issues, they will be violating the law and risking fines and imprisonment. Again, public workers could seek mass working-class support in such situations and press forward with their demands. But suppose that public employers, like those in private industry, offer more money in exchange for managerial control. Will union leaders, no matter how radical, be able to resist this offer when the alternative is a long, drawn-out, and uncertain struggle for worker support for more radical demands?

A Challenge to Radicals

Despite the formidable difficulties, public sector unions do have radical potential. They offer the best hope, I believe, for moving the labor movement away from "pure and simple," economist unionism, and they offer some hope as the basis for the formation of a radical political party. Naturally, they will not fulfill their promise on their own; that will have to be the result of an active participation and leadership by radicals, especially those who are public workers. We must do everything that we can to make our union locals democratic and responsive to the members, and we must also propagandize in an open and nondogmatic way for the kind of public sector unionism envisioned in this paper. We must try to get our co-workers to see the necessity of demanding things that benefit workers and of forming the alliances with other workers so that the government will be required to construct budgets that contain these things. Ultimately, we know that for this to happen the nature of the government itself must change, but it will only be through patient, day-to-day organizing among all workers that the working class as a whole will see this too. Radical public workers can begin this process in their unions now. We have nothing to lose.

Notes

1. *Economic Report of the President,* 1978, p. 257.
2. Ibid., p. 296. See also Barbara Cottman Job, "More Public Services Spur Growth in Government Employment," *Monthly Labor Review,* 101(1978):3–7.
3. *Economic Report of the President,* 1978, p. 296.
4. AFL membership fell from around 4 million in 1921 to about 2 million by 1933 (Daniel Quinn Mills, *Labor-Management Relations* [New York: McGraw-Hill, 1978], pp. 87–88).
5. Cited in David Brody, "The Expansion of the American Labor Movement: Institutional Sources of Stimulus and Restraint," in *The American Labor Movement,* ed. David Brody (New York: Harper & Row, 1971), p. 120.
6. For a general treatment of labor in the 1920s see Irving Bernstein, *The Lean Years, A History of the American Worker: 1920–1933* (Baltimore: Penguin, 1960). Paternalism included the formation of company unions, company houses for certain workers, profit-sharing, etc. For some details from the steel industry, see David Brody, *Steelworkers in America: The Nonunion Era* (New York: Harper & Row, 1969), pp. 80–124.
7. Robert Justin Goldstein, *Political Repression in Modern America* (Cambridge, Mass.: Schenkman, 1978), pp. 103–92.

8. Ibid., p. 183.
9. Ibid., pp. 183–91.
10. For specific examples see Katherine Stone, "The Origins of Job Structures in the Steel Industry," *The Review of Radical Political Economics*, 6 (Summer 1974):113–73; Harry Braverman, *Labor and Monopoly Capital* (New York: Monthly Review Press, 1974); and The Work Relations Group, "Uncovering the Hidden History of the American Workplace," *The Review of Radical Political Economics*, 10 (Winter 1978):1–23.
11. Brody, *Steelworkers in America,* pp. 214–62; Melvyn Dubofsky and Warren Van Tine, *John L. Lewis: A Biography* (New York: Times Books, 1977), pp. 203–21.
12. James Weinstein, *The Decline of Socialism in America: 1912–1925* (New York: Monthly Review Press, 1967); Goldstein, op. cit., pp. 137–92.
13. This is the conclusion of labor historian Sidney Lens's, "Disorganized Labor," *The Nation*, 228 (Feb. 1979):206–09.
14. Mills, op. cit., p. 96. These percentages exclude members of employee associations, many of which function as labor unions. However, including them would not change the downward trend. See also "Unions Growing But Not Keeping Up," *Dollars and Sense* (Sept. 1978):6–8.
15. The most important reforms would have made it more difficult to discharge workers for union activity and potentially very costly for an employer to bargain in bad faith. *The Labor Reform Act of 1977*, 95th Cong., 2d. Sess., H.R. 8410, 1978.
16. Thomas Ferguson and Joel Rogers, "Labor Law Reform and Its Enemies," *The Nation*, 228 (Jan. 1979):1, 17–20.
17. See, for example, "California's 13 Hits CETA Jobs," *Dollars and Sense* (Oct. 1978):6 and *The Guardian,* especially May to August 1979.
18. General Motors and other corporate giants, for example, have been hiring anti-union consultants to help them keep their nonunion plants and workers unorganized. See "Big Brother in the Workplace," *Dollars and Sense* (March 1979):17.
19. This has been most apparent in the printing trades where newspaper owners have declared all-out war on union work rules and have won significant victories over the unions in Washington, D.C. and several other cities. In July 1979, Westinghouse Corporation demanded that union workers begin to pay into their pension funds. The company had made 100 percent of these payments for twenty-five years.
20. Ferguson and Rogers, op. cit., p. 17; Paul Johnston, "The Promise of Public-Service Unionism, *Monthly Review*, 30 (Sept. 1978):17. However, a lot of unorganized workers throughout the country would like to be organized. Thomas A. Kochan, "How American Workers View Labor Unions," *Monthly Labor Review*, 102 (April 1979):23–31.
21. In 1960 unions won 59 percent of all representation elections; in 1970

the figure was 56 percent; and by 1977 it had fallen to 48 percent. Unions also have been losing more decertification elections: 69 percent in 1960, 70 percent in 1970, and 76 percent in 1977. "Unions Growing But Not Keeping Up," op. cit., p. 7.

22. For general histories of the rebirth of the labor movement in the 1930s, see Dubofsky and Van Tine, op. cit., pp. 181–388; Irving Bernstein, *Turbulent Years, A History of the American Worker: 1933–1941* (Boston: Houghton Mifflin, 1970); Jeremy Brecker, *Strike* (San Francisco: Straight Arrow, 1972), pp. 144–220.

23. Mills, op. cit., pp. 90 and 94; *American Labor Movement*, ed. David Brody, p. 136.

24. Ray Marshall, "Unions and the Black Community," in *American Labor Movement*, ed. David Brody, pp. 138–57; James J. Kennealy, *Women and American Trade Unions* (St. Albans, Vt.: Eden, 1978), pp. 154–77.

25. Dubofsky and Van Tine, op. cit., p. 326.

26. Alice and Staughton Lynd, eds., *Rank and File* (Boston: Beacon Press, 1973).

27. Dubofsky and Van Tine, op. cit., p. 251 ff.

28. The next few paragraphs are taken from Michael Yates, *Public School Teachers' Unions in Pennsylvania* (Ph.D. dissertation, University of Pittsburgh, 1976), pp. 50–75.

29. Jack Stieber, *Public Employee Unionism* (Washington, D.C.: Brookings Institution, 1973), pp. 23–30.

30. See, for example, George N. Schmidt, *The American Federation of Teachers and the CIA* (Chicago: Substitutes United for Better Schools, 1978), pp. 50–54.

31. Stieber, op. cit., pp. 194–99.

32. John O'Neill, "The Rise and Fall of the UFT," in *Schools Against Children*, ed. Annette Rubinstein (New York: Monthly Review Press, 1970), p. 175.

33. Material in this paragraph is taken from Yates, op. cit., pp. 190–92.

34. Sterling D. Spero and John M. Capozzola, *The Urban Community and Its Unionized Bureaucracies* (New York: Dunellen, 1973), pp. 179–82.

35. Dubofsky and Van Tine, op. cit., pp. 300–38.

36. Taft-Hartley placed restrictions upon strikes, picketing, and boycotts. For details see Richard Hurd, "New Deal Labor Policy and the Containment of Radical Union Activity," *The Review of Radical Political Economics*, 8 (Fall 1976):32–43.

37. Goldstein, op. cit., pp. 231–398.

38. For details from the auto industry, see William Serrin, *The Company and the Union* (New York: Knopf, 1973).

39. James Weinstein, *Ambiguous Legacy, The Left in American Politics* (New York: New Viewpoints, 1975), pp. 57–86. As Communist Party leader Earl Browder put it, "Everything that organizes and activizes

the working class and its allies is progress toward socialism," Earl Browder, *The People's Front* (New York: International Publishers, 1938), p. 148.

40. Stieber, op. cit., p. 32.
41. Steve Zeluck, "Three Months After the UFT Strike," in Rubinstein, op. cit., p. 217.
42. Schmidt, op. cit., pp. 31–38.
43. Mark Maier, "Public Sector Labor Relations," Chapter 17 of this volume.
44. Ibid.
45. Brecher, op. cit., pp. 233–62.
46. Miners interviewed by students of mine invariably expressed the sentiment that FDR wanted them to join the union.
47. The Work Relations Group, op. cit., pp. 7–15.
48. New Deal social security and labor legislation are examples. See Frances Fox Piven and Richard A. Cloward, *Poor People's Movements* (New York: Pantheon, 1977), pp. 41–180.
49. This was the strategy of the IWW.
50. Brecher, op. cit., pp. 233–62.
51. Ibid.
52. The Editors, "Debt and the Business Cycle," *Monthly Review*, 30 (June 1978):1–12.
53. James O'Connor, *The Fiscal Crisis of the State* (New York: St. Martin's Press, 1973), pp. 40–63, 221–60.
54. Johnston, op. cit., pp. 9–10.
55. Public workers have been supported by the public many times, even in economic strikes. For an example, see Yates, op. cit., p. 188.
56. At times it will be necessary and possible to seek support from sympathetic people outside of the working class, such as professionals and owners of small businesses.
57. AFSCME, in a series of ads in newspapers and magazines, has begun to criticize military expenditures along these lines. For useful information on the priorities of the federal budget and some alternatives, see Study Group on the Budget, Institute for Policy Studies, *The Federal Budget and Social Reconstruction* (New Brunswick, N.J.: Transaction, 1978).
58. About half of all state and local government workers remain unorganized. "State and Local Government Employees in Labor Organizations," *Monthly Labor Review*, 101 (August 1978):43–44. Even in large cities, many municipal workers make much less than $1,000 per month. *Statistical Abstract of the United States* (Washington, D.C.: U.S. Bureau of Census, 1978), p. 323.
59. Johnston, op. cit., p. 16.
60. Maier, op. cit.

16. Public Sector Workers and the Crisis of Capitalism

Martin Hart-Landsberg, Jerry Lembcke, and Bob Marotto

The Importance of the Public Sector at the State and Local Level

On the surface, the growth of the U.S. economy throughout the 1950s and 1960s appeared to give testimony to the fact that the growing involvement of the capitalist state, financed by deficit spending, could provide political legitimation for capitalism and support private capital accumulation.[1] Interestingly, the greatest increase in public sector employment and debt have occurred at the state and local level, not at the federal level. State and local government employment, for example, increased 210 percent from 1950 to 1978, compared with an increase of only 43 percent at the federal level. Debt increased almost seventeen times over the same period at the state and local level, but only doubled at the federal level.

This rapid growth was necessary because state and local governments are most directly involved in the provision of accumulation services (roads, sewers, utilities, etc.) and legitimation services (education, welfare, health, etc.). They are the level of government in greatest contact with and most accessible to the

Martin Hart-Landsberg teaches economics at Lewis and Clark College in Portland, Oregon; Jerry Lembcke is a sociologist living in Madison, Wisconsin; Bob Marotto is doing graduate work in sociology at the University of California at Santa Cruz. This paper is an expanded and updated version of "Public Employees: Digging Graves for the System?" which appeared in *U.S. Capitalism in Crisis,* published by URPE in 1978.

majority of the people. Their need to rely on debt to finance the growth in these services, however, was primarily due to certain historical conditions and structural limitations.[2]

In the early post-World War II period, many areas (particularly the Northeast and Midwest) experienced a sizable in-migration of poor, unskilled workers, demands by Third World people for adequate social services, and demands by business and citizens for increased services of all kinds. All of these pressures necessitated ever-increasing expenditures.

Problems, however, existed on the revenue side. Because of political realities, there were certain limits on the speed and size of tax increases. Governments were unable to match revenue to expenditures, since higher tax levels could, and often did, encourage corporations and wealthy families to leave urban areas, and the working class could not be squeezed indefinitely without severe political consequences for elected officials. For most local governments, deficit financing was the only way that expenditures and social peace could be maintained.

With the economic problems of the 1970s, however, all levels of government faced new and serious challenges. The situation came to a crisis in the 1970s: inflation drove costs up, while the recession lowered revenues and increased demands on the government. State and local governments found their need to borrow greatly increased by the two-way squeeze.

This time, however, forces combined to limit the governments' ability to raise additional funds: financial institutions refused to lend more money for fear of seeing ever-mounting debts go unpayed; workers already under attack from inflation and recession resisted new increases in taxes. Under this pressure governments reduced spending to bring it in line with revenues. Deficit financing could no longer be relied upon to paper over the problems generated by capitalism.

The 1970s recession produced sizable unemployment and budget cuts in many urban areas. The subsequent recovery was too weak to substantially improve the situation. Government officials realized that urban stability and peace could not be maintained forever under depressed economic conditions. Economic revitalization was necessary and, according to most officials, could only be achieved through private investment and activity. Given this perspective, state and local governments found themselves with two interrelated tasks: spending on some programs had to be cut back, and the private sector had to be encouraged to increase investment and create new jobs.

Translated into concrete policy, this meant a reduction in legitimation services (health, education, welfare). Cuts in this area were most logical, since they did not harm private capital. In fact, by reducing benefits, local governments could encourage more workers to accept low-paying and unsafe employment. At the same time, governments sought to increase accumulation services so as to attract new capital. By increasing infrastructural activity, the state was helping to socialize business costs among workers, thereby directly increasing private profits. If deficits were to be reduced, cuts in legitimation had to be greater than increases in accumulation.

State and local governments are now competing with each other to demonstrate to banks their "fiscal responsibility" (by restricting overall budget deficits) and to corporations their willingness to provide attractive and profitable options. Reductions in corporate tax rates and less restrictive environmental and occupational safety regulations are now common parts of state policy. So, too, are such projects as industrial parks, whereby the state purchases land, builds facilities, and trains workers for interested corporations, all at the taxpayers' expense.

The bidding war between states has become so serious that even the *Wall Street Journal* was forced to comment. Discussing the recent Pennsylvania-Volkswagen negotiations, its editorial noted:

> The host government will put up $40 million to buy an unused plant for the auto firm to lease; it will spend $30 million on highway and rail links to the plant; it will waive 95% of local taxes the first two years and 50% the following two; it has arranged for employee training. Not content with all this, the auto company is sticking at paying 9% interest on a $135 million tooling loan.
>
> Pennsylvania officials argue that the complex leaseback agreement and the economic activity generated by the VW Rabbit plant will rapidly pay back the subsidies. We certainly hope they are right. But the best test of such judgments is the amount of private capital attracted, and that is largely absent in this case. The $135 million loan under discussion would come from pension funds of school teachers and other state employees.[3]

Examples of similar state support for private accumulation can also be found in the Sunbelt. According to Brad Heil:

Over the past ten years Sunbelt cities, in conjunction with their respective states, have increasingly made use of financial-aid incentives in order to attract industry. Typically, a municipality will sell bonds to purchase a site and build a plant for a particular company, usually to the company's specification. It is then leased to the company for a period of time sufficient for rental payments to cover principal and interest on the bonds.

The industrial-aid bond is often accompanied by an offer to train the required work force to meet the firm's specifications at public expense, and several years of immunity from property taxes. South Carolina's worker training program, for example, trained the 700 employees of Georgetown Steel plant while the plant was being constructed. When the plant opened, production started the first day. Cities in Mississippi carry this process one step further. According to *U.S. News and World Report:* "If a new factory does not work out as well as hoped, Mississippi will conduct plant lay-out studies, management analysis, and product or marketing surveys to correct errors. The state maintains a computerized listing of available sites, vital facts on 350 communities, and the names of 10,000 graduates of the state universities as potential employees."[4]

While local government strategy is designed to respond to immediate economic pressures, the rearrangement of the state's priorities and the further expansion of state and local governments into the process of private capital accumulation also works in support of capital's struggle against the growing stagflation. By reducing the state's deficits through cuts in legitimation services, the state supports capital's fight against inflation. By increasing its involvement in the provision of infrastructural services, the state supports capital's attempt to reinvigorate investment and production.[5] Given the magnitude of the crisis facing capitalism, however, these are only small props to the system and unlikely to reverse current downward trends.

The severity of service cuts and the impact of continuing hard times has, not surprisingly, brought resistance to state and local government policy. This resistance has included struggles by public sector workers and community groups around jobs, wages, housing, health care, education, and other social services. Both the crisis and the fight-back are bound to grow. Given cohesion and direction, this struggle could become an organized political force challenging capitalism's power to govern. The key element to this development is a progressive trade-union movement. Because of their current position in the U.S. political economy, public sector workers can play an important role in that movement.

The Crisis at the State and Local Levels

Because of their numbers, composition, and structural location in the economy, public sector employees play a crucial role in the current political and economic crisis in the United States.

Size

Contrary to media propaganda about a sprawling Washington bureaucracy, growth at the federal level has been comparatively small; over 90 percent of the growth in public sector employment has occurred at the local level.

Furthermore, during the post-war period employment at the public sector level has grown twice as fast as it has in the private sector. While private sector employment has fallen during each post-war recession, local government employment has grown every year except 1951. During the 1970s recession, for example, while private sector employment fell 3 percent, local government employment rose 4 percent.

Given capitalism's inherent instability, it is not surprising that public sector employment and the state's activity have grown in both good times and bad. While current calls for state fiscal responsibility may temporarily slow this growth, the present size and long-term pattern of growth suggests that they will remain an important and sizable factor in the U.S. political economy.

Composition

While size is important, the racial, sexual, and class composition of state and local government workers are also significant. In the 1960s, the fastest growth occurred in areas employing predominantly Third World and women workers. Table 16-1, which provides data for the five largest Standard Metropolitan Statistical Areas (SMSAs), shows that the fastest growing categories are ones that have above-average percentages of Third World and women workers. In welfare services, for example, 69.3 percent of all work-

Table 16-1   Full-time public sector employees in five largest SMSAs by sex, race, and ethnic group, 1974

Public sector department	Percent employed			Total employees
	Women	Blacks	Hispanics	
Police	10.2	12.7	3.9	121,047
Fire	1.5	4.9	1.8	39,894
Utilities and transport	11.7	36.2	5.8	97,668
Public welfare	69.3	44.7	6.4	76,708
Financial administration and general control	46.2	15.1	4.7	66,444
Streets and highways*	8.2	16.7	7.6	32,424
Sanitation and sewage*	3.5	27.5	2.1	33,851
Hospitals and sanitariums	63.5	44.4	10.8	120,889
Health	59.4	39.3	—	4,276
Natural resources*	14.6	22.2	8.9	22,557
Corrections†	27.6	29.0	—	5,416
Housing‡	23.9	37.8	15.0	21,006
Other	36.7	31.4	6.1	96,381
Total	33.0	28.0	5.0	754,142

Source: Employment Profiles of Women and Minorities in 23 Metropolitan Areas, 1974, U.S. Equal Employment Opportunity Commission. SMSAs include New York/New Jersey; Chicago; Los Angeles/Long Beach; Detroit; and Philadelphia/New Jersey. Data for Hispanics is only provided for first three SMSAs.

* Includes data for only four SMSAs; Hispanics, two.
† Includes data for only two SMSAs; Hispanics, none.
‡ Includes data for only three SMSAs; Hispanics, one.

ers are women, 44 percent are Black, and 6.4 percent, Hispanic, compared with overall averages of 33 percent, 28 percent and 5 percent respectively.

One result of such growth is that by the mid-1970s, Black workers had a higher participation rate in the public sector than in the private sector in many large urban areas. Table 16-2 shows that in the largest urban areas, almost twice as many Blacks are employed in the public sector as in the private sector. In New York City and Los Angeles, state and local governments employ over one-fourth of all Black workers.[6] While the figures are not as dramatic in terms of female and Hispanic workers, participation rates

Table 16-2   Full-time public and private sector employees in five largest SMSAs by sex, race, and ethnic group, 1974

| | Percent in private sector | | | Percent in public sector | | |
SMSA	Women	Blacks	His-panics	Women	Blacks	His-panics
New York/ New Jersey	40.9	15.0	8.9	32.6	31.0	7.3
Chicago	37.8	15.1	6.9	32.3	32.6	2.9
Los Angeles/ Long Beach	36.5	9.1	16.4	35.4	21.1	10.1
Detroit	28.0	18.8	—	38.8	29.2	—
Philadelphia/ New Jersey	35.9	14.8	—	32.4	29.5	—
Total	36.3	14.3	7.5	33.0	28.0	5.0

Source: Employment Profiles, op. cit.

for both groups of workers in the public sector are now almost identical to that in the private sector.

These trends are very important. Racism and sexism remain great blocks to working-class unity and must be struggled against as part of the process of building a progressive trade-union movement. The heavy concentration of Third World workers and the substantial percentage of women workers in the state sector means that organizing efforts among state sector workers will be more likely to confront these issues directly, and in a way that encourages ties to issues and constituencies currently outside of narrow trade-union political work.

The class composition of the state and local public sector work force also argues for its key significance: most are employed in blue-collar, proletarian occupations. Over half are in service-maintenance, skilled crafts, clerical, and paraprofessional jobs. If fire fighters and teachers are added, we find that nearly two-thirds of this work force is proletarian.[7] This is obviously important, since it encourages greater class consciousness and solidarity with other workers in opposition to the needs of capitalists.

Structural Location within the Economy

While the political importance of organizing workers in both the accumulation and legitimation sectors of the state work force has increased, this increased importance stems from different, and in some sense, opposite, developments within each of these two functional sectors.

Very generally, Table 16-3 shows that during the period 1962-1972 public sector employment in state and local government grew more rapidly in areas of legitimation than accumulation. During the 1973-1977 period, however, while growth slowed in all legitimation functions, it increased in four out of six accumulation functions. In order to draw out the political implications of this development, we undertake a separate analysis of each sector.

Accumulation. The apparent shift of state employment priorities to accumulation services is very important. The expansion of the

Table 16-3   Percentage growth in local public sector employment by job category

	1962–1972	*1973–1975*	*1973–1977*
Legitimation functions			
Welfare	10.9	6.3	4.6
Health	9.3	5.3	4.2
Education	7.3	3.1	2.5
Hospitals	4.3	1.4	1.8
Sanitation	1.4	− 0.8	− 0.6
Accumulation functions			
Highways	1.0	0.4	− 0.5
Sewage	3.7	5.9	4.6
Housing & urban			
renewal	2.2	15.5	5.4
Airports	5.0	5.9	2.9
Water transportation			
& terminals	− 0.6	7.7	3.9
Local utilities	1.4	4.6	2.7

Source: Data compiled from Table 3 of the *Public Employment* series for given years, U.S. Department of Commerce, Bureau of the Census.

state's involvement in areas of infrastructural services such as garbage collection, urban renewal, and public utilities diminishes the necessity for private investors to provide capital for production of these services, thereby freeing private capital for profit-producing investments.

Table 16-3 indicates that the shift-to-accumulation functions seem to accelerate during periods of recession. In the 1973-1975 period, when the state was forced to respond to an overall downturn in the private economy, it did so by making dramatic, if relative, cutbacks in all areas of legitimation. Welfare, for example, grew at an annual rate of 10.9 percent during 1962-1972 but slowed to a rate of 6.3 percent during 1973-1975. This reduction occurred despite the fact that, with tens of thousands of additional workers thrown out of work, there was undoubtedly an increased demand for welfare services. During the same period, we find an increasing rate of growth occurring in all but one of the accumulation functions. The changes in housing and urban renewal (2.2 percent to 15.5 percent) and water transportation and terminals (-0.6 percent to 7.7 percent) were the most spectacular.

When the 1973-1977 period, which included a recession (1973-1975) and a growth period (1976-1977), is examined in its entirety, the trends indicated above are moderated. That is, during the growth period, it appears that employment weakened somewhat in *both* legitimation and accumulation. When the recession period is compared to the 1962-1972 period, however, the great disparities that existed between growth rates in legitimation and accumulation functions in the earlier period are eliminated. That is, while legitimation functions were growing much more rapidly during 1962-1972 than accumulation functions, they have very similar growth rates over the 1973-1977 period.

In describing these trends, we obviously do not mean to imply that all capitalists share a simple-minded goal of expanding the state's accumulation services. There are, in fact, examples of the exact opposite policy being pursued (Cleveland being a recent example). Capitalists will most likely seek to overcome the current crisis by maintaining a flexible strategy. At times they will no doubt find it more profitable and politically advantageous to argue for private subcontracting of existing state services. In our opinion, however, developments over the next several years should sharpen and clarify the trends discussed above.

The Proposition 13 movement has put workers in local government legitimation functions on the "hit list." Welfare and education will very likely suffer employment losses. Concurrently, capitalism has a long-term crisis to solve, and there is every indication that the state will play a prominent role in the provision of infrastructural necessities. In fact, it seems likely that after free-market, balance-the-budget policies prove to be successful only at deepening recession, the state will be drawn into even greater and more direct involvement in investment and production decisions.

The political importance of the state's increasingly large role in accumulation functions has three facets. First, such an expansion means an increase in blue-collar employment in state and local governments.[8] These workers, both skilled (electricians, carpenters, machine operators) and unskilled (laborers on construction and maintenance crews), will be drawn from private sector employment. They are likely to bring with them a degree of union consciousness and experience traditionally lacking where public-employee associations and anti-unionism have prevailed.

Second, while it is doubtful that *any* sector of the working class, private or public, is in a position to singularly paralyze the economy by withholding its labor, public sector workers in transit, bridge control, sanitation, communications, and utilities perform tasks that are essential for capital accumulation.

Finally, but perhaps most importantly, these workers, essential for capital accumulation, now enter into direct relations with the state. Unlike the private sector, where market mechanisms mask the class nature of the political economy, conditions in the public sector are established by explicitly political processes. This difference and the unique position of (all) state workers has been summarized by Paul Johnston:

> The private-sector worker is a direct employee of capital. Labor-power is sold to capital as part of the process of accumulation involving the production of commodities to be sold on the capitalist market. What is to be produced is defined by the demands of that market.
> The public worker, on the other hand, works for government or state-power. Labor-power is sold to the government for the production, not of commodities, but of "social use-values" which are goods or services defined as useful to society at large by those who hold state power. What is to be produced is determined through *political* decisions, not by economic "laws" of the market.[9]

This development constitutes an "interpenetration of economic base and political superstructure" which is a substantial alteration in the social relationships of production. The false consciousness attributed by Marx to the freedom of labor and commodity exchange on the market can thus be overcome. While politics may not be in command in this new alignment, political struggle is nonetheless always present, increasing the likelihood that state workers will raise political and qualitative demands in addition to economic ones.[10]

Legitimation. While the significance of state involvement in accumulation lies in its increasing structural centrality and employment growth, workers involved in legitimation are significant because, while remaining crucial to the continuation and transformation of capitalism, they are under attack. Because of the state's attempt to restore fiscal solvency, occupations concerned with providing legitimation have been the hardest hit by layoffs since the 1970s. These were, of course, the very occupations that grew most rapidly during the 1960s. This development has important consequences. First, the gatekeepers of capitalist ideology—teachers and social workers—are themselves being victimized. Second, social control previously exercised through complicated channels of legitimation is now being supplanted with less subtle mechanisms such as police repression. We can take the educational system as an example of what is happening to legitimation services. Education and teaching practices have largely been geared to cultivating both the technical and psychological foundation necessary for the reproduction of the class structure. As Gintis and Bowles argue in their powerful work, *Schooling in Capitalist America:*

> The economic system is stable only if the consciousness of the strata and classes which compose it remains compatible with the social relations which characterize it as a mode of production. The perpetuation of the class structure requires that the hierarchical division of labor be reproduced in the consciousness of its participants. The educational system is one of the several reproduction mechanisms through which dominant elites seek to achieve this objective. . . . The education system reproduces the capitalist division of labor, in part, through a correspondence between its own internal social relationships and those of the workplace.[11]

In respect to the direct ideological function, capitalism has remained unshakable, partly because its agents—teachers—have for several generations been ideological products of that very system. In recent years, however, their conditions have deteriorated considerably. Teaching, once marginally a profession, is now more akin to other white-collar wage work. They have become what sociologists call the "dirty workers" of American society—workers paid to manage the tensions created by an irrational and exploitative society. Their work has shifted from the intellectual realm to social control.[12]

The degradation of their work has had many repercussions. Among these are undoubtedly shifts in popular consciousness among teachers regarding the nature of their work and its relation to other sections of the working class.[13] Through the process of proletarianization, teachers have become more open to unionization. By 1972, nearly 2 million of the nation's 3 million teachers belonged to some sort of collective-bargaining organization. They also conducted 50 percent of the strikes in the public sector. This militancy is not only a powerful example for students (most of whom are working class), but is a direct assault on an important pillar of capitalist ideology—anti-unionism.

Welfare workers, also involved in legitimation services, have normally not only carried out the technical aspects of making the welfare system work (by assisting clients through the bureaucracy, keeping the necessary logs on the clients' status, and counseling the clients), but have also acted as ideological props of classical liberalism. These programs retard the formation of a progressive movement by directing the attention of workers away from the system and toward the victims. The welfare system also reinforces the myth that even though the national political economy has imperfections that cause "personal hardships," it takes care of those who are temporarily disadvantaged.

Welfare workers are, like teachers, induced through training programs to accept liberal myths surrounding the welfare programs. At best they become buffers between the power structure and their clients and, at worst, actual proponents of free-enterprise liberalism.

As with teachers, welfare workers have been hard-hit by cutbacks; their relationship with the system is shifting to that of victim. They are now being thrown into the ranks of the unemployed and brought into closer structural alignment with their clients. The fact that many of the unemployed welfare workers are Third World only reinforces the potential for coalitions with former clients, many of whom are also Third World.

In struggling for their own jobs, state legitimation workers necessarily raise demands concerned with provision of goods and services that are of a qualitative, noneconomist nature. This, in the words of Boris Frankel, "is because most state workers such as teachers, health workers, and social workers are struggling over conditions of work and services which directly affect their object of production—that is, other people (students, pensioners, the sick). Every attack upon the definition and organization of education, health, or transport is a struggle over social relations in a way that narrow wage demands in private factories are not."[14]

The current attack on legitimation workers thus gives the socialist movement an important chance to win the support of individuals with valuable skills and experience, as well as to build and strengthen ties between groups of people that do have a basis for a shared vision and struggle.

Control of pension funds.   One final dimension of the structural location of public sector workers needs to be discussed. Public-employee pension funds, which serve as a mechanism of capital accumulation, but which are generated by all state sector workers, accumulation and legitimation, give added weight to the political importance of this body of workers.

As Rifkin and Barber point out:

> Pension funds are a new form of wealth that has emerged over the past thirty years to become the largest single pool of private capital in the world. They are now worth over $500 billion and represent the deferred savings of millions and millions of American workers. Pension funds at present own 20–25 percent of the equity in American corporations and hold 40 percent of the bonds. Pension funds are now the largest source of investment capital for the American capitalist system.[15]

Approximately $78.4 billion in pension funds belong to state and local government retirement systems; 92 percent of these funds are invested in nongovernment (private) securities. Government workers are thus a major source of private investment capital and strategically positioned in the capital accumulation process to affect its political direction.

Until very recently, however, public-employee pension fund management has been carried out by professional and private investment institutions. As a consequence, public funds have been used to bankroll the expansion of private corporate enterprises, which in turn have wielded this economic leverage in their own interest, not the public's. Rifkin and Barber point to the flight of capital from the Northeast as a case in point. Specifically, they argue that pension funds of public employees in Northeastern cities have been invested in companies that have closed their operations in that region and opened new operations elsewhere, thereby eroding the economic base upon which the jobs of Northeastern state and local government workers are dependent.

Union members and leaders in public sector unions are beginning to wake up to the fact that by investing in private enterprise, they are digging their own graves. In New York, for example, leaders of several public-employee unions agreed to bail the city out by purchasing $240 million worth of Municipal Assistance Corporation bonds. While this was a controversial move, in that it came too late to be more than a stop-gap measure and seriously jeopardized the retirement futures of thousands of New York public employees, it did break the ice. Since then, unions have mobilized the economic leverage of pension funds against J. P. Stevens and, most recently, against the continuance of investments in South African apartheid.

To date, the exercise of pension-fund control by unions has been mainly of a protest or defensive nature. An offensive program entailing union control over pension-fund investment has yet to be developed. Rifkin and Barber suggest that social and political (as well as economic) criteria be applied to investment decisions. The social impact of an investment in low-cost housing, for example, may be more desirable in the long run than an investment in corporate stock that, while paying a higher immediate return, underwrites runaway shops. Public-employee pension funds could also be used for the acquisition of fixed capital assets abandoned by private enterprise. Mill and factory closures often threaten whole communities, including workers in public sector jobs. Pension funds could be used to purchase these properties, thereby stabilizing the local economy and breaking the structural nexus of capitalism—private ownership of productive capital.

Finally, whether union control of pension funds will contribute to a socialist transformation depends on whether unions can act in concert, and whether their action is part of a larger, theoretically conceived socialist strategy. Given the conservative character of present union leadership, however, the formulation of that broader strategy will have to be undertaken by union members and political activists.

The Left and the State Sector

Heretofore, the left has generally dismissed public sector workers as part of a labor aristocracy that benefits directly from a welfare state built upon imperialism, or as a nonrevolutionary segment of the new working class.

A socialist movement could not advance without the participation of manual workers in basic industries. We question, however, whether a socialist movement without the mobilization of public sector workers is tenable. Given their increasing involvement in accumulation and their continuing importance for legitimation (which is key to the ability of private sector workers to develop revolutionary consciousness and organization), it appears that the left can no longer ignore the sizable population of state and local public sector workers.

The heyday of unionism was the 1930s. Excluded from the union movement until 1935 by a combination of its own dual-unionist strategies and political repression, the left reentered the union movement on the crest of its own wave of organizing in the late 1930s. The CIO broke into new industrial areas. Organizing, which the left did better than anyone, was the order of the day; leadership was earned, not bought. The left in the 1930s did not gain control of existing unions or wrest leadership from the reactionary AFL leaders; it built its own unions as part of the CIO drive and consequently found itself organically linked with these unions.

While the parallel between the industrial sector in the 1930s and the public sector today is imperfect, similarities do exist. The public sector is critical to the country's political economy and to its crisis; its workers are militant and underorganized. It is, therefore, in the public sector that new unions can be and are being built.

The public sector offers special opportunities for organizing the unorganized and unionizing the organized. In 1970, 26 percent of state and local government workers were organized, but only 9 percent were actually in unions. The remainder were in associations. In 1974, 1,492,000 out of a total 11,754,000 (12.7 percent) of state and local workers were in AFL-CIO unions across the country.

Public employees threaten the labor establishment. If 12 million public workers are to enter the House of Labor, the labor bureaucrats want them under their wing or not at all. Public-employee unions, however, want some autonomy and are attempting to carve out structures similar to the industrial union department within the AFL-CIO. Consequently, a new bureaucratic structure is developing. Each newly organized union creates new positions in the union structure: local officers and delegates to AFL-CIO central labor councils and state and national conventions. Positions within these unions are likely to be filled by people who have proven their mettle in organizing; in unions organized by the left, they will be filled with leftists.[16]

Progressive public sector union members have historic opportunities to make links with social-democratic forces within labor. Included in the latter are many of the former CIO unions still influenced by social-democrats like Victor Reuther and the organization that came together around the candidacy of Ed Sadlowski for the presidency of the Steelworkers early in 1977. While the progressive character of this political tendency has severe limitations (anticommunism, elitism, and inadequate analysis of imperialism) and should not be confused with the left, which was purged from the labor movement in the 1940s, it is nevertheless distinguishable from the right-wing faction of the AFL-CIO.

With Meany's passing, old questions of control are arising within the AFL-CIO, questions raised at all levels of the organization. Wounds lingering from days before the merger, and from in-house fights are already opening, partially because of the added presence of public sector unions. Coalitions can be built on a host of local, regional, environmental, and foreign-policy issues, which have already split the labor establishment. Public sector unions are a new factor in the power equations; if their strength is joined with progressive forces in labor, the environment for leftists to raise important questions and political positions would be greatly enhanced.

Fortunately, the ability to forge militant and progressive unions is greatly advanced by the fact that much of the left is organically rooted in the public sector. The New Left movement primarily energized people who were headed for academic, paraprofessional, or other jobs found most often in the public sector. While some

New Left strategies have taken people into private industry and the Communist Party and some Trotskyist groups still have strong roots in basic industry, most radicals of the 1960s movements are in or on the fringe of the public sector. Consequently, they tend to see themselves as apart from the grass roots of industrial workers' organizations. For these radicals, organizing unions in their own work places and using these unions as vehicles to legitimately enter the labor movement is a most expedient way to accomplish links with other segments of the working class.

Public and Private Labor Unity

The growth of union militancy in the public sector has brought to the surface some contradictions between public and private sector workers that must be addressed by the left. When, for example, public sector workers demand pay raises, private sector workers suffer tax increases. In turn, private sector workers rebel, as in San Francisco, to defeat state workers' demands.[17] We believe, however, that the same dynamics that have produced this contradiction have also provided conditions within which greater working-class unity may be achieved.

Before unionization, the interest of public and private sectors could easily be pitted against one another. At one time, public sector workers produced for less pay than private sector workers, enabling services necessary for capitalism to be shifted to lower-paid workers. This acted as a drag on the wages of private sector workers and cost them jobs. Then, as public sector workers organized, government agencies began letting jobs to nonunion private employers on a contract basis. Now, with both public and private sectors being organized, these divide-and-conquer strategies can be thwarted; their affiliation with common labor organizations (local labor councils, for example) contributes to conditions of cooperative and empathetic, rather than competitive, relations.

Bringing public workers—close to 20 percent of the U.S. labor force—into the union movement will strengthen labor per se. A chief weakness of the U.S. working class has always been an ideology that does not understand, and often rejects, the principles of class solidarity and unionism. For many people, involvement in the labor movement is an education. Questions about the history of their organizations, popular wisdom about unions and working-class culture, class struggle, and socialism, will be asked. This, too, will offset much of the intraclass strife heightened by unionization of the public sector.

The relations of those who work for and those who are dependent on the state provide another counterbalance to intraclass antagonisms.[18] Clients of welfare workers and teachers, for example, are most often from private sector, working-class families. Conflicts arising from tax appropriations, which pay the wages of public sector workers, may be addressed in worker-client relations that determine the allocation of tax monies. Unemployed workers, retirees on welfare, and AFDC parents, for example, share with these workers an interest in having tax monies spent on social services, not on B-1 bombers. Coalitions built around these issues, especially with the organized political force of public sector unions, can influence the allocation of resources. These coalitions will only materialize, however, when working-class activists recognize the necessity for such coalitions.

> When this notion—which is essentially that of a socialist unionism for the public sector—is placed into the framework of the need for political power, then we will understand that the community too has an interest in what is produced (or, more precisely, that different parts of the community have varying interests in what kind of public sector is produced). . . . Activity of this kind will fill in more of the content of socialist unionism in the public sector, or public-service unionism, and will help to lay the basis for the strategic concept of the "labor/community alliance."[19]

Demands need to be made for public expenditures on services and products that are needed by both private and public employees and that also create jobs for the unemployed. Whereas taxes spent on defense benefit only the workers in the defense industry, taxes spent on mass transit create jobs for both public and private sector workers while also rationalizing the transportation system. Struggles around such programs also allow workers to confront issues of imperialism and U.S. foreign policy. Likewise, expanded educational and health programs (rather than welfare) could potentially employ millions in this country in both the private and public sector, while immensely increasing the quality of life. In short, we believe the contradiction between public and private sector workers is not as much an inherent feature of capitalism as it is a carefully orchestrated divide-and-rule strategy that is likely to continue until it is challenged by progressive organizing strategies.

For structural and historical reasons, public sector workers are advantageously situated to influence the resolution of capitalism's latest crisis, but the political future of the public sector union movement remains undecided. Capitalism's crisis is long term; its throes present new challenges, new contradictions, and new opportunities. The state's changing role in the capitalist political economy is a frontier; we can ill afford to neglect the political potential inherent in organizing the public sector work force.

Notes

1. We are using the terms accumulation and legitimation quite generally here. State services that are primarily directed at reducing private costs of production are called accumulation services. State money spent on sewers, roads, communication, energy, and industrial parks obviously supports private capital accumulation and growth, since individual capitalists get certain necessary costs paid for by the rest of the population—primarily the working class.

   State-supported legitimation services are designed more to ensure that private profits and capitalism will be safe rather than to directly subsidize private capital accumulation. Legitimation services are meant to reduce or mask the worst aspects of capitalist inequality and exploitation. If successful, such services "legitimize" the operation of capitalism for large sectors of the population and thus weaken movements that challenge the system.

   An overemphasis on legitimation is definitely not in capital's interest, since it means that valuable resources are being diverted from profit-making activities. An overemphasis on accumulation can also be dangerous for capital, since the working class may come to realize that private wealth is being accumulated directly at their expense. Few services can be classified as either pure accumulation or legitimation; yet, the distinction is of real and useful value for analyzing state priorities and policies in different periods.

2. James O'Connor's *The Fiscal Crisis of the State* (New York: St. Martin's Press, 1973) established the groundwork for much of the work done on the growth of debt-financed state activity and the resulting fiscal crisis.

3. *Wall Street Journal*, Aug. 17, 1976.

4. Brad Heil, "Sunbelt Migration," *U.S. Capitalism in Crisis*, Union of Radical Political Economics (New York: URPE, 1978).

5. On a theoretical plane important questions regarding the development of the state in advanced capitalist countries are being debated. Recently several scenarios have been sketched that address state involvement in production and accumulation. One forecasts institutional arrangements, similar to the RFC of the New Deal, which would provide equity capital for private investment. Another suggests increasing state involvement in production itself. The former is presented in Felix Rohatyn's "Wall Street Call for a New RFC and State Planning" in David Mermelstein's *The Economic Crisis Reader* (New York: Vintage, 1975) and Alan Nasser's "The Twilight of Capitalism: Contours of an Emerging Epoch" in the *Insurgent Sociologist*, 6 (Fall 1975). Eric Olin Wright's "Alternative Perspectives in the Marxist Theory of Accumulation and Crisis," in the same issue of the *Insurgent Sociologist*, suggests the latter scenario. For more recent essays on the subject, see the journal *Kapitalistate*. To date, this enquiry has chiefly addressed the institutional configurations manifested by state growth. In the analysis presented in this paper, we have concentrated on trends in state and local government employment.

6. *Employment Profiles of Women and Minorities in 23 Metropolitan Areas, 1974*, U.S. Equal Employment Opportunity Commission. In New York/New Jersey 26.9 percent of 368,631 total Black workers are employed by the state and local government. 26.9 percent of 149,459 total Black workers are employed by the state and local government in Los Angeles/Long Beach.

7. The occupational distribution of full-time employees in state and local government for the five largest SMSAs surveyed in 1974 are as follows: officials and administrators, 4.3 percent; professionals, 15.9 percent; technicians, 5.7 percent; protective services, 18.2 percent; paraprofessionals, 8 percent; office clerical and skilled craft, 6.8 percent; service maintenance, 16.5 percent. Ibid.

8. This is a difficult trend to document. Data on occupational categories does not exist in the regular government publications on public sector employment. The relative size of the service-maintenance and protective-services categories in [7] indicate the substantial numbers of blue-collar workers in public sector employment.

9. Paul Johnston, "The Promise of Public-Service Unionism," *Monthly Review*, 30 (Sept. 1978):3. It is on the basis of this relationship that Jonhston urges the adoption of a corresponding political unionism that promotes strategic "labor/community alliance."

10. Boris Frankel, "On The State of The State," *Theory and Society*, 7 (1979):199–242. Reference has been made, in other works, to the "fusion of base and superstructure." We suggest the reader see Rich Deaton's "The Fiscal Crisis and the Public Employee" in *Our Generation*, 8 (Oct. 1972).

11. Herb Gintis and Sam Bowles, *Schooling in Capitalist America* (New York: Basic Books, 1976), pp. 204–05.

12. Lee Rainwater, "The Revolt of the Dirty Workers," in *Crisis in American Institutions*, eds. Jerome H. Skolnick and Elliot Curry (Boston: Little, Brown, 1973).
13. James Rinehart, *The Tyranny of Work* (Toronto: Longman, 1975), p. 115.
14. Boris Frankel, op. cit.
15. Jeremy Rifkin and Randy Barber, *The North Will Rise Again* (Boston: Beacon Press, 1978), p. 10.
16. The Industrial Union Department is a parallel structure at the top of the AFL-CIO that was established at the time of the merger in order to give the CIO industrial unions some autonomy in the craft-union-dominated AFL-CIO. Similarly, the public-employee unions seek independence from private sector domination through the creation of a parallel structure, which will run from top to bottom. While the basic groundwork for this was laid in 1974, the exact form this new structure will take is being struggled over at all levels. It's an important issue and one the left should not be ignoring.
17. For a more detailed evaluation see "Lack of Public Support Proves Vital: San Francisco Workers Strike Out," *Dollars and Sense*, 18 (Summer 1976).
18. O'Connor develops this analysis in op. cit., chap. 9. Especially important are "Movements of State Workers" and "Movements of State Clients," pp. 236–46.
19. Johnston, op. cit., pp. 8 9.

17. Public Sector Labor Relations

Mark H. Maier

Management Tactics in Union Formation

Public sector labor relations have changed dramatically in recent years. Strikes by public employees, rare before 1960, are now frequent headline news. And large unions of public workers have emerged, where prior to 1960, there were none. One needs to go back to the formation of industrial unions during the 1930s to find a period comparable in union growth and activity.

Accompanying labor militancy during both these periods was new labor legislation. In 1935 the federal government passed the National Labor Relations Act (NLRA) which granted private sector workers the right to join unions of their choice. The act specifically excluded public sector workers from its jurisdiction. They were not only unprotected from management reprisal against union activity, but in many states public workers were prohibited altogether from joining unions. Beginning with Wisconsin in 1962, however, states began to pass legislation similar to the NLRA. At present over forty states permit city and state government employees to join unions.[1]

Most traditional accounts of labor relations describe the ways in which labor legislation makes it easier for unions to organize.[2] The NLRA, for instance, took away from management such tactics as company unions. What traditional interpretations ignore, however,

Mark H. Maier teaches economics at the College of New Rochelle, New Rochelle, New York. This chapter is based on his doctoral dissertation, "The City and the Unions: Collective Bargaining in New York City 1954–1973," New School for Social Research, 1980.

is how management has influenced the legal framework for union recognition and bargaining in order to increase its power over workers. Several large corporations, including U.S. Steel and General Motors, were prepared to accept the formation of unions as an alternative to the violent confrontations with militant workers that occurred between 1933 and 1937. Then, as today, most contracts included no-strike clauses which bound union leaders to help prevent wildcat strikes.[3]

Less has been written about public sector unions, but the case studies presented in this paper suggest that management has used similar tactics and for the same reasons.[4] Management was able to influence the writing of public-employee labor legislation so that the impact of unionization was minimized. Since the same officials were frequently involved both in writing labor laws and in negotiating with public workers, it is not surprising to find that labor laws are biased in favor of management. Three kinds of tactics appear to have been most successful.

Favoritism toward Certain Unions

Most state laws prevented management from picking the union of its choice, a company union, but it was possible for management to tilt the process of union recognition toward certain unions or certain types of unions. Their tactics included adjusting the timing of elections and gerrymandering unit determination so that a particular union would win an election. Continued dominance by that union could be ensured by a procedure called "exclusive representation,"[5] which prevented workers from forming a new union within a unit previously granted to the jurisdiction of another union. Furthermore, competition between unions could be reduced by rules that required large jurisdictional units. In this way there were only a few unions dealing with a city or state government.

Restricting the Scope of Bargaining

Most public sector labor legislation limited the kinds of issues that labor and management could bring to the bargaining table. In particular, workers were prevented from even discussing a wide range of issues concerning work rules and the kind of services provided by workers. In addition, the law frequently prevented unions from bargaining over topics usually permitted in negotiations, such as wages and benefits, if that union did not represent all the workers who could make claim to contract improvements won by that union.

These restrictions did not prevent management from bringing work-rule changes to the bargaining table. In recent years many unions have accepted "productivity deals," in which increased wages and benefits have been granted in return for union acceptance of changes in work rules.

Union Leadership Assistance in Enforcement of Contracts

As mentioned above, almost all contracts contained no-strike clauses. In general, they made union leadership responsible for work stoppages, even for wildcat actions not sanctioned by the union. When the contract included productivity deals with changes in work rules, union leaders were expected to help management in the enforcement of these rules.

Case Studies of Management Favoritism

Four examples of management influence on workers' choice of union representation are presented below. Usually management control was indirect, involving labor laws that tended to favor one union over another. The New York City transit case and the examples from Philadelphia and Cincinnati illustrate this approach. In one instance, however, the case of the New Orleans police, management tried outright to refuse recognition to one particular union.

New York City Transit

One of the most vivid examples of how a public employer used a union to its own ends took place in New York City transit labor relations between 1947 and 1958. In a series of representational elections and contracts, the city assured the domination of Michael Quill in the Transport Workers Union over competition from other unions and from other potential leaders in the TWU.[6] The arrangement began in 1947 when New York City Mayor O'Dwyer offered Quill as large a contract as he needed to defeat the "reds" in the union.[7] The city then assured victory for the TWU over competing unions by conducting an election among all workers in the transit system. Other unions were strong among certain groups of workers, but no union could compete with the TWU on a systemwide basis.

Why was the city so eager to help Quill and the TWU become the exclusive bargaining agent for transport workers? Quill himself summed up the situation: "The elimination of splinter groups in the representation elections and the new contract promise greater stability in dealings between labor and management than have been known for years."[8] Quill tried to keep his promise by establishing highly predictable negotiating routines. At the end of every other year Quill would threaten a subway strike, only to settle late on New Year's Eve. Quill's strike threats were only bluster; according to a New York State labor leader, the union's "proof of responsibility" was the fact that "the TWU has often threatened strikes, but never has called one."[9]

Philadelphia

Philadelphia city workers faced a situation similar to that of New York City transit workers. After a strike by street department workers in 1939, the city wanted to find "responsible representatives" to sign an agreement for the workers. A district council of the American Federation of State, County, and Municipal Employees was formed and quickly recognized. Since then, the city has refused to deal with any other union for nonuniformed Philadelphia workers. When formalizing the arrangement in 1957, the mayor noted: "Municipal management has been plagued with wasteful union competition over grievances and a lack of centralized union responsibility required for stable and efficient collective bargaining."[10]

Cincinnati

Cincinnati, too, was a trend-setter in allowing city workers to join unions—and in granting exclusive bargaining rights to one union for all nonuniformed workers. From the 1930s onward, AFSCME and the United Mine Workers competed to organize Cincinnati workers. In 1960 Cincinnati recognized AFSCME as the sole bargaining agent because, according to the Cincinnati personnel officer, "it did not want the city to serve again as a battleground between two rival groups." The same official reported that "the union and the department heads worked well together," at least until 1969, when union members hooted down an agreement presented by their leaders and forced the union to go out on strike until a pay increase was won.[11]

New Orleans

In New York, Philadelphia, and Cincinnati, management successfully limited the type of union that would be permitted to act as the workers' representative in collective bargaining. Management has not always been successful in dictating this choice. In 1979 the mayor of New Orleans sparked a police strike when he refused to recognize the Police Association of the International Brotherhood of Teamsters, their chosen agent, opting instead for recognition of the Fraternal Order of Police. New Orleans police went on strike, disrupting the Mardi Gras celebration until the mayor backed down and recognized the Teamsters.[12]

Large or Small Unions

One management demand is common to all of these examples: insistence on large, unified bargaining units. One would have thought that management would be interested in fragmenting the labor movement into competing groups. Instead we find management creating large and potentially powerful unions. Has management adopted the union slogan, "In unity there is strength"?

The answer to this apparent paradox is that management *usually* prefers no unions or small competing unions. But when workers are demanding union recognition, single-unit representation may be the best way for management to limit the power of workers because with only one union to deal with, competition between unions for a better settlement is eliminated.

In recent years most cities have adopted the large-unit strategy of recognizing one union operating under carefully written rules for collective bargaining—a practice endorsed by most management consultants. An example from New York City history shows just such a strategic shift.

In 1954, Mayor Robert Wagner, Jr., proclaimed that New York City workers had "full freedom of association to negotiate the terms and conditions of employment." But in the ten years that followed, only transit and sanitation workers were able to negotiate contracts with the city. An official explained how Wagner limited union powers:

> Wagner . . . would just pick up the phone and call the people over at the Department of Labor and tell them who to certify and who not to certify.
>
> There was a conscious policy of Wagner's to get a lot of unions involved rather than trying to create one strong union. Of course, what this did was to fragment generally the strength of union power within the city, while at the same time keeping the various unions happy by giving them all a little piece of the action.[13]

In addition to playing one union off against another, Wagner designed the rules for collective bargaining, so that unions could not negotiate with the city about any issue unless they represented a majority of workers affected by the proposed change. For example, even though AFSCME represented clerical workers in the welfare department, they could not bargain over wages because they did not represent a citywide majority of clerical workers. Also, issues such as pensions, working hours, and vacations, which were covered by the city's civil service plan, could not be negotiated until a union represented a majority of the over 200,000 nonuniformed workers. As long as the city kept unions evenly matched, and thus relatively weak, it was impossible for any union to win victories for its members on issues as basic as pay and benefits.[14]

In 1966 the city was forced to change its strategy: rules were drawn up accepting AFSCME's District 37 as sole bargaining agent for nonuniformed city workers. There were these reasons for the change in strategy.

First, Mayor Wagner's divide-and-conquer policy had one undesirable effect on management. It forced unions into competition with one another, usually on the basis of militancy. As a result, there was a great increase in the number of strikes during the early 1960s. It was hoped that recognizing one union would reduce the high incidence of strikes.

Second, Wagner's policy, which denied any one group the right to negotiate benefits outside of the civil service system, had been overturned by city welfare workers. After a month-long strike, welfare workers won pay increases and benefits in excess of those in effect for other civil service workers. The city was fearful of similar demands from other small groups of workers. Citywide negotiations would end this leapfrog effect.

Finally, District 37 won citywide recognition because of an extremely well-run organizing campaign, which featured the union's militancy. In 1965, with the assistance of many civil rights leaders, District 37 won a dramatic victory over a chief rival, a Teamster's local, in elections among hospital and clerical workers. As a result, District 37 won representation rights for nearly half of the city's workers, which allowed them to negotiate a citywide contract on all civil service benefits.[15]

Scope of Bargaining

Once unions were accepted into the framework of public sector labor relations, management strategy shifted to setting the rules for collective bargaining. One specification insisted upon by many city and state governments was limitation of the scope of bargaining. In thirty-two states legislation establishing collective-bargaining rights for public employees requires that negotiations be limited to wages, benefits, and working conditions. In the private sector similar language was used by the NLRB to describe *mandatory* topics of bargaining, those issues which management and labor must be willing to negotiate. But, while the NLRB has banned only a few issues from bargaining such as those that violate the law, many public sector laws *limit* collective bargaining to wages, benefits, and working conditions. The restrictions have been further increased by narrowly defining what is meant by working conditions. The New York City Collective Bargaining Law, for example, specified that workers could not bargain over hiring, firing, determination of the level of service, or the organization and technology of work.[16]

One effect of the narrow scope of bargaining was to reduce possible cooperation between public sector workers and consumers. Teachers sometimes could not bargain over class size. Social workers could not discuss what they considered to be oppressive features of the welfare system. And transit workers could not negotiate to reduce fares.

An additional limitation on the scope of bargaining was imposed in combination with rules for unit determination. Some unions were prevented from negotiating over otherwise permitted topics such as wages and benefits by the requirement that the union represent all workers who might potentially be affected by the change. Social workers in New York City were forced to merge with a larger union, District 37, in order to be able to bargain over work hours and vacation days. By New York City law, rules for these benefits were supposed to be uniform for all city civil service workers.[17]

Productivity Deals

Usually management wants to restrict the scope of bargaining in order to reserve for itself as many decisions as possible. In recent years, however, many public employers have tried to expand contracts to include discussion of the work process in the form of "productivity deals." Union demands for higher wages were accepted only in return for assurances that the union would accept changes in work-place practices. Such agreements are not new. The 1955 New York City transit negotiations forced the union to accept an end to pay for the first day of sick leave before wage increases were considered. And, in the private sector, arrangements such as the 1963 Kaiser Plan for steel workers attempted to link wages directly with productivity.[18]

During the 1970s, however, there was an unprecedented emphasis on productivity in the public sector. Consulting firms, such as the Rand Corporation, and business groups, such as the Committee for Economic Development, proposed increased productivity as an answer to urban problems. In the newspapers their high-technology solutions were stressed—"fast water" for fire fighters and computers for police. But a close look at these studies reveals that two strategies dominated their plans: public sector work should be contracted out to low-wage workers in the private sector, and public sector workers should be forced to speed up their work through the use of productivity rates and cutbacks in personnel.[19]

Sanitation collection is the city job most frequently singled out for contracting to the private sector. The immediate payoff for cities is obvious: the private sector contractor paying workers the least and offering them the fewest benefits will make the lowest bid. Jobs will have been transferred from unionized and relatively high-paid city employees to those paid low wages by the contractor. But city management gains another benefit, as a Brookings Institution report explains. "While there have been few general (or almost general) strikes by public employees, there have been some. A recent one in San Francisco was made less unbearable because the city does not collect refuse. The garbage men are unionized but they did not join the strike."[20]

The second thrust of productivity programs, speedup, is illustrated by looking at the highly touted 1976 New York City productivity program. At the height of the cutbacks in services, city unions agreed that workers would receive cost-of-living pay increases only if the raises could be matched by increases in output. The result was speedup. Most of the plan involved cutbacks—for example, four secretaries promised to do the work formerly done by six others involved quotas. Asphalt crews agreed to fill more holes per day.

Unions Help Prevent Strikes

At first it may seem that productivity deals are unnecessary. If collective-bargaining rules say that management has the right to control the work process, why should management bother to bring any proposed changes to contract negotiations? The answer is that management needs worker cooperation for every job, even if it is only an agreement not to stop production with a strike or a slowdown. The situation is especially grave for management of public services such as police, fire, or social work, which rely on a large amount of worker self-motivation. In both the private and the public sectors, management has tried to enlist unions to help guarantee that jobs get done by boosting worker morale and preventing work stoppages. Almost every contract contains a clause stating that the union will not strike or otherwise interrupt production for the duration of the contract. Unions are thus legally responsible to keep workers from striking.

Public sector unions have an additional burden. In all but two states, all strikes by public sector workers are illegal, even after the expiration of a contract. For the most part, employers have been able to count on public sector union leaders to suppress strikes. Given the number of public sector strikes in recent years and the impression given in the media that many are led by firebrand union officials, it may not be obvious that union leaders oppose strikes; but a study of major public sector strikes shows just such a pattern. In New York, Cincinnati, Memphis, and Washington, D.C., recent strikes took place at the insistence of the rank and file over the opposition of union leaders. During the 1978 Washington, D.C. bus strikes, for instance, the *Washington Post* reported "Union Loses Control of Workers." Despite pleas by union leaders and contempt-of-court citations against individuals identified as leaders of the strike, bus drivers went on two wildcat strikes that year.[21]

Unions have not always been able to deliver on their promises of stability in labor relations. Despite recognition of the "responsible" Transport Workers Union in New York City, there were over twenty strikes or slowdowns in the transit system between 1950 and 1957—instigated, for the most part, by rank-and-file groups within the TWU. The most disruptive strikes were led by the Motormen's Benevolent Association, which twice stopped the subways, once on the hottest day of the year in 1956, and again for several days in 1957. The city was able to defeat the MBA by using court-imposed fines, until December 1957 when the Transit Authority was caught bugging the MBA's headquarters. In those pre-Watergate days, this invasion of privacy brought newspaper and public opinion to the MBA's side. The following year the city was forced to grant workers in the transit system bonus payments and restore pay for the first day of sick leave. In return, the MBA agreed to drop a court suit concerning the bugging and affiliated itself with the TWU, thus maintaining TWU's exclusive bargaining rights.[22]

Summary

Labor law is usually portrayed as the protector of workers' rights. The claim is true to a degree. Prior to laws passed in response to worker militance in many states, workers had no recourse if they were fired for joining a union. Moreover, workers had only an informal say about their wages and working conditions. But the way in which collective bargaining is structured also limits the power of workers. Now that most public sector employers are forced to accept unions, how can workers force management to accept unions that are responsive to the rank and file? Some strategies are suggested by the examples in this article.

1. Workers can struggle to maintain independent caucuses within the large bargaining units dictated by employers.
2. Workers can keep union leaders accountable to membership.
3. Workers can demand the right to bargain over a broad range of issues at the negotiating table.
4. Workers can demand the right to strike both during a contract and after its expiration.

Most of these strategies are blocked by labor laws. Laws can be changed, of course, but frequently governments enforce laws selectively. In Cincinnati, unions have been recognized for almost twenty years despite a lack of state enabling legislation. In New York City, welfare workers won unprecedented gains by going outside the civil service system. And in many states where fines against public sector strikers are supposed to be mandatory, the penalties are quite often not enforced. In all these instances, government officials were forced to find ways to overlook the law when they were faced with militant workers.

Notes

1. For a summary of current legislation, see Thomas A. Kochan, "Correlates of State Public Employee Bargaining Laws," in *Public Sector Labor Relations*, eds. David Lewin, Peter Feuille, and Thomas Kochan (Glen Ridge, N.J.: Horton, 1977).
2. See, for example, Derek C. Bok and John T. Dunlop, *Labor and the American Community* (New York: Simon & Schuster, 1970).
3. For discussion of this period, see Richard Hurd, "New Deal Labor Policy and the Containment of Radical Union Activity," *Review of Radical Political Economics*, 8 (1976):32–43 and Frances Fox Piven and Richard Cloward, *Poor People's Movements* (New York: Pantheon, 1977).
4. The major books in the existing literature are Lewin et al., op. cit., Sam Zagoria, *Public Workers and Public Unions* (Englewood Cliffs, N.J.: Prentice-Hall, 1972), and Sterling Spero and John Capozzola, *The Urban Community and Its Unionized Bureaucracies* (New York: Dunellen, 1973).

5. Although exclusive representation is common to both private and public sector U.S. labor relations, it is not universal. In several European countries, for instance, unions compete to represent employees at the same work place.

6. Contracts were actually signed from the Board of Transportation and the Transit Authority, but these agencies were controlled by state and city political leaders.

7. See L. H. Whittemore, *The Man Who Ran the Subways* (New York: Holt, Rinehart & Winston, 1973) and Peter Freund, "Labor Relations in NYC Rapid Transit" (Ph.D. dissertation, New York University, 1964).

8. *New York Times,* July 9, 1954, p. 1.

9. *New York Times,* Dec. 27, 1957, p. 8.

10. *New York Times,* Feb. 14, 1957, p. 1.

11. Donald Heisel, "Anatomy of a Strike," *Public Employment Review,* 30, No. 4 (1969):226–32 and *New York Times,* Jan. 6, 1969, p. 34; Jan. 6, 1970, p. 29; Jan. 17, 1970, p. 15; Feb. 4, 1970, p. 15; June 6, 1970, p. 40.

12. *Washington Post,* Mar. 5, 1979, p. 6; *New York Times,* July 21, 1978, p. 11; Feb. 11, 1979, p. 26; Feb. 26, 1979, p. 15; Mar. 6, 1979, p. 12.

13. Raymond Horton, *Municipal Labor Relations in New York City* (New York: Praeger, 1973), pp. 36–37.

14. See Mark H. Maier, "The City and the Unions: Collective Bargaining in New York City 1954–1973" (Ph.D. dissertation, New School for Social Research, 1980).

15. Ibid., pp. 207–10.

16. *New York City Record,* "Consolidated Rules of the Office of Collective Bargaining," Jan. 11, 1968.

17. Maier, op. cit., p. 185.

18. See Richard Betheil, "The ENA in Perspective," *Review of Radical Political Economics,* 10, No. 2 (1978):10–11.

19. Maier, op. cit., pp. 213–16.

20. H. H. Wellington and R. K. Winter, *The Unions & The Cities* (Washington, D.C.: Brookings Institution, 1971), p. 104.

21. *Washington Post,* July 21, 1978, p. 1.

22. Maier, op. cit., pp. 141–43.

18. Contracting Out: Attrition of State Employees

Suzanne Sankar

Contracting Out

As the fiscal crisis deepens, local governments are contracting out more and more work to private sector human-service agencies. This trend has implications for both clients and workers. A case in point is the State of Massachusetts Department of Mental Health.

Since the 1960s the department has had a policy of deinstitutionalization, which has shifted mental-health services from the state hospital to the community. In many cases this has improved the quality of care. Most community programs and services are provided through the "contracting out" mechanism; that is, services the state deems necessary are bought from local human-service providers, which in turn employ their own staff to provide services for patients from a given locality. The programs are administered by local human-service providers or vendors, which are under the governance of local boards made up of consumers and community members. Thus, the programs are subject to both community and state government control.

Each community can exercise its influence in deciding what type of deinstitutionalization programs are necessary for a particular community. In many areas, patients formerly treated exclusively in state mental hospitals are now offered alternatives such as day

Suzanne Sankar is a social worker at the Somerville Mental Health Center and was a member of United Human Service Workers and the Commonwealth Newsletter Collective at the time this article was written. Parts of this article appeared in *Commonwealth Newsletter*, No. 1, April 1979.

treatment, partial hospitalization, emergency crisis intervention, and supervised living situations. The state's policy of deinstitutionalization has created a more comprehensive network of services and at the same time has increased community control of the delivery of mental-health services.

Before deinstitutionalization, the state hospital system undeniably had a poor track record in providing quality human services. However, the provision of quality care is not the main reason for deinstitutionalization and contracting out. In fact, the state government is using a client-centered liberal argument to mask their attempts at dismantling public sector unions. This obviously has implications for workers' job security as well as for the continuity and quality of care for clients.

The Massachusetts Department of Mental Health employs approximately 12,400 workers in institutional and community settings, including custodial and maintenance workers, mental-health workers, nurses, social workers, psychologists, and psychiatrists. The workers are represented by several different public-employee unions, together called the Alliance. Until twelve years ago many of these workers were unorganized. The Social Workers Union, Local 509 of SEIU, was not organized until 1969 and didn't begin representing some Department of Mental Health social workers until 1975.

In response to the growing strength of these public sector unions, the State of Massachusetts Department of Mental Health developed an attrition plan in 1977 to cut back the number of state employees providing direct human services: the year-end goal of the department was a work-force reduction of 3000. A department memo carefully spelled out the intent of the attrition plan:

> The Department should minimize its role as a direct service provider and expand its role in the formulation and enforcement of regulations, policy making, planning, monitoring and evaluation of mental health and retardation services. The long range effect of this proposal would be the complete conversion of all delivery of service in the community to contracted human service providers.[1]

The department has in effect made long-range plans to dismantle the unions representing workers in the Department of Mental Health. In doing so, a new unorganized work force is being created, as the state is now beginning to contract with the private sector to provide these services.

A more recent statement of policy underscores the department's intent. Robert Okin, the Massachusetts Commissioner of Mental Health, discussed the department's plan to create a network of services to replace the state hospital system. He lists three factors that hinder the efficient financial operation of the state hospital system: "the constraints of the civil service system, the hospitals' difficulty in influencing the collective bargaining process and the rigidity of the line item budget structure."[2]

His statement implies that two systems that protect workers are responsible for the financial insolvency of the state hospital system. His solution for getting around these "constraints" is to create an alternative care system in the community, one that will not be burdened by unions or civil service. A network of community services may benefit clients of mental-health services, but it clearly weakens public sector unions, whose membership will dwindle under this plan. What, in fact, will be the effect on new contract employees who work in nonunionized, community-based programs?

When state employees leave their job, the positions are converted to contract positions. The next workers hired to fill the vacancies are not state employees but employees of a mental-health association or of a private vendor. Although these new workers would be providing services comparable to those of their unionized co-workers, in some cases they would be receiving wages considerably lower than state wages. They often receive fewer vacation days, sick days, and holidays than state workers. Health insurance is not provided or, when it is, workers pays up to 50 percent of the premium. Furthermore, most contract employees receive no pension, whereas state workers are eligible for the state employee retirement plan. Also, most contract employees have no job security. An employee is hired for only one year at a time. Community programs can fold from year to year, depending on the whim of the legislature, department, or vendor.

A contract employee also finds that paychecks do not come on time. Delays in state payments to vendors and mismanagement of payroll funds by vendors can result in weeks of payless paydays for contract employees. In the summer of 1978, over sixty contract employees in one mental-health center went for weeks without pay. Because the contract employees are isolated from one another in scattered community settings, they have little clout in demanding their pay. By comparison, in July 1978 when state workers were threatened with payless paydays, the unionized workers organized to strike if they were not paid. Workers were paid only one day late. This kind of organized action is virtually impossible for non-unionized workers.

Contract employees face another problem: it is difficult to identify management. Often, the supervisor is also on contract and experiencing the same repressive working conditions, benefits, and salary scale. Attempts to identify the vendor as employer are frustrated, as the vendor often claims the department or legislature really holds the purse strings.

The professional identification and independence of the contract employee is seductive, but the realities of the work as described above are the same as for other workers. Increased concern for efficiency has led the state to the use of contracts to cut back services and cut out state workers from their direct employ. The contracted employer in effect makes the lowest bid for providing services. In most cases the employee has no role in contract negotiations and suffers as a result.

Fighting Back

In December 1978 the union stated its concern about contracting out. "The two largest issues for DMH workers to face are contracting out and deinstitutionalization. Will the state jobs go to non-state employees? Will private agencies run state programs, and how will this be decided? Who is working for whom once vendors enter state agencies?"[3]

This union identifies contracting out as a major problem, which threatens its own dismantling. Like other state worker unions, its response has been legislative. Local 509, AFSCME Local 93, IBEW Local 123, and the Massachusetts Nurses Association have co-sponsored legislation spelling out certain guidelines for the contracting out of positions. Included in these guidelines is a statement that work or services being contracted are not currently being provided by state employees. This is an important piece of legislation, but it has not yet helped workers newly hired in contract positions.

Professionalism for human-service workers is a particularly big stumbling block to unionizing. Even though wages and benefits for most such workers are lower than those of their counterparts in education and are much lower than those of the organized worker in monopoly-sector industry, human-service workers cling to their professional identity, a perspective that is rated and strengthened by strong professional organizations such as the National Association of Social Workers. Most pass their work lives as salaried employees of state or private agencies, maintaining their identity as professionals. Although this does not keep workers from unionizing or forming alliances with one another, it hampers the process of forming a worker identification. The tenacity with which many such workers hold on to their professional status can partially be attributed to their class background. Many are from working-class backgrounds, and their ascent to professional status is jealously guarded. Other workers from middle-class backgrounds are sensitive to their low rung on the professional ladder (compared to doctors and lawyers) and use "professionalism" to defend their fragile social position. All these factors, along with the basic negative messages relayed about worker alliances and unions, undermine human-service workers' allegiance to unions.

However, in Massachusetts contract employees of private human-service agencies and mental-health associations are beginning to organize themselves. One case in point was an organizing drive in a large mental-health association. Over fifty human-service workers worked for the association as contract employees. Characteristic of many contract workers, these workers received less pay and fewer benefits than unionized co-workers. They were scattered in several small community settings. In 1978, their plight as nonunion workers was underscored by weeks of payless paydays. Paraprofessionals and professional workers began talking about their shared problems as contract employees and began discussing the need for a union. Representatives of each community program began to meet regularly to discuss the kind of union representation they needed and issues of professionalism versus worker identification. The group agreed to contact the state social workers' union. This union met with the contract employees but stated that they were unable to take on the jurisdictional battle they anticipated in making the first attempt to bring contract employees into the union. They did, however, suggest other unions, specifically a large, established union already representing public sector employees. Contract workers' representatives spoke with this union and made an agreement with the union to begin organizing human-service workers in their association. Because of complicated hiring and funding procedures for contract employees, union card signing was stalled, and the union drive was ultimately unsuccessful. However, since the passage of Proposition 2½ the same Mental Health Employees Association has begun to talk about organizing again. Additionally, employees of the Greater Lawrence Mental Health Association did in fact wage a successful union struggle and are now members of District 65 of the United Auto Workers. At the Boston, April 1981 "Human Services in a Good Society" conference, workers in mental-health associations statewide reported on several new union struggles.

United Human Service Workers and their newsletter, *Commonwealth*, are no longer in existence, although many of its former members stay in close contact and remain active in human-service worker issues.

Notes

1. Department of Mental Health memo to John Buckley, secretary of Administration and Finance, and Jerald L. Stevens, secretary of Human Services, from Joseph Finnegan, deputy commissioner of Mental Health, Aug. 23, 1977, p. 4.
2. Jean Dietz, "Okin's Push on Mental Health, *Boston Globe*, Dec. 30, 1979, pp. 13–14.
3. Susan Phillips, "Which Way Mental Health?" *Local 509 News*, Dec. 1, 1978, p. 6.

19. Union Organizing in Day Care

Andrew McCormick

Day-care workers in Massachusetts have for years suffered from low wages, high child-to-staff ratios, and poor working conditions. People working in day-care, in addition to their principal function of planning and implementing the curriculum, are asked to fill many other roles, such as cook, housekeeper, secretary, and family worker. There are almost always evening meetings and parent conferences to attend. All of this is expected of people who are paid less than public school teachers. But now workers are tired of the same old story and are organizing to change their lives. The Boston Area Day Care Workers United (BADWU) has worked closely with District 65 of the United Auto Workers in Massachusetts and has hired an organizer to do it.

Associated Day Care Services (ADCS) is one of the largest day-care providers in Massachusetts. It comprises seven day-care centers in the metropolitan Boston area: five in Boston, one in Cambridge, and one in Chelsea. A total of 105 employees are eligible for union membership. Despite the fact that salaries at ADCS are better than most day-care salaries, they need improvement. In 1979, when the organizing drive began, teachers' salaries started

Andrew McCormick is a social worker, a former employee of ADCS in Cambridge, and a member of United Human Service Workers, an organization working to build worker-client alliances and unions in the human-service field.

This article is an expanded version of one that originally appeared in *Commonwealth*, the newsletter of United Human Service Workers. It chronicles the steps that were taken to organize the workers at Associated Day Care Services in metropolitan Boston.

at $7500 per year, and teacher assistants at $6000 per year. They worked a thirty-five hour week, year-round.

ADCS has developed personnel practices and benefits that are better than most other day-care agencies.

Because of these advances for workers there is much less turnover among staff in ADCS centers. This has encouraged a significant amount of complacency in the agency, but it also provided us with a solid base for organizing.

Our task was to organize all seven centers. The National Labor Relations Board determined that all the centers comprise one shop, which is responsible to the central office staff. Because of this ruling we had to organize very diverse centers in widely separate areas of the city into one cohesive unit.

Impediments to Unionization

Several issues arose during the course of our organizing effort that became obstacles to building unity. Some were common to all human-service organizing: the funding process for human services, the need for higher salaries, and the concept of professionalism. Others were particular to ADCS: for example, resentment toward unions and a sympathetic management.

The Department of Social Services (DSS) funding mechanism was by far the most serious problem we faced. Through the Purchase of Service process, whereby agencies contract for the right to deliver day-care services, the DSS is able to maintain control of expenditures by not increasing the payments for contracted services. This kept a cap on spending for the years 1976–1979. In 1979, workers received a wage increase and day-care centers still had to cut back on their materials budgets. Many workers have expressed hopelessness that a union could do anything for them because they would have to fight the state. They believe that the DSS will not increase the contract payments, because the state legislature will not increase the appropriation for day care. Although difficult, changing the state budget priorities is not impossible. Budget decisions are highly political and require that day-care workers be more visible politically to ensure that their needs are met.

The main demand of all the agency staff has been higher salaries. Because of the nature of the DSS contracts, organizing solely around issues of wage increases would be foolhardy and unattainable. Although there was an immediate need for a raise, this goal was the most difficult to achieve in the short run.

A very difficult impediment to unionization was the issue of professionalism. The term is ambiguous and often leads to confusion when it is raised in discussions among human-service workers. One definition of "professionalism" relates to competency in work performance, a goal of all workers, whether they work in day care or in a steel mill. People want to take pride in doing a good job and want to feel that their work is of professional quality.

However, when elite professional organizations and social-service administrators speak of "professionalism," they are referring to a "code of conduct" or ethics that requires workers to control their behavior within arbitrary limits or to sacrifice their own needs in favor of their clients'. The ideology of professionalism is frequently used to seduce workers into believing that their interests are the same as those of management. This is, of course, true to the extent that both parties want to serve the clients well. However, this belief serves to undermine workers' incentive to unionize. A union is a viable way for workers to get the conditions and materials they need to do a professional, competent job.

The conflict around professionalism caused a serious problem during our drive. Many day-care workers identify with the elementary school teacher as their professional model. Because of this, some workers did not want to join a blue-collar union such as District 65. This was particularly strong in one ADCS center. Since District 65 had already been chosen by BADWU to organize in day care, our organizers decided to go along with them; but the staff at one center wanted to join the American Federation of Teachers (AFT). This created a splinter during the organizing drive. However, the problem was short lived. After a meeting was held at the center with AFT representatives, the AFT said they were not interested in organizing in day care. In fact, they thought day care should be part of the public school system and that they could organize workers as teachers at that time. The drive was solidly with District 65 after that.

Workers in ADCS were very wary of the union because of some leftover ill-feeling toward Local 1199 of the Hospital Workers

Union, which had attempted to organize in day care five years ago. Many of the workers remembered that the drive with Local 1199 was unsuccessful and none of the ADCS centers were brought into the union. The discouragement in one center was so strong that they refused to even hold a meeting until there was some show of support from other centers.

Another impediment peculiar to ADCS was the sympathetic management of the agency. This, combined with a high degree of loyalty among staff members, made many workers reluctant to organize. The agency worked hard to provide quality day-care services under the DPW contract. They were concerned about the workers and often gave public tribute to them. There was also a high level of honesty concerning the agency's financial situation, and the staff was given raises when the money was available. Nevertheless, people felt the need to take direct action on their own behalf and not to rely on the administration to negotiate with the DSS or state legislature.

Many workers had misconceptions about unions that had to be resolved. Several believed that union drives were filled with hostility and would make enemies of the administration. Others were fearful of a strike being called against their will. It was vital that the democratic character of the union be conveyed to them.

Strategy

The particular nature of the funding mechanisms for day care, and the ambiguous question of who the boss really is, forced us to develop both a short-term and a long-term strategy. In the short run we focused on the noneconomic benefits of unionizing and identified the agency administration as the employer. We stressed the importance of collective bargaining for better working conditions, job security through grievance procedure, and the benefits that come from worker solidarity. We combined this with a demand for the District 65 Security Health Plan to be paid for by the agency, and a small salary increase. All of these demands are negotiable within the agency structure and within the contract limitations.

Demands such as wage parity with elementary school teachers must be part of a long-term struggle against the state. Because the state legislature appropriates funds to private day-care providers, the employees of these agencies are in a position similar to that of state employees vis-à-vis the state. However, they do not get the benefits of the state employees' union. As more day-care centers are organized into District 65, we will develop a day-care local, which will be able to lobby the legislature and the Rate Setting Commission for increases in the allotment for day-care services. Workers familiar with the DSS day-care regulations understand the necessity of this strategy, although they would rather not wait. They recognize that the first step of organizing the workers must be accomplished.

To overcome the impediments we encountered within the agency, principally the discouragement toward unions and the benevolence of the administration, we organized in our strongest centers first. After we had two centers signed up, the witholding center was very happy to have a meeting and in fact responded very well. We allayed peoples' fear of making enemies among the administrative staff by reassuring them that we were not organizing out of a sense of antagonism toward the administration, but rather because it is important and valuable for them as workers to organize; that, in fact, they were doing something good for themselves, and not something bad to the administration.

Process

The key ingredients to organizing in an agency like ADCS, where people have been employed for ten to fifteen years in some cases, are time and trust and the recognition among the workers of the need to have a union. In this case we worked from the existing democratic organization called the Inter-Center Council (ICC), a representative body of workers from the agency. Representatives agitated in their own centers around the need for a union and the benefits it would bring. My own position as representative for two years and chairperson for one year gave me credibility among the workers and an opportunity to develop trust.

In our situation the ICC representatives acted as an organizing committee and set up meetings at the centers with key people. An organizer from District 65 accompanied me to these meetings to explain the union's commitment to day care. These contact people then arranged staff meetings so that everyone could talk with the union representative. These meetings were held in peoples' homes and on occasion in the centers. People were free to ask any questions they might have had. This created an atmosphere of dialogue, so that workers did not feel that the union was being thrown at them. A staff member from an already organized center also accompanied the union organizer to each meeting. This provided continuity to the agencywide effort and a friendly face reinforcing the organizer.

We found this to be very important. The workers wanted to see someone they knew who could talk about their needs and the benefits of the union. They also appreciated the "official" presence of the union representatives, which gave their meetings a greater sense of value. They felt important because this person came out to talk to them.

The meetings were also used to have people sign union cards. It worked differently at different centers. In some cases, when one person signed at the end of a meeting everyone else did also. In others people exercised their independence and said they wanted to wait. We received cards from these people a few days later. Here our contact people were vital. They reminded people of the need to sign the card as a first step in getting a union.

When we had 60 percent of the staff signed up, a representative group of employees met with the executive director to seek recognition. However, after meeting with agency board members, he informed us that we would not be recognized without first proving our majority status through an election. So we filed for an election with the National Labor Relations Board.

The Campaign

The administration's first strategy was to propose separate voting units for professional (social workers and teachers) and nonprofessional (teacher assistants, cooks, and secretaries) staff members. In the election the professional unit would be asked if they wanted to join the nonprofessional unit to form a single bargaining unit. We accepted this distinction for voting purposes only. Our support among the professional staff was high, and we knew everyone wanted to be together. Many staff members were angered by the administration's attempt to split us up. The issue served to strengthen our solidarity.

We proposed an early voting date. However, the administration wanted a late date to allow plenty of time for an anti-union campaign. They countered with a proposal to exclude the secretaries in each of the centers on the basis that they are "confidential employees." We rejected the idea, because we wanted the secretaries in the unit. We compromised on a seven-week period before the election in exchange for the inclusion of secretaries.

During the seven weeks the agency sent letters to all of the employees' homes and made visits to several day-care centers. Their focus was to convince the staff that there should be no "third party" influencing the good relationships between administration and staff. This argument had little impact on us. We considered the District 65 staff member as an aid to us and we constituted the union, not a third party. On the contrary, we considered the agency attorneys to be the third party. Their advice changed much of the normal operating procedures of the agency, including asking the staff representative to withdraw from the Personnel Practices Committee.

Because the period between the time we agreed on the election and the date itself was so long, we had to be sure to maintain our solidarity. To do this we held general meetings every other Friday afternoon to discuss the mailings, plan strategy, and offer support to one another. There was a high level of commitment among many staff members and attendance at the meetings was good.

It all paid off on December 13, 1979, when we chose District 65, UAW, to represent us by a vote of 66–30. There was no question of our strength.

Conclusion

Since the election we have selected representatives from each center and one from the union offices to make up the negotiating committee. The committee worked during the contract negotiations to compile input from workers to develop a list of demands. After eight months of difficult negotiations, a contract was signed with the agency board of directors. The agency remains hostile to the union, and preservation of the union's gains will be a continuing challenge.

Since Associated Day Care Services is one of the largest day-care providers in Massachusetts, unionization here will go a long way toward increasing the potential for other centers to organize and will strengthen the ability of District 65 to lobby the legislature. Already there have been two exciting developments as a result of union organizing in day care. One center was able to add $6000 to its DSS contract allotment to pay for the District 65 health plan, which the workers had negotiated with the administration. When the administrator told the DSS that the union had negotiated this benefit and would raise hell if they did not get it, the DSS agent relented.

In addition, day-care administrators through the Massachusetts Association of Day Care Administrators have planned a special meeting on unionizing in day care. The meeting is *not* to organize to stop it, but rather to explore how they can be part of it. The administrators are in many senses also employees and receive no extra benefits from their position, except a slightly higher salary. They do, however, have hiring and firing power which to this time has made them ineligible for inclusion in the bargaining unit. They are now becoming aware of the benefits of the union to their staffs and in their negotiations with the DSS and therefore want to work cooperatively with the union.

ADCS is now part of District 65 and is now able to support the organizing efforts of smaller day-care centers, several of which have begun organizing and may soon join the ranks of organized workers.

20. Proposition 13: Fighting Cutbacks in Alameda County

Gregory Topakian and Laura Henze

The Setting

By the winter of 1977–1978, the Jarvis-Gann campaign had obtained the sufficient number of signatures to qualify the statewide property tax-limitation initiative for a June 1978 California election. The well-financed and organized campaign was aided by people's growing dissatisfaction with escalating inflation, rising property-tax payments, and the announcement in the spring of 1978 of a surplus in the state's revenue collections. By June, support for the initiative from most sectors of the population was overwhelming, and Proposition 13 passed by a two-to-one margin.

The property tax is the major source of revenue for local governments in California. There are fifty-eight counties, over 400 cities, and almost 6,000 school and special districts that set a property-tax rate for properties in their jurisdiction. In pre-Proposition 13 California, the average property-tax rate paid was $10.32 per $100 of assessed value.[1]

Proposition 13 placed a limit on the combined property-tax rate in California at a maximum of $4 per $100 of assessed value.[2] The impact of the initiative on local government revenues was dramatic. Prior to Proposition 13, local governments had collected $11.3 billion from the property tax; after its passage, approximately $5

The authors lived in Alameda County from 1976 to 1980. Greg Topakian now teaches economics at Boston University. Laura Henze works at the Industrial Cooperative Association in Somerville, Massachusetts. Both are members of Solidarity, a socialist-feminist network.

billion was to be collected. The state legislature drew up a formula to stipulate the share of the $5 billion that was to be apportioned to each county, city, school district, etc. All would suffer revenue losses; all were thus faced with the task of preparing new budgets for the upcoming 1978–79 fiscal year. Decisions would have to be made regarding cutbacks in public services and new revenue sources.

Upon passage of the initiative, segments of the population most threatened by the loss of revenues—such as public employees and clients of community programs—began to organize informally in cities and counties throughout California. These groups discussed possible strategies to take in the face of imminent cutbacks at the local level. Led by coalitions in Sacramento, Los Angeles, and Alameda, a few statewide mobilizations were organized in the weeks following the passage of Proposition 13. The demonstrations called for a large portion of the state's surplus revenue to serve as bail-out funds for local governments.

Most local governments waited for the announcement of the bail-out program before making decisions on cutbacks. In Alameda County, which includes Oakland, Berkeley, and eleven other cities, the board of supervisors acted quickly. They announced that 1100 county workers, over 20 percent of the county work force, would be laid off, and funding for over 100 community programs would be reduced by 20 to 40 percent.

In this context, the Alameda County Labor-Community Coalition emerged. The coalition's first action was to hold a rally of over 100 organizations. Those participating included labor-union locals, the Chicano, Black, and Asian communities, women, the disabled, and the elderly. Enthusiasm was high among the participants in the fight-back coalition.

With the announcement of the state bail-out program, coalition members prepared an alternative budget for the county, which included 100 percent funding for community programs and no layoffs for county workers. Rallies and demonstrations at the county administration building continued through August, as did active mass participation in the public hearings on the new budget. These efforts proved to be partially successful. When the 1978–79 budget was finally approved in late August, 600 to 700 workers had been rehired and community programs faced a cutback in funding of only 10 percent. However, both the unions and the community agencies faced contract negotiations with the county in February 1979.

Reformulation and Regroupment

The fall months provided time to evaluate the summer campaign and to formulate future strategies. In Alameda County, a smaller number of people than had been active during the summer took up these tasks. The coalition developed a basic political perspective in order to inform its goals and strategy.

The coalition's analysis involved two main points. First, the recurring fiscal crises of the public sector should be perceived as one part of the generally stagnating U.S. capitalist economy in the 1970s. Second, while Proposition 13 had addressed legitimate concerns of people over inflation and high taxes, it provided a facile solution tinged with latent racism and sexism. The initiative basically blamed "lazy" public sector workers and excessive spending programs for the fiscal crisis.

This analysis suggested that public sector taxing and spending issues would continue to be on the political agenda. It recognized the need for building an organizational structure to provide a collective memory and continuity to these struggles. For California, the political perspective envisioned building a people's coalition on taxing and spending issues that would embrace and defend progressive spending priorities and tax reform.

Two strategic organizations were suggested. The first was to put forward a concrete alternative on taxing and spending issues, which could serve to fight the facile cutback mentality of the right. The second was to build the general movement: to help organize threatened communities to struggle against cutbacks imposed by local governments.

The argument for the first orientation was that an articulated progressive alternative could provide the theoretical basis for unity among the different sectors of the population that would support progressive taxing and spending. Furthermore, it could serve as a common unifying demand for local organizations involved in fighting cutbacks throughout the state. To further these goals, a committee was formed in the early winter of 1978 to begin research on a possible statewide initiative embracing the principles of progressive tax reform and spending priorities.

The argument for the second orientation was that organizing at the local level was the key to building an authentic fight-back movement. The aim of the fight-back was to actively involve people in their struggles, to prevent cutbacks, to increase community awareness about the impacts of Proposition 13, and to challenge the legitimacy of current local government priorities.

The Alameda County Cutbacks and the Labor-Community Coalition

Community agencies arose out of the turbulence of the 1960s, as different communities organized to provide sorely needed services for their members. Over the years, community-based organizations (CBOs) have grown in number and sophistication. They have their own independent administrations and staff and seek grants and contracts to provide services otherwise not available. Services range from localized health and mental care, to child care, care for the elderly, crisis counseling, drug and alcohol abuse counseling, etc.

In Alameda County, approximately 100 CBOs receive funded contracts from the county board of supervisors. They provide services to the Black, Asian, and Spanish-speaking communities, women, the disabled. and senior citizens, as well as to the more general public. Funding for CBOs constitutes 1 to 2 percent of the total county budget. The funds received by these organizations are generally associated with the general revenue-sharing monies the county receives from the federal government.

In 1972, revenue-sharing funds replaced the patchwork system of categorical grants, which had previously funded the CBOs. The revenue-sharing funds, unlike categorical grants, enter the county's general fund and can be allocated to a wide variety of uses. There is no guarantee that such funds will be allocated to the community agencies. It is also not neccessary that CBO funding come only from revenue-sharing monies.

The county is, of course, responsible for a wide range of functions: judicial, police, health and sanitation, social services, and public assistance. Alameda County's over 5000 employees are represented in collective bargaining by three locals of the Service Employees

International Union (SEIU). As a result of Proposition 13, county workers have had to struggle over cutbacks, hiring, and wage freezes, as well as over general work-place issues.

While the potential for united opposition to county implementation of cutbacks exists, relations between the county employees and the CBOs are not very well developed and are strained by the divide-and-conquer strategy adopted by the board of supervisors. In addition, some of the county workers believe that the CBOs serve as scab labor, by providing mechanisms for contracting-out services at below-union wage rates.

At the close of 1978, the county began its forecasts of revenues and expenditures for the 1979–80 fiscal year. A $32 million deficit was projected for the county's roughly $400 million budget. With contract negotiations upcoming in February, community agencies were immediately placed on the chopping block, and the unions were promised a tough stance in their attempts to break the wage freeze.

The coalition sought to intervene in the county's budget decisions and placed demands on the board of supervisors for continued funding for the CBOs and for good-faith negotiations with the county workers. The basic strategy of the coalition was to attempt to build a united front among the community agencies and between the CBOs and the union. The coalition felt that the union's efforts could most likely be influenced by the agencies if there was a continuous dialogue between the two groups, and *if* the CBOs could first be united into a viable and powerful force.

The coalition's structure included an outreach committee and a media committee. The outreach committee developed a communication network among the agencies and started making regular phone calls to the staff of the agencies to help them organize their constituencies. Petitions, suggestions, and news updates were made available to the agencies; smaller meetings were called to help prepare selected agencies to speak with a united voice at public hearings. A key point of strategy adopted by the coalition was that there would be no back-room bargaining or lobbying on behalf of individual agencies. The media committee coordinated talk shows, press releases, and conferences.

In February, a rally attended by 400 people was held at the county administration building. A highly enthusiastic crowd entered the building for a public hearing with the supervisors. Attempts by the board to pit one agency against another were constantly rebuffed by agency spokespersons, who insisted upon the need and interdependence of all the services. Contrary to the county's initial plans, continued funding for the CBOs was granted through June.

This obstacle surmounted, the coalition began a process of evaluation in order to help inform its next struggle: continued funding through fiscal year 1979-80. This process was interrupted by notices of termination received by a number of agencies in late March. Just one month after the high point of the February rally, demoralization began to surface as the agencies were put on the defensive. General meetings were not as well attended; a rally later in the spring generated a much weaker showing and lower level of enthusiasm than previous rallies.

Terminations of over thirty agency contracts were set for June 30. A series of packed public hearings induced the supervisors to postpone terminations until August 1, when the new bail-out funds to be received from the state for the coming fiscal year would be known. The coalition planned a series of mass actions for late July. After consultations with county workers, about 100 community members who regularly utilize the CBOs went to three selected county centers. They noisily and visibly demanded comparable services and revealed the inadequate staffing and resources at the county centers.

A rally was held the following day. County workers, still without a contract, complemented this action with a one-day strike. Six people were arrested at a sit-in at the board of supervisors' chambers following the rally. The entire sequence of actions received widespread and sympathetic coverage in the press. Nevertheless, on July 31—despite an overall increase in the county budget from the preceding year—more than thirty community agencies were officially eliminated from county funding, and the remaining agencies recieved partial cutbacks in funds.

Evaluation and Prospects

Despite the ultimate termination of about thirty community agencies, there were some partial successes for the coalition's campaign.

Cutbacks slated for the summer of 1978 were significantly reduced after an organized outcry by employee and community organizations; imminent cutbacks for CBOs were postponed throughout the 1978–79 fiscal year; a few agencies originally scheduled for termination were re-funded; and the general awareness and militancy of a number of the CBOs and their constituencies increased significantly.

From the point of view of building a coherent organization of the agencies and their communities, there were, of course, shortfalls. CBOs representing a number of specific constituencies, including the Black community, never really communicated with the coalition after August 1978. Some turned to lobbying and individual bargaining efforts to try to secure funding.

For the agencies continuing to participate in the coalition, it was difficult to regularly integrate them into the actual decision-making process. In part, the general demoralization and the scrambling-to-stay-alive attitude within the CBOs made it difficult for them to attend regular meetings. However, it is fair to say that the coalition was unable to suggest concrete, responsible, non-trivial tasks to people who wanted to help but did not want to participate fully in the coalition's committees.

Finally, it is not clear how many people, other than CBO staff and regulars, were reached by the campaign. The size of the outreach committee meant that coalition members had to call the staff of agencies and rely upon the staff in turn to mobilize their clients. Agency staff participating in the leadership of the coalition were much more successful in mobilizing their constituencies to participate in mass actions. It is unclear whether other CBO staff were less experienced, less successful, or simply not as committed to the idea of mass organizing as a form of political pressure.

It is impossible at this time to evaluate the role of the proposed statewide initiative. With a goal of generally building a movement for progressive taxing and spending, such a campaign could help politicize the public and also help to unify local struggles. However, as the Alameda County experience has demonstrated, it was not merely a lack of revenues or a lack of an alternative plan that eventually doomed the community agencies. Rather, it was the lack of a more highly developed, active, and enthusiastic movement of people who could fight for the agencies in particular and for an alternative in general.

Notes

1. In California, property is assessed at 25 percent of market value.
2. In addition, the assessed values of properties were rolled back to their 1975–1976 levels. Increases in assessed value are limited to 2 percent per year, except upon resale, when properties are reassessed at 25 percent of market value.

Part VI

The Crisis in Political Perspective

21. The Far-Right Plan for 1980

Sasha Lewis

"All we want is a chance to run the country." It sounds like the name of a bad country-western tune, but it's the theme song of the New Right's operation to take control of Congress in 1980.

It all started in 1974 as Watergate was crashing around Nixon.

Three men—a deposed Nixon appointee from Harvard, a timid Texan, and a Colorado political tactician—launched a plan to save the nation for free enterprise, the Bible, and the memory of Senator Joe McCarthy. Howard Phillips was the man Nixon had chosen to dismantle the war on poverty. Richard A. Viguerie had first gotten his political feet wet in Texas Senator John Tower's early campaigns and had gone on to raise money for Young Americans for Freedom. (It was there that he discovered he was too timid to ask for money in person and began to solicit funds through direct mail.) The third member of the team was Paul Weyrich, who had arrived in Washington as a press aide to ultraconservative Colorado Senator Gordon Allot and gone on, with backing from fellow Coloradan Joseph Coors, to create the Heritage Foundation—a right-wing "alternative" to the liberal Brookings Institution.

Their original plan called for a vigorous third-party effort rising from the ruins of the GOP and led by a Reagan-Wallace ticket in 1976. The basis of the new party was to be an organization called The Conservative Caucus (TCC), directed by Phillips and funded by Viguerie's efforts. When Reagan and Wallace ended up going

Sasha Lewis is an author and is currently executive director of the American Human Rights Fund, a nonprofit corporation dedicated to improving the status of human rights for all people in the United States.

their separate ways in 1976, the three made a last-ditch effort to control a national political party in an attempted coup in the Wallaceite American Independent Party. The AIP showed the trio and their aides the door, and the dreams for a third party went underground. It was probably the best thing that could have happened for Phillips, Viguerie, and Weyrich, who have since come to be known as the troika behind the New Right

It was the worst thing that could have happened to liberals. Had the threesome succeeded in taking over the AIP or creating a legitimate third party, it would have been much easier to follow their activities in the years to come. But like a snake (Viguerie likes to compare his direct-mail techniques to having a water moccasin as a watchdog: the snake is deadly and leaves no footprints), an underground third party leaves few tracks in the public record.

Viguerie had spent ten years creating the most extensive list of right-wing contributors in the nation, starting out, in 1964, by hand-copying the names and addresses of the Goldwater contributors. He made a business out of his operations and kept on building his list from clients like Billy James Hargis's Christian Crusade, the Anti-Communist Book Club, John Ashbrook's 1972 race against Nixon, and finally in 1973, George Wallace. The Viguerie list, now handled by a 300-employee operation, numbers 5 million individual contributors to right-wing, conservative, and Christian causes. Within a few months in 1974 the Viguerie list raised $250,000 for Paul Weyrich's new Committee for the Survival of a Free Congress (CSFC) and helped elect 15 percent of the victors in the 1974 races.

On yet another front, North Carolina Senator Jesse Helms in 1974 had inspired the creation of an outfit called the American Legislative Exchange Council (ALEC), which organizes meetings of right-wing state legislators and drafts model legislation for right-wing causes.

By the end of 1974 the New Right had built the key components of a political party: a policy arm (the Heritage Foundation), a national campaign committee (CSFC), a grass-roots organizing committee to develop campaign volunteers and candidates (TCC), and a state legislative arm to groom candidates for higher office (ALEC). The operation also had a political strategy. Described by Howard Phillips as "organizing people's discontent," it was based on a three-pronged assault: (1) tough-minded political pragmatism— if an issue or campaign doesn't work, dump it and go on to something that does; (2) loyalty to issues before political parties; (3) a set of issues guided not by an overriding philosophy of government but by movements that stir passions in grass-roots Americans.

In 1975 the operation expanded significantly and began reaching out to single-issue "anti" constituencies: anti-gun-control, antibusing, anticommunist, antitax, anti-ERA, and anti-union. Where there weren't special-interest organizations already spending money and organizing people for elections, the New Right created them. Where groups existed, the New Right tried co-opting them. In addition, the New Right created a second national multi-issue political action committee, the National Conservative Political Action Committee (NCPAC). NCPAC has a milder tone than CSFC's harsh anticommunist line and is more attractive to contributors not yet ready to believe in the imminent takeover of government by Marxists.

By 1976 the New Right had helped to elect almost 25 percent of the U.S. House of Representatives. Amazingly, almost no one commented on the phenomenon—it was still tough to follow the water moccasin's path. But the New Right was well aware of its achievement. An early 1977 TCC flier proudly displayed a *Chicago Tribune* article that began with the statement, "A group of conspirators is meeting here this weekend to plan a takeover of the United States Congress through a 'guerrilla strategy.' " The same leaflet states TCC's goal: "1980—Conservatives Achieve Dominance Over the Policies of the U.S. Congress."

By the end of 1977, New Right Republicans had won upset victories in all three special elections for the U.S. House of Representatives: TCC organizer Arlan Strangeland in Minnesota's seventh district, which pundits felt was safely in Democrat-Farm-Labor Party hands; John E. Cunningham in Washington's seventh district, which all observers had agreed was a safe Democratic district; and Robert Livingston, who was the first Republican to win in 104 years in Louisiana's first district. By the beginning of 1978 the New Right was big news and reporters were swarming around Richard Viguerie, the New Right money-man, for interviews. "All we want is a chance to run the country," Viguerie boasted to the Charlotte North Carolina *Observer*, "and that is beginning to happen."

In 1978 the New Right raised more money than either labor or big business. It scored several key upset victories and backed nearly 40 percent of the successful candidates in the U.S. House of Representatives. In early 1979, the New Right backed yet another special-election upset victory, Bill Royer, for the California seat left vacant by the slaying of Congressman Leo Ryan in Guyana.

As the numbers add up today, the New Right victories mean 168 members of the House who can generally be counted on to vote the New Right line on issues it considers important: against gun control, against school desegregation by busing, against affirmative action, against labor-law reform, and against abortion (Weyrich and Phillips are known to be extremists on so-called family issues—everything from gay rights to ERA and abortion. Viguerie, meanwhile, is never far from his Bible). Most of the 168 are Republicans, but there are a growing number of Democrats in the New Right camp.

New Right strength in the U.S. Senate has picked up as well due to their success in retaining right-wing senators in office and adding to their ranks through upset victories. There are now a minimum of twenty-four senators who will predictably vote the far-right line and six additional "conservatives." This is only four short of the number needed to block treaty ratification, and only eleven votes short of the margin needed to prevent cloture of a Senate filibuster, and stifle legislative action. Meanwhile, most of the remaining liberal senators are up for reelection in 1980 and are beginning to run scared.

New Right power in both houses of Congress is already dragging some moderates and even weak-kneed liberals down the right line on some votes. Just a few months ago Congress did what was once unthinkable: both houses, by surprising margins, voted in favor of a legislative amendment that would allow prayer in public schools. On June 7, the Senate, where New Right strength is the weakest, cast forty-six votes in favor of legislation that would have ended school busing.

New Right gains in Congress, thanks to the Federal Elections Commission, are fairly easy to tabulate. Success in the fifty state houses and legislatures is more difficult to measure because of the variety of campaign finance disclosure laws operative in the different states. But the New Right can claim at least two governors: John Dalton, elected in Virginia in 1977, and Massachusetts Democrat Edward King, elected in 1978. Another measure of New Right strength in the state houses is the fact that in 1979 two New Right groups, ALEC and Gun Owners of America, stopped the move to ratify the District of Columbia Representation Amendment dead in its tracks by promising to deliver thirteen states that would enact resolutions opposing ratification.

But the trail of the underground third party is becoming harder to follow as the troika incorporates more of its own front organizations: tax-deductible research and education foundations to support the studies needed for congressional races and lobbying activities, tax-deductible public-interest legal corporations, countless local political-action committees (one NCPAC employee claimed to have organized seventy-five of them in 1978 alone), national lobbies like the new American Life Lobby, and yet more national special-interest political-action committees. Meanwhile, former employees of CSFC have gone on to boost the operations of other far-right political organizations such as the Life Amendment PAC, which includes Paul Weyrich among its advisers and former CSFC staff member Barbara Baroody among its key employees. There's also an outfit called Christian Voice, one of whose key leaders is a former assistant CSFC director, David Troxler. Although CV calls itself a public-interest lobby and denies any ties to Richard Viguerie, its list of advisers is drawn entirely from the New Right ranks of Congress. Its avowed aim is organizing fundamentalist Christians and Mormons for political action on what it believes to be "moral" issues including abortion, inflation, and SALT II.

The New Right has grown so much it is difficult to label it, as did the *Chicago Tribune*, a "conspiracy." Instead of a dozen or so right-wing leaders who met weekly beginning in 1976 to organize strategy and, in the words of Howard Phillips, "divide up the tasks to be done," the meetings now are reported to include from thirty to forty people. And the New Right congressional delegation, as it grows in size within both political parties, also grows more difficult to keep in line. The *New Right Report*, a kind of public house organ published by Viguerie, frequently lashes out at members who deviate from the hard-core New Right line in their votes, threatening on occasion to replace them with true believers during the next election.

And, as the New Right expands, it becomes harder for journalists to trace the real activities of the operation. The New Right brought in two stunning upset victories in the 1978 Senate races: the defeats of Thomas McIntyre in New Hampshire and Dick Clark in Iowa. Reporters covering the races sought a simple explanation and blamed the upsets on the Right-to-Life movement. The anti-abortionists indeed were instrumental in the strategy to oust the two

senators, but their opponents—both advisers to Christian Voice—
Gordon Humphrey, a New Hampshire TCC director, and Roger
Jepsen were recruited by the New Right machine, financed by the
New Right machine, and followed campaign strategies laid out by
the New Right. To the surprise of no one familiar with the New
Right as an underground third party, both Jepsen and Humphrey
have become key New Right leaders on a variety of issues ranging
from opposition to recognition of the People's Republic of China
and lifting economic sanctions against Rhodesia to favoring school
prayer.

Early this year the New Right began its campaigns against some
senators up for election in 1980, including George McGovern. An
opponent, Dale Bell, former TCC organizer and NCPAC consultant
is already campaigning in South Dakota. Meanwhile, NCPAC has
launched a newspaper ad campaign against McGovern, depicting
him handing over the United States to a Chinese soldier, reading,
in part, "McGovern supports a sellout of Taiwan and the United
States. Can you support a senator who would sell out your interests?" Alarmed, McGovern has declared the campaign against
him to be the "work of a hard-core extremist."

But liberals should expect below-the-belt campaign tactics in
1980. As Paul Weyrich says, "We are no longer working to preserve
the status quo. We are radicals, working to overturn the present
power structure."

Some New Right Leaders and Organizations to Watch in 1980

The Conservative Caucus (TCC)

Titular head: former New Hampshire governor *Meldrim Thomson,*
a member of the John Birch Society national council and possible
candidate in 1980 either for the American Independent Party presidential slot or for the senate seat now held by Democrat John A.
Durkin. (The National Conservative Political Action Committee
[NCPAC] has already begun an oust-Durkin media program.)
Thomson, in 1978, had considered running for the U.S. Senate
seat then held by Democrat Thomas McIntyre, but bowed out in
favor of political neophyte and state TCC director *Gordon Humphrey.* (Humphrey went on to win an upset victory.)

Aside from his ties to TCC and NCPAC, South Dakotan *Dale Bell*'s drive for the Senate also benefits from an anti-McGovern campaign by the New Right's Life Amendment Political Action Committee (LAPAC).

Louisiana State Representative *Louis "Woody" Jenkins*, another TCC organizer as well as a leader in the New Right's American Legislative Exchange Council (ALEC) may run against the more moderate Senator Russell B. Long in 1980. Jenkins made a good showing in the 1978 U.S. Senate race.

Committee for the Survival of a Free Congress (CSFC)

Among CSFC's advisers in the U.S. House of Representatives are: *Charles Grassley* (R-Iowa), whose speaking tours have included the "white right" organization Liberty Lobby; *Steve Symms* (R-Idaho), who has reportedly been a booster of the John Birch Society; *Lawrence P. McDonald* (D-Georgia), another member of the Birch Society's national council; and *Robert Dornan* (R-California), a lifetime morality crusader who, under public pressure, had to fire an aide who had earlier worked for a Birch Society magazine.

Grassley may run against Iowa's Senator John Culver, a Democrat, in 1980. Culver is another on LAPAC's hit list and is reportedly already the target of NCPAC media attacks.

Symms may run against Idaho's Frank Church, another LAPAC (and NCPAC) target. (NCPAC was, in late spring, exploring an oust-Church media campaign.)

McDonald, apparently discontented as a member of the lower house, may try running against the more moderate Senate incumbent, Herman Talmadge.

Dornan, meanwhile, may surface as an opponent to California Senator Alan Cranston, but there is already some competition for this honor.

American Legislative Exchange Council (ALEC)

Current ALEC chairman is *Woody Jenkins*. First vice chairman [sic] is *Donna J. Carlson*, a member of the Arizona House of Representatives and a regular Birch Society speaker. Second vice chairman is *H.L. "Bill" Richardson*, a California State representative, former Birch Society member, and head of the New Right's Gun Owners of America. Richardson made an ill-fated run against

U.S. Senator Alan Cranston in 1974, and many Golden State natives expected him to make another try next year. However, Congressman John Rousselot has already announced for the seat and has gone so far as to drop his longstanding membership in the Birch Society in preparation. While Rousselot has remained aloof from the New Right, he has apparently struck a bargain with Richardson—Rousselot will try for the Senate, and Richardson will try for (and probably win) Rousselot's seat in Congress.

Update

The article above was written in early 1979 and was meant to be predictive of trends in the New Right camp. It is actually quite interesting to review the article, post-election, to see just how well the clandestine third-party model of New Right performance worked. It was, of course, extremely early to make predictions about specific 1980 elections, as the 1978 Congressional elections had only recently been completed. In the normal functioning of the two-party system, such predictions would generally be totally impossible because fratricidal struggles within the two parties must be resolved through the primary process and the peace-making that follows.

As the article points out, one of the benefits accruing to the New Right is that it functions as a third political party, without the need to perform the rituals of democracy by which the two parties are bound; hence, its efficiency is enhanced, as is its predictability. So let us undertake a test of the model as described in my article. I should add one caveat. In general, the New Right groups mentioned had averaged about a 60 percent "hit" rate in their earlier congressional wins. Such a success rate is fairly high when compared to that of other special-interest groups (Americans for Democratic Action, for example).

General Success

The New Right did surprisingly well in the 1980 congressional elections. Through a variety of circumstances, including some stupid moves by liberal politicians, the New Right and its friendly ally, the Moral Majority, managed to nearly decimate progressive spokespeople in both houses of Congress. This, coupled with a Reagan presidential victory— even though the New Right can never make a claim that Reagan is "their" man—have set an ultraconservative tone in federal government for many years in the future. Several key appointments must be made during the Reagan term, and these will fall into conservative hands. So it might be said that there was, in 1980, a reactionary revolution.

The New Right has certainly attempted to take credit for this counterrevolution and, to a great degree, is taking advantage of this claim, regardless of its legitimacy. Most of the Reagan administration's proposals in foreign policy, in budget programs, in law-and-order areas, are familiar reading to those who follow the work of the Heritage Foundation. It is reported (with a great deal of justification) that the Heritage Foundation wrote the Reagan program.

Specific Elections

- Meldrim Thomson chose not to run for the New Hampshire Senate seat.
- Lawrence P. McDonald chose not to run for the Senate.
- Robert Dornan chose not to run, holding onto his house seat by a grim margin.
- Bill Richardson apparently remained content with his state seat and also chose not to run for national office.
- Congressman Rousselot was apparently talked into staying in the lower U. S. House; his name recognition was not such that it would have been of much help in a statewide race.

So much for predictions that did not materialize. Now for those who actually ran: both Charles Grassley (R-Iowa) and Steve Symms (R-Idaho) did well in unseating their opponents. Of the liberal senators targeted for defeat by the New Right coalition, Culver, McGovern, Javits, Bayh, Cranston, and Church—the big six—only one survived the 1980 onslaught.

Senator Cranston had the benefit of a large state requiring a great deal of expense for name recognition alone, yet even the challenge to him was significant enough for his aides to take extra precautions. New Right political advisers began a frontal attack on the senator's age. Cranston advisers had the good sense to face the challenge directly, and his voice, for what it is worth to progressive causes, can still be heard in the U.S. Senate.

In summary, the New Right claims victory in five of six contests. Had New York's Javits stepped aside in favor of the progressive Holtzman, a New Right victory in New York could have been avoided. So the true batting average in 1980 was maintained at about six in ten. Even some of these may be credited to the unexpected Reagan coat-tail effect, lowering the New Right's average even further.

Nonetheless, a major element of the administration has accepted the New Right victory and is following its policies, seriously considering its suggestions, and even mouthing its slogans. New Right agitators also got their share of political appointments. Although the facts may show clearly that their victory was largely symbolic, the symbolism was significant enough for it to be taken as gospel by a majority of both the legislative and executive branches of government.

The lesson here, then, is that the current political system is subject to manipulation by relatively small groups of people working in combination toward similar ends and using modern propaganda and fund-raising technnology, as well as standard sources of conservative money. It is not a lesson progressives should run from. It is a lesson we may learn to our own advantage.

22. The Ideology of the New Right

Allen Hunter

Most conservative ideology demands the rolling back of social services provided by the welfare state. Right-wing groups tend to
combine economic and social conservatism to justify relaxing government regulation of business and cutting back the social wage.
This essay will address the ideology of the New Right's coherent
attack on the public sector.

The New Right is only part of the right wing in the United States
today, of course, but it has promoted and nurtured a popular
combination of ideological impulses so effectively that it is now
prominent in mass conservative political activity. For that reason
we focus on the New Right here rather than on the more intellectually rigorous conservative positions such as those of the neo-
conservatives and conservatives in the pages of *The Public Interest*
and *Commentary*, or in such institutions as the American Enterprise Institute or the Hoover Institute.

The New Right, along with most other groups on the right today,
supports conservative policies in three areas: economic retrenchment, social conservatism, and an anti-Soviet military buildup.[1]
They believe that economic vitality requires cutting back many
social services and ending government regulation of business.[2]
They link the stimulation of profitable investment and the increase
in worker productivity with these cutbacks. In their arguments for

Allen Hunter is an editor of *Radical America*. He is currently teaching
sociology at Hampshire College and writing about the pro-family politics of the
New Right. Special Thanks to Linda Gordon, Mary Jo Hetzel, Robert Horwitz,
and Jim O'Brien for their suggestions, criticisms, and general encouragement.

increasing worker productivity, many of their social and economic views connect. Many conservatives—not without good reason— argue that a welfare system that supports those who do not work fails to provide the coercive incentives that "encourage" worker productivity. They are convinced that revitalizing the market and worker productivity requires a renewed cultural emphasis on self-restraint and hard work, tax incentives for capital, and a relaxation of environmental, health, and safety regulations.[3]

The New Right's program for achieving these goals is a combination of supply-side economics and a thoroughgoing social traditionalism. The economic policies Reagan proposed in the first months of his administration and the sweeping provisions for social conservatism contained in Senator Paul Laxalt's proposed omnibus Family Protection Act are the main ways that these two are crystallized today. The New Right holds that the free market and traditional family morality are mutually sustaining and necessarily connected.

It is important to look at the New Right on three levels: as a political and cultural sensibility, as a series of conservative, single-issue social movements, and as an organizational core led by a small number of organizers and strategists. The strategy of its leadership is to mobilize popular support from people interested primarily in single issues, such as abortion, by appealing to common sensibility. Recognizing that this is a period with decreasing activism in the two main parties and decreased interest in party politics, it seeks to mobilize political energy—for both electoral and other ends—through the social movements that have arisen outside party structures.

The New Right arose as a sensibility within a series of single-issue social movements before it recognized itself as a New Right. Retrospectively, however, one can consider many of these early social movements as New Right in spirit. Examples of early articulations were evident in the speeches by Richard Nixon, Spiro Agnew, and George Wallace in the 1968 presidential election. The earliest social movements were the opposition to busing, sex education, abortion, the ERA, taxes, and by the mid-1970s, gay rights. In 1974, the four core organizations of the New Right—Richard Viguerie's direct-mail fund-raising company, RAVCO, Howard Phillips's Conservative Caucus, Paul Weyrich's Committee for the Survival of a Free Congress, and John "Terry" Dolan's National Conservative Political Action Committee—began consciously co-

ordinating their organizational activities. Since a number of other
organizations have been taken over or established, and many of
the single-issue movements have been drawn into the New Right's
domain. In 1977 the New Right leadership began to draw together
the various social movements into a "profamily" coalition, and since
1979 have been closely collaborating with the conservative fundamentalists in the Moral Majority and similar organizations.

A number of senators and representatives consider themselves
in or close to the New Right, and some people close to Reagan
have had similar ties to it. Senator Paul Laxalt is prominent among
Reagan's close associates. Senator Jesse Helms, perhaps the most
articulate and forceful elected spokesperson for the New Right,
acts as a conservative conscience on the right of Reagan. Lyn
Nofziger is now Reagan's liason with political groups; he was formerly a leading New Right activitist and publicist.[4]

The Attack on the Public Sector

New Right views might be labelled a diffuse petty bourgeois ideology. (This traditional class terminology is imprecise and must be
modified eventually, but now we lack new categories which are
exact and generally understood.) The ideology is deliberately diffuse
because it aims to draw together many social strata and classes by
masking certain conflicts of interests. It is petty bourgeois because
it is explicitly procapitalist while not particularly supportive of big
business. The New Right appeals to small business interests against
the interventions and oppressiveness of bigness—big government,
big labor, big business. It claims to defend the permanently employed members of the white male working class against the lower-
paid, irregularly employed, radical, and national minority segments. It is petty bourgeois, again, because in its procapitalist
perspective it incorporates and acclaims the production-sector managerial strata, while excluding and excoriating the welfare-sector
professional and bureaucratic strata. The petty bourgeois outlook
is the ideological basis upon which the American "people" are
drawn together. The New Right's ideology is thus an expression
of its right-wing populism. In this way the ideology not only defines
a legitimate middle America against the extremes but also defines
the righteous portions of the middle strata.

Important for the ideology is the manner in which elements of the middle classes—broadly understood—are included or excluded from a group considered society's "producers." The middle is drawn together against the extremes above (big business, big labor, big government) and below (welfare clients, Blacks). A number of elements in the New Right sensibility are used to separate "the people" from their enemies: racism, antistatism, sexual repressiveness, religiosity, moral indignation, patriotism, free-market individualism and the work ethic, and conspiratorial thinking. Around these and other concerns a dichotomy is created between those who live right and those who do not. Those who do are included in middle America and those who do not are excluded. Many of the dichotomies are overlapping and mutually reinforcing. Social and cultural traditionalism combine with an ethic favoring free enterprise and the marketplace. Both aspects of the New Right ideology are brought to bear against the liberal state.

To understand the emergence of this sensibility, one must recall that a shift in the political form of class alliances took place between the 1960s and the 1970s. In the 1960s the liberal, professional sections of the middle strata were in a tacit alliance with corporate liberal capitalists and with the social movements of the underclass—mainly in the civil rights and welfare-rights movements. This alliance, politically situated within the Democratic party, cohered around the Great Society programs. Left out were the white portions of the working and lower-middle classes—the backbone of the New Deal electoral coalition—especially white Southerners and Northern urban "ethnics" in the inner cities and newer suburbs. Thus there was a tension between major groupings inside the Democratic Party that manifested polarizations within the larger society.

Various factors led corporate interests to reject the liberalism associated with the Great Society programs. Concern about inflation was important. Inflation was caused by President Johnson's unwillingness to risk political support by raising taxes while continuing social spending at home and increased military spending for the war in Vietnam. The world economic crisis of the 1970s and the need for U.S. business to reassert its competitiveness internationally led it to shift away from spending for social programs and toward increasing the profitability of investment. The establishment of the Trilateral Commission was indicative of this shift. These former corporate liberals no longer believed that governmant could simultaneously stimulate economic growth and deliver increased levels of welfare programs. They believed that renewed emphasis on profitability, necessary in the economic recession, demanded that welfare programs be cut back. They now characterized the strivings of such movements as the civil rights or welfare-rights movements as excesses of egalitarianism at the expense of liberty.

This reversal in the uses of the state could not be accomplished through the existing political coalition. Cutbacks in the public sector could not be sold to the public through a coalition based on the expansion of public services. Thus corporate interests shifted toward an alliance with production- and accumulation-oriented managerial groups, small business, and the sections of the New Deal coalition that were not part of the Great Society coalition. Since many of the actual policies of the corporate conservatives were (and are) against the interests of the working class, these policies had to be presented in ways that occluded class antagonisms. Attacking the state, particularly the distant, unresponsive bureaucracies of the federal government, was a crucial element in eroding support for the regulatory and social-wage elements of the state, and for building support for the progrowth and military-spending elements.[5]

But it was not only a political shift by liberal capitalists that led to the demise of the New Deal coalition. The links between class and political formations are not that tight. In 1968 conservative forces within both the Democratic and Republican parties manipulated the growing tensions in the New Deal coalition. The economic liberalism that bound them together was no longer as politically important for many people as the social issues—especially race—which divided them. There were many indications of this weakness. As Kevin Phillips, who had been active in Richard Nixon's 1968 presidential campaign, wrote, "The principal force which broke up the Democratic (New Deal) coalition is the Negro socioeconomic revolution and the liberal Democratic ideological inability to cope with it. . . . The Democratic Party fell victim to the ideological impetus which had carried it far beyond the programs taxing the few for the benefit of the many (the New Deal) to programs taxing the many on behalf of the few (the Great Society).[6] In 1968 both Nixon and Wallace exploited the fissures they saw developing within the Democratic electoral coalition. Wallace used racist populism, Nixon used anti-Establishment rhetoric that mixed attacks on liberals with racism. As the quote from Phillips suggests, Nixon and Agnew linked racial backlash, the incipient tax revolt, and resentment against big government to win votes from socially conservative Democrats. In attempting to create a significant split between liberal professionals, minorities, and youth on the one hand, and Southern whites, Northern white ethnic workers, and small business on the other hand, conservative politicians also exploited cultural issues. Phillips argued that the Republican Party should also use populist rhetoric to mobilize "resentment of the blyth [sic] nihilism of the children of the affluent society."[7] This resentment should not be directed, in Phillips' argument, against consumerist distortions of cultural change. Rather this resentment of cultural change should be directed against liberals and the state. "The emerging Republican majority spoke clearly in 1968 for a shift away from the sociological jurisprudence, moral permissiveness, experimental residential, welfare, and educational programming and massive federal spending by which the Liberal (mostly Democratic) Establishment sought to propagate liberal institutions and ideology—all the while reaping growing economic benefits."[8] Together, racism and the opposition to cultural liberalism (and radicalism) were translated into votes for conservatives.

The 1968 presidential campaign was pervaded by the notion of a silent majority (or a real majority, or a middle-class majority) of hard-working, sober, tradition-minded patriots fed up with welfare handouts, "peace creeps," hippies, Black militants, and street crime. The emphasis that both George Wallace and Richard Nixon placed on law and order and respect for the flag, signaled the invocation of "the people" against the "interests" allied in the Democratic Party. Youth, Blacks, and others struggling against economic and cultural oppression were portrayed as united with elite "interests" in society. It is the sum of these and other resentments and indignations on the part of those who felt left out and offended by the Black, youth, antiwar, and women's movement that characterized the emergence of a New Right sensibility as a political force.

The New Right's political strength was drawn in large part from a series of *hostilities:* hostility to the racial advancements allegedly made by Blacks at the expense of whites; hostility to youth cultures that were anti-work ethic and oppositional in many respects; hostility to liberal sexual practices that offended moral traditionalists. There was an operative distinction, however unspoken, between the now-traditional New Deal aspects of the welfare state, which dealt with basic economic needs, and those of the Great Society which, it was felt, were directed more to remedying inequality, particularly racial inequality. Uniting all these hostilities was anger at the bureaucrats and professionals who administered these programs. It was these liberals who led the advance toward cultural nihilism and who disdained and walked over the traditionalists of the silent majority. All these hostilities were channeled into a general desire to curb the state, a.k.a. "big government," for its insensitive smothering of individual enterprise and initiative. There was enough truth in these arguments that they worked extremely well to mobilize many traditionalists, who were also economic liberals, against liberalism and the welfare state.[9]

A dynamically presented, coherent liberal program for economic revival might have succesfully kept some of these economic liberal/social conservatives who voted for conservative candidates in a liberal coalition. But it is doubtful that any program could have kept the whole coalition—of labor, liberals, minorities, *and* corporate interests—together.

Following the strategic suggestions of Phillips, William Rusher, the publisher of *National Review*, presented a more fully developed ideology that spoke to social and economic conservatism. Written in 1975, his book *The Making of the New Majority Party* did not call for reviving the Republican Party but for creating a *new* party, based on thoroughly conservative principles, without the burden of liberal "Eastern" Republicans. He estimated that there were more socially conservative Democrats who could be won to a new party than economically conservative but socially liberal Republicans. This pragmatism and anti-elite populism are among the distinguishing features of the New Right organizations and their strategy. The social base of the new party—and here we see the economic concerns presented under the guise of social and moral concerns—was to be society's producers, who were rightfully indignant at the increasing power of the nonproducers. Rusher's work illustrates well the relationship between the New Right's ideology, its electoral strategy, and its political arguments for attacking the public sector. The ideology was clearly constructed to help bring distinct groups into a new coalition. Economic conservatives in the Republican Party, capitalists, managers, independent small-business people, and white working-class people in the Democratic Party, Southern whites, Northern urban ethnics should recognize their fundamental agreements, their common interests, he argued, in their opposition to liberalism. The attack on the public sector

. itself becomes clearer as Rusher lays out the structural basis for that new coalition:

> The basic economic division in this country is no longer (if it ever was) between the haves and the have-nots. Instead a new economic division pits the producers—businessmen, manufacturers, hard-hats, blue-collar workers, and farmers—against the new and powerful class of nonproducers comprised of liberal verbalist elites (the dominant media, the major foundations and research institutions, the educational establishment, the federal and state bureaucracies) and a semi-permanent welfare constituency, all coexisting happily in a state of mutually sustaining symbiosis.[10]

Crucial to the division between producers and nonproducers is the manner in which the middle strata are divided. One important division is between society and the state. For Rusher, the members of the unrighteous, liberal New Class employed by or defending the welfare state are excluded because they use their control of the state to assist other excluded groups to the detriment of the producers in the moral, social bloc. The dichotomy between society and the state thus creates images by which the New Class is excluded from the "real America": as functionaries of the state administrative apparatus they are not *of* society but *against* society.[11]

In a second distinction, between producers and nonproducers, Rusher elaborates on the role of the state and the New Class. Here he shifts from a reasonably accurate *description* of the social bases for a new coalition to a conspiratorial, and only very partially accurate, *analysis:*

> Under the leadership of the verbalists, post-war liberalism moved far beyond the New Deal's simple favoritism toward the poor and conciously promoted the growth of an entirely new (and also nonproducing) welfare constituency; a vast segment of the population that was no longer seriously expected to (and in fact does not) play any constructive economic role, but exists simply as a permanent parasite on the body politic . . . carefully tended and forever subtly expanded by the verbalizers as a justification for their own existence and growth.[12]

Rusher here ties together a number of themes into a neat conspiratorial package. For Rusher, social struggles by the working class, Blacks, women, and other social groups have nothing to do with the development of social-welfare programs—social security, aid to families with dependent children, expanded welfare roles, for instance. Only the selfish and instrumental use of the state by the New Class "verbalists" has led to the increase in welfare pro-visions. He does not view women or Blacks as agents of history capable of fighting for their own needs but as the undeserving and unproductive recipients of benefits that destroy society.[13] A term like "parasite on the body politic" is a crude biological metaphor by which the legitimate and illegitimate elements of society are distinguished.

The critical focus on the state and the emphasis on the right-eousness of society's producers (as defined by Rusher) established the basis for a cross-class collaboration to challenge the power of the New Class and its underclass, immoral allies. From both eco-nomic and social conservatism, criticisms are leveled against the New Class. The latter group is alleged to favor its nonproductive welfare clients over hardworking members of the working class, struggling shopkeepers, and capitalists who risk their capital in job-creating ventures. The cultural values of the New Class favor Black nationalism, sexual liberation, and women's liberation at the ex-pense of middle Americans, who live in stable families, and are morally upright, and hardworking.

Rusher consistently understands the advantage in linking social and economic conservatism.[14] He also underscores the importance of the work ethic in joining them:

> The economic conservative is dedicated to the proposition that ener-gies of men are the root source of all real wealth, and hence that work is one of society's highest values. But the social conservative, too, is a believer in the virtue and value of work. He is no free-loader; on the contrary he is inclined to be contemptuous, if not downright resentful, of social parasites who make a career out of government money—be they welfare payments or academic grants.[15]

Racism, anti-intellectualism, and economic individualism inform Rusher's appreciation of hard work. Neither here nor elsewhere in his book does he mention any intrinsic values for wages and profit.

While the attack on the New Class and liberalism has been the main New Right focus in domestic affairs so far, the possibility of renewed witch-hunts should not be discounted. The current push to link all terrorism to Soviet machinations and the hints that opponents of nuclear power have engaged in terrorist actions sug-gest an attempt to manufacture a Red Scare. Currently liberals are the main enemy, but even with liberals it is possible to question loyalty. Former secretary of the treasury and "energy czar" William

Simon wonders if those with the wrong attitude toward basic values are really American. "An American who is hostile to individualism, to the work ethic, to free enterprise, who advocates an increasing government take-over of the economy or who advocates coercive socialization of American life is in some profound sense advocating that America cease being America. He is advocating values that are not American and are philosophically antithetical to America itself."[16] Such a view surely fits with conspiratorial, rather than historical, explanations of the increasing power of those termed the New Class. The right argues that the New Class, while not communist, is collectivist, statist, antigrowth, and culturally modernist—not, in Simon's eyes, American virtues.

We can now see how the combination of social and economic conservatism lends itself to a broad range of criticisms of the welfare state. The New Class is charged with using the welfare state both to stifle economic growth and to stimulate social change. The New Right would have the state do just the opposite, support economic dynamism and social stasis. Thus William Simon argues: "Today our state is simply a redistributionist machine run amok, in which a relatively small group of people keep taking the wealth out of everybody's pockets and redistributing it for a variety of purposes that they alone deem important. . . . So what is actually going on is an attempt to level all people."[17] And Jesse Helms complements Simon in writing: "Our first priority in holding back the waves of statism that threaten to engulf us all must be to renew the honor and dignity and prestige of the family. The family as prior right to that of any government. Almighty God is the author of the family and the Lord Jesus Himself grew up subject to his human household."[18]

Against the state, which they believe divides people into unisexed, atomistic individuals, the New Right places "the people" who live together in traditional nuclear families, who use the military power of the nation-state to execute the American mission in the world, but who decline to use the welfare state to satisfy their material needs. The populist imagery works to mask class divisions; to deny that the state serves class interests; and hence to deny the legitimacy of the state's addressing immediate economic needs.

The social and economic conservatisms in their ideology are mutually reinforcing in numerous ways. Their pro-family morality supports the antiwelfare animus against single women on welfare (often envisaged as Black) supporting children born out of wedlock.

Their belief that individuals are responsible for their fate and that they freely enter into contractual relationships reinforces their hostility to regulation of health and safety in the workplace.[19] Their view that parents should control the sexuality of their teenage daughters leads them to oppose contraceptive counseling for teenagers or the availability of abortions for minors without parental consent. Their belief that the family is the only moral institution for sexual intimacy strengthens their oppositon to government legal aid or medical services for gays and lesbians.

The market system is presented as a netural entity, a mode of human interaction that, like the family, is God-given and outside history. New Class environmentalists who seek to impose restrictions on growth in the name of ecological or human medical considerations are elitist, no-growth fanatics who seek to preserve their access to nature at the expense of jobs for society's producers.[20] The pleasure-seeking of cultural liberals who "consume" nature is unfavorably juxtaposed to the profit- and wage-seeking work of cultural conservatives who produce wealth through the market economy. The right's support for government subsidies of nuclear power is an obvious place where their market ideology conflicts with their orientation toward profitable economic growth. Yet the dichotomy between no-growth fanatics and economically realistic producers masks this inconsistency a bit. Also, the appeals to national chauvinism in the name of "energy self-sufficiency" and allusions to the political volatility of the Middle East also lend support to the pronuclear appeals.

The social conservatism constantly facilitates cross-class support for anti-working-class policies. As British Marxist Stuart Hall has argued, the "cross-class conception of the family as a 'refuge' carries a particular weight and intensity when the world from which the family forms a 'refuge' is the daily experience of class exploitation in production and work."[21] The (partially accurate) attack on the manifold ways the state intervenes in family life is used to relieve capitalist economic relations of reponsibility for the travails of family life.

The Moral Crusade

In addition to providing a general critique of the public sector, of public sector spending, and of the control of the state and society

by the New Class, the New Right also attacks particular institutions
in the public sector. Even though most of the antistate rhetoric
focuses on big government, the federal agencies, the large bureaucracies, the regulatory commissions, and so forth, many of the
actual targets of the New Right are closer to home. Again, while
so much of the rhetoric is addressed to the redistributive elements
of social spending, many of the actual targets of the attacks on the
public sector are people who "produce" services in the public
sector. Thus, under the guise of attacking the distant, bloated bureaucracies of Washington and the supposed parasites on welfare,
the New Right is actually a part of a much broader attack on the
services delivered through local and state governments as well as
by the federal government. We can see important examples of this
in New Right views of the schools, particularly in relevant provisions of the Family Protection Act. I will focus on attacks on sex
education and public sector unionism to show how moral traditionalism and anti–working-class policies can be wrapped in the
respectability of defending the rights of citizens and parents.

   Since 1968 opposition to sex education has been a salient political
issue for social conservatives and conservative fundamentalists.
Given original impetus by the Reverend Billy James Hargis and
his Christian Crusade, and the John Birch Society's Movement to
Restore Decency (MOTOREDE), the attack on sex education continued through the 1970s and has gained energy since the creation
of the Moral Majority as a political force and Reagan's election.[22]
The Moral Majority is currently organizing a campaign against the
use of the feminist book *Our Bodies, Our Selves* in public schools,
arguing that it promotes homosexuality, sexual liberation, per-
versity, and premarital sex as legitimate practices. While conservative Catholics and Protestants may disagree about the role of
nonprocreative sex in marriage, they agree that premarital sex,
abortion, and contraception are wrong. They see sex education as
part of the process through which such a liberal sexual ethic is
taught.

   The attack on sex education in public schools is of course part
of a general attack on liberalism in sexual matters, on anti-author-
itarianism among youth, on feminism, on reproductive freedom for
women. It is also, however, part of a more general attack on liberalism in the schools. Sex education (along with, for example, the
United Nations, collectivism, and internationalism) is taught at the
expense of patriotism and self-reliance. As one opponent of sex

education wrote, "My conviction is that when you talk about sex instruction, you are talking about the family. When you are talking about the family, you are talking about the home. When you are talking about the home, you are talking about the country. When you are talking about the country, you are talking about survival. So the issue is a life-and-death matter." Communists, and now the New Class, are labeled "change agents," intent on subverting the moral fiber of the youth.[23] Thus sexual restraint (and ignorance) are tied to defense of America as is the individualism of the market place.

The opposition to sex education has mostly been organized locally, bringing pressure to bear on local school boards. It overlaps with the concern about textbooks, "sexy" or "immoral" books in school libraries, and liberal "indoctrination" in social studies. In some states, such as Texas, where textbooks are chosen at the state level, the right-wing critics of textbooks try to impose traditional views of sexuality, sex roles, and family life along with their lobbying for textbook presentations of creationism (to counter the dread secular ideology of evolution), Americanism, and individualism.

The proposed Laxalt Family Protection Act is an attempt, oddly inconsistent with their localist and states' rights arguments, to make educational policy at the national level through the power of the purse: if school districts do not abide by the provisions of the act, they will lose federal grants. There is no specific item in the bill about sex education, but there are bases for opposition to liberal sex-education materials and courses in it. For instance, the bill opposes any program that "promotes courses of instruction or curriculum seeking to inculcate values or modes of behavior which contradict the demonstrated beliefs and values of the community."[24] Or, again, federal money would be denied districts that "would tend to denigrate, diminish, or deny the role of differences between the sexes as it has historically been understood in the United States."[25] The work that feminists have done to change the male bias in textbooks would be reversed and sex education would be chastity education.

Another provision of the Laxalt bill points to the New Right opposition to public sector unionism. Federal funds would be denied a school district "which required the forced payment of dues or fees as a condition of employment for teachers."[26] The right has long been opposed to the closed shop. The New Right now uses the pro-family ideology as a guise for opposing teachers' unions.

The main organization promoting anti-labor legislation and lobbying is the National Right to Work Committee (NRTWC), founded in 1955 but close to the New Right since the early 1970s. Supplementing the work of the NRTWC is the Public Service Research Council (PSRC), which is directed against public sector unionism particularly. The PSRC was organized in 1973 and has been close to the New Right from its inception. It has various public fronts, including the Americans Against Union Control of Government (AAUCG), which lobby at the state level, and the Public Service Legal Defense Foundation, which provides legal services for individuals opposing closed shops. In the recent past public sector employees have been organizing unions at a rate that far surpasses workers in the private sector. In fact, with the percentage of workers in unions generally declining, it is only the rise in public sector unionism that has kept it from falling more precipitously. Restricting its work to the public sector, the PSRC is able to deploy arguments against unions that are not readily applicable for private sector unions. These are worth noting, for, once again, they show how the anti-working-class strategy of opposition to unionism can be cloaked in arguments about the rights of citizens. Noteworthy here is the manner in which existing structural divisions between workers in the public and private sectors are played upon in a conservative manner, and the divisions are heightened and given cultural and political importance as a way of denying public sector workers their rights.

One of the arguments against public sector unions contrasts an extremely unfavorable portrayal of unions to a most generous portrayal of representative government. "Public sector union bosses used a variety of tactics in their effort to subvert the will of the public which desires a greater voice in its government, and for more efficient government at less costs."[27] The capitalist rationality of labor morality as a mechanism for lowering costs and increasing control of a work force (hire and fire people as needed) is here linked to the right of the public to achieve fiscal and other control over its public work force. There are, in fact, tensions and conflicts between citizens and their employees in the public sector. But to deny that the people employed by the government have rights as workers, as well as in their status as voters and taxpayers, is to deny the tension by favoring some amorphous, nonworking, "public." Not only does this view exaggerate the degree to which unions are unresponsive to their members and the public, but it certainly distorts the degree to which the public actually controls government. Most local governments are hardly more responsive to the citizenry than union leaders are to their memberships. In terms of the schools, however, the PSRC argument combines the rights of citizens and parents. Citizens have the right to fiscal control of the schools, which is harder when unions fight for pay increases. With demographic shifts and declining enrollment in schools, unions demand that teachers have a say in the "reduction-in-force" procedures. As parents, many people are upset at their lack of control over the content of their children's education; such control should not be in the hands of union leaders in New York City. Here the rights of parents are evoked against bureaucratic unions, and at the same time the virtues of small-town America are defended against the sins of urban-based New Class bureaucrats.

Clearly parents lack control over their children's education. But that problem owes as much or more to the kind of administrative control exercised by people working for the supposedly representative school boards as to the teachers' power. Further, there are many reasons why schools do not work well or are not responsive to parents. The presence of a union may make it harder to fire a really lousy teacher; it may also make it harder to fire a good teacher who defies the administration. But as difficult as parental control of educational content and quality of teaching is, the introduction of anti-union ideology seeks to pit parents against teachers in a manner that diverts attention from many other causes of poor education. This is part of the New Right's opportunism, for many parents really are concerned with better education. Ironically, New Right programs offer them merely a repressive requirement for teaching traditionalist content, while denying teachers and other employees basic rights as workers.

The New Right Ideology

In the 1950s and the 1960s the right mainly attacked communism; indeed anticommunism was virtually the identity of the right. Liberals were smeared as fellow travelers or dupes. Today, by contrast, criticisms of liberalism predominate. The antiliberal focus is in some ways more accurate than anticommunism, for liberalism is the prevailing form in which most of the developments the right abhors have been delivered. For the right, liberalism promotes two seemingly antagonistic, pernicious trends: atomization and collectivism. Both of these are understood to have come about as political penetrations of society by the state, in turn due to the influence of the intelligentsia. In addition the right attacks many aspects of cultural modernism promoted or defended by liberals as a consequence of their moral relativism and secularism.[28] Let us look at each of these elements in turn.

The New Right associates atomization with what it considers unwarranted extensions of civil rights and civil liberties. Examples of this are the Voting Rights Act, the right of women to have abortions, the equal rights amendment, the rights for minors, the increased protection given free speech that has legalized the spread of pornography, and court decisions that have given greater rights to the accused. Second, they oppose the liberalism of the welfare state, which they associate with collectivism. They attack state intervention as inconsistent with those principles of classic liberalism that they do accept, and as subversive of capitalist and traditional social relations. They distinguish, as we have seen, between Great Society welfare liberalism with its redistributive programs and the New Deal which provided a basic floor for welfare. They argue that welfare liberalism is replacing equality of opportunity with equality of outcome. It is thereby interfering with the economic and ethical features of the market in the name of a specious egalitarianism. They also attack welfare liberalism for creating state intervention in the private lives of people and the moral structure of society in such areas as the socialization of children and the relations between the sexes. The attack on the welfare state thus combines the cultural and economic concerns of the right.

The opposition to the atomizing effects of extending civil rights and civil liberties and the collectivist qualities of the welfare state are interwoven in the New Right's criticisms of the public sector. The New Right opposes functions of the state that it views as hostile to market forces. In this way it not only blames the liberal uses of the state for the decline of the market, but it also blames on liberalism many features of modern society inextricably connected with the development of capitalism. In destroying the market incentive among workers and capitalists alike, the state has suppressed the dynamism of the economy, stifled the development of the nation's riches, rewarded the indolent, and punished the industrious.

The state alone is blamed for inflation (monetary and fiscal policies), collapse of the work ethic and productivity (welfare policies that reward the unproductive), and the decline of industrial efficiency (overregulation by government). Second, the welfare state is charged with interfering in the private lives of "the people." It has taken away from people the right and ability to regulate their own lives, the socialization of their children, the integrity of the educational process, the stability of the traditional nuclear family. The state has forced on people undesired social changes.

Related to the attack on the state is the New Right's critique of the politicization of society, which in turn is blamed on intellectuals, a self-serving and power-hungry elite. This critique is based on a conceptual error in much conservative ideology, an error which conflates many different historical processes—social, economic, even diplomatic and military. For an historical explanation they substitute a conspiracy theory with a villain, the intelligentsia. In accounting for the decline of the market and civil society as self-regulating mechanisms, the conservatives ignore the rise of giant corporate enterprises, the decline of religion as a hegemonic belief system, the changes in the socialization of the young, and challenges to traditional authority, to name but a few relevant factors. The characterization of the problem is reduced to the politicization of society, and the explanation to a single elite.

It is worth quoting at length a clear statement of this position. In his introduction to a recent collection titled *The Politicization of Society*, the conservative economic historian R.M. Hartwell wrote:

> Politicization can be defined as that now pervasive tendency for making all questions political questions, all issues political issues, all values political values, and all decisions political decisions. . . . Politicization can now be seen in the relationship between all people in a society: between parents and children, between teachers and pupils, between professors and students, betweeen employers and employees, between producers and consumers, between races, between sportsmen, indeed men and women. Where once individuals saw their problems as private and sought private solutions for them, now they seek political solutions. . . .
>
> Politicization thus takes the manifest form of increasing the power of the state, of increasing political power as against all other forms of power in society, of increasing the power of the politicians and the bureaucrats as against the power of individuals, private institutions, and voluntary associations. . . .

Since the market is no longer allowed to function freely, the state must decide what to produce and how to distribute that production; since the family as a social unit has declined because of the erosion of parental responsibilities largely as a result of state action, the state must decide about education, health, behavior, and all other aspects of growing up and earning a living; and finally, since the state decides what values should prevail in society, and ensures that such values are embodied in legislation and enforced by bureaucracies, the state has increasingly replaced the church in determining how we should behave. Politics is now religion.[29]

With politics as the new religion it is not politicians but intellectuals who are the new priests. Hartwell argues, and the New Right implies, that the historic agency propelling this politicization is the intelligentsia, whose self-interested members oppose the market "because it does not reward them according to their own estimation of their obvious social worth." Intellectuals, today the leading element in the New Class in conservative demonology, "play leading roles in the bureaucracies of the state, as advisors, experts, and administrators, and increasingly the power of the state means increasing the power of the intellectuals. Their 'cult of the powerful state,' therefore, is not disinterested, even though their own self-interest is well rationalized."[30]

Not without insight, Hartwell's ringing condemnation is nonetheless but a more intelligent version of the positions developed by Phillips, Rusher, Helms, and others of the New Right. However important intellectuals and the explosion of knowledge have been in the recent past, their power is greatly exaggerated here.

Nevertheless, the role of intellectuals, bureaucrats, and other professionals are critical political questions today. The instrumental arrogance of such groups in their delivery of "services," and the hierarchical, bureaucratic organization of the service sector angers many of its "clients."[31] (Although oddly enough the groups most victimized by the service sector are usually those of the "underclass"—the welfare poor, for example—excluded by the New Right coalition.) Working- and middle-class anti-intellectualism is often a "class response" to [the] unequal distribution of knowledge."[32]

The deepest and most influential aspects of the New Right criticism of liberalism cannot, however, be categorized on the basis of traditional political principles. New Right propaganda grows from a deeper, less intellectual sensibility that is part of an aesthetic and even emotional revulsion against liberalism and modernity. Their reaction is punitive, sexually repressive, racist, and antifeminist in part because they are responding to fears of a complete disintegration of social cohesion. These fears pervade their propaganda and function like webs connecting the many issues raised by the New Right over the past decade. They are similar to concerns about loss of community, family, church, and other "mediating institutions" expressed by neoconservatives, and to the antifeminist, anti-youth cultural conservatism of such "leftist" cultural critics as Christopher Lasch.[33]

The fears, and the problems which produce them, are real. The proposed solutions, however, are very limited, embracing repression as the only antidote to what rightists view as the individualist, licentious excesses of modern culture. The parts of classic liberalism they approve are for men, not women. They think that the family should be run by men according to custom, and that the social bonds between men and women and children in the family ought to be regulated by traditional and religious morality, not by contractual relations worked out by the particular individuals involved. They juxtapose an image of legitimate patriarchal authority in the family to one of instrumental, individualistic self-seeking by men and especially by women at the expense of the family, love, intimacy, and children. They do not juxtapose male supremacy, sexual inequality, and sexual repression to more equal and sharing relationships between men and women. They believe in the complementarity of sex roles in the family and society at large. They hold that sexual equality leads to unisex promiscuity, lack of complementarity, and the collapse of social bonds necessary for society.

They fear that the very kind of selfish individualism and instrumentality that they admire in the economy will invade the family, sexual relations, and all situations of warmth and comfort. Not attracted to forms of community and solidarity, love and intimacy, other than those of the so-called traditional family, parental power, and male dominance, they want to recapture an idealized family of the past. Exalting the virtues of individualism for men in the marketplace, they understand that such self-seeking can only exist as long as it is sustained by more generous and accommodating behavior; this role is assigned to women because it has been theirs historically, because it is God's will, because it is in their genes. They argue that the family and hierarchal gender/generation re-

328 Crisis in the Public Sector

lations are natural and godly. Liberalism is unnatural and ungodly because it knows no limits, and subverts proper and necessary absolutes in its specious pursuit of relativism and humanism.

The opposition to liberalism is tied to the view that families, traditional male-headed families, are the basic units of society. Men should go out and seek wealth as individuals; women should stay at home as wives (or also work for wages if necessary to support the family, but not for reasons of career advancement or personal satisfaction), and raise girls to be like themselves and boys to be like their fathers. The work ethic, sexual repression, and a punitive view of those who fail or do not live according to these norms, follow. Thus the current administration's definition of the "truly needy" excludes most people who have true needs. To deliver to those needs would, in the view of the New Right, reward the undeserving at the expense of the deserving.

In summary, five general tendencies within New Right thought about the state and the public sector stand out. First, the New Rightists link criticisms of welfare liberalism to criticisms of the further extension of classical individualist liberalism; both forms of liberalism now seem to them to undercut a social stability which, in their view, can only be based on traditional forms of authority and hierarchy. Second, they tend to identify the noxious aspects of the state with its welfare functions and support those aspects of big government which administer the military establishment, the police establishment, etc. Third, they attack the New Class for self-aggrandizement at the expense of economic growth and domestic tranquility. Fourth, in their attacks on big government and the New Class, they set up a major dichotomy between society and the state which fits their populist appeal: "the people" constitute society in opposition to the New Class and its allies who represent the state. Fifth, and extremely important for the cohesion of New Right ideology, they accuse the state of simultaneously forestalling and promoting change. The state supresses desirable economic growth and forces undesirable changes in private life and social relations. Against this reprehensible behavior of the state the New Right calls for domestic stability and economic dynamism. The New Right, in other words, is for nuclear families and nuclear power. In both demands the New Right is responding to genuine popular sentiment against simultaneous loss of cultural control and loss of economic security. The right-wing appeal manipulates such sentiment, possibly effectively in terms of short-run and electoral victories. Whether it can retain widespread support on the basis of an actual program remains to be seen.

Notes

1. The right-wing libertarians are the exception insofar as they oppose the coercive control of personal behavior implied by social conservatism and also militarism because it strengthens the state.
2. It has often been properly pointed out that capitalists actually support regulation because it tends to decrease the debilitating aspects of intracapitalist competition. But, especially since the late 1960s, rules and regulations have been implemented that capitalists generally oppose, namely, those aimed at reducing the social impact of business. For an important discussion of this issue, see David Vogel, "The Inadequacy of Contemporary Opposition to Business," *Daedalus* (Summer 1980): 47–58.
3. See also, for example, "Thatcherism and the Welfare State," *Marxism Today* (July 1980): 8.
4. For more about the organized New Right, see: Richard A. Viguerie, *The New Right: We're Ready to Lead* (Falls Church, Va.: The Viguerie Company, 1980); Alan Crawford, *Thunder on the Right: The "New Right" and the Politics of Resentment* (New York: Pantheon, 1980); Thomas J. McIntyre, *The Fear Brokers* (New York: Pilgrim, 1979); William A. Hunter, *The "New Right": A Growing Force in State Politics* (Washington, D.C.: Conference on Alternative State and Local Policies & the Center to Protect Workers' Rights, 1980); and Allen Hunter, "In the Wings: New Right Ideology and Organization," *Radical America*, 15(1981):113–38.
5. Many working-class people support cutbacks of those very services which were originally won through struggles of the working class itself. This is an issue which merits serious attention. For an important analysis of the turn to the right in Britain, see Stuart Hall, Chas Critcher, Tony Jefferson, John Clarke, and Brian Roberts, *Policing the Crisis: Mugging, the State, and Law and Order* (New York: Holmes and Meier, 1978). An American left-liberal critique is contained in Willard Gaylin, Ira Glasser, Steven Marcus, David J. Rothman, *Doing Good: The Limits of Benevolence* (New York: Pantheon Books, 1978) and an important British socialist perspective on the issues can be found in The London Edinburgh Weekend Return Group, a working group of the Conference of Socialist Economists, *In and Against the State* (London: Pluto Press, 1980).
6. Kevin Phillips, *The Emerging Republican Majority* (New York: Doubleday, 1970), p. 37.

7. Ibid., p. 467.
8. Ibid., p. 471.
9. The decline in the political salience of economic issues and the rise of social issues, the shift from cultural liberalism to cultural conservatism, and the increasing significance of splits in the Democratic Party have been noted by many commentators. Studies of cultural conflict around race and youth that are sympathetic to the white urban working class include Patricia Cayo Sexton and Brendan Sexton, *Blue Collars and Hard Hats: The Working Class and the Future of American Politics* (New York: Random House, 1971); Peter Binzen, *Whitetown, USA* (New York: Random House, 1970); and Richard M. Scammon and Ben J. Wattenberg, *The Real Majority* (New York: Coward, McCann & Geoghegan, 1970). For more critical evaluations, see Richard E. Dawson, *Public Opinion and Contemporary Disarray* (New York: Harper & Row, 1973); and for the 1972 presidential election, Samuel Lubell, *The Future While It Happened* (New York: W. W. Norton, 1973). Important studies that show the role of these shifts in public opinion for electoral politics are Walter Dean Burnham, *Critical Elections and the Mainsprings of American Politics* (New York: W. W. Norton, 1970); Everett C. Ladd, Jr., "The Shifting Party Coalitions—1932–1976," *Emerging Coalitions in American Politics,* ed. S. M. Lipset (San Francisco: Institute for Contemporary Studies, 1978); and Robert Lekachman, "Troubles of the Welfare State," *Dissent,* 26, No. 4(1979):414–29. Two useful articles that place the shift toward conservatism and the disarray in the Democratic Party in a political economic context are David Gold, "The Rise and Decline of the Keynesian Coalition," *Kapitalistate,* 6(1977):129–61, and M. Brian Murphy and Alan Wolfe, "Democracy in Disarray," *Kapitalistate,* 8(1980):9–25. For a general historical treatment of the post-World War II period that is very sensitive to the shifting cultural and political currents, see Godfrey Hodgson, *America in Our Time* (New York: Doubleday, 1976).
10. William A. Rusher, *The Making of the New Majority Party* (Ottawa, Ill.: Green Hill, 1975), p. 14.
11. The term "New Class" is most often used today to refer disparagingly to the professionals and bureaucrats of the welfare state, their intellectual defenders and cultural modernists. It is a term with a long lineage on the left that has recently been appropriated and modified by neoconservatives on the right. Irving Kristol in *Two Cheers for Capitalism* (New York: Basic Books, 1978) and in earlier journalistic writings is usually credited with having done the most to promote the term. For a critical discussion of neoconservative thought, see Peter Steinfels, *The Neo-Conservatives: The Men Who Are Changing America's Politics* (New York: Simon & Schuster, 1979). For a neoconservative collection of essays, see B. Bruce-Briggs, ed., *The New Class?* (New Brunswick, N.J.: Transaction, 1979). For a historically sound

analysis of the New Class, see Alvin Gouldner, *The Future of the Intellectuals and the Rise of the New Class* (New York: Seabury, 1979).

12. Rusher, op. cit., p. 33.

13. Many students of the right wing have noted its proclivity for conspiracy theories of history. Currently the New Class is the center of the conspiracy for many on the right. The attack on the New Class allows the right to explain undesirable cultural and economic changes and the growth of the state without reference to the dynamics of the capitalist economy or the legitimate strivings of subordinate groups in society. The right holds that New Class secular humanists are responsible for almost all threats to "middle America."

14. Rusher believes that such a coalition has been a potential majority party since the 1950s. See also the views of conservative intellectuals as expressed by George H. Nash, *The Conservative Intellectual Movement in America Since 1945* (New York: Harper & Row, 1976), especially chapter 6.

15. Rusher, op. cit., p. 93.

16. William E. Simon, *A Time for Truth* (New York: Readers Digest, 1978), p. 47.

17. William E. Simon, "Inflation: Made and Manufactured in Washington, D.C.," *imprimis*, 8, No. 7(1979):3.

18. Jesse Helms, *When Free Men Shall Stand* (Grand Rapids, Mich.: Zondervan, 1976), pp. 119–20.

19. For a criticism of OSHA that plays to individualism and property rights as sacrosanct and bound together, see George V. Hansen, "OSHA: A Nightmare about to End," *Can You Afford this House?*, ed. David Treen (Ottawa, Ill.: Caroline House, 1978), pp. 74–81.

20. The link between environmentalism and the New Class is a ploy used time and again by the right. The problems that enviromentalists raise have to be considered on their own merits and not dismissed because of who raises them. Also, there is a tendency to lump all kinds of environmentalism together and tie health and safety measures into the same package and then *still* claim that these are only the concerns of a small elite.

21. Stuart Hall et al., op. cit., p. 145.

22. Mary Breasted, *Oh! Sex Education!* (New York: Praeger, 1970) is still the best treatment of the early sex education controversies.

23. Sam Campbell, quoted in Ibid., p. 147.

24. *Family Protection Act*, 96th Cong., 1st Sess., S. 1808, 1979, p. 3.

25. Ibid., p. 4.

26. Ibid., p. 3.

27. *Annual Report*, Public Service Research Council, 1978, p. 3.

28. For a litany of complaints against liberalism see Viguerie, op. cit., pp. 1–5. For a more intellectually sustained right-wing conservatism of many aspects of liberalism, see M. Stanton Evans, *Clear and Present*

Dangers: A Conservative View of America's Government (New York: Harcourt Brace Jovanovich, 1975).

29. R. M. Hartwell, "Introduction," *The Politicization of Society,* ed. Kenneth S. Templeton, Jr. (Indianapolis, Ind.: Liberty Press, 1979), pp. 14–15, 24.

30. Ibid., p. 18.

31. Yet it is also a conservative position to highlight the forms of domination in public bureaucracies and not criticize the hierarchical organization of production, for example, in private enterprises.

32. Stuart Hall et al., op. cit., p. 152.

33. The neoconservative position on "mediating institutions" can be found in Peter L. Berger and Richard John Neuhaus, *To Empower People: The Role of Mediating Structures in Public Policy* and Michael Novak ed., *Democracy and Mediating Structures: A Theological Inquiry,* both published by the American Enterprise Institute for Public Policy Research, in 1977 and 1980, respectively. The main proponent of cultural conservatism from the left is Christopher Lasch, *Haven in a Heartless World: The Family Besieged* (New York: Basic Books, 1977) and *The Culture of Narcissism: American Life in an Age of Diminishing Expectations* (New York: W. W. Norton, 1978). For a left perspective more oriented toward political activity and less toward cultural criticism that still retains the conservative view of "mediating institutions," see Harry Boyte, *The Backyard Revolution: Understanding the New Citizen Movement* (Philadelphia, Pa.: Temple University Press, 1980).

23. Beyond Liberalism

Mary Jo Hetzel and John Brouder

The Sources of the Fiscal Crisis

It is important that groups fighting current austerity policies dispel some of the myths about who is to blame for the fiscal crisis. While explanations put forward by conservative government and business leaders and popularized by the media point to escalating demands by greedy public workers and welfare recipients or to liberal governmant mismanagement, the actual sources of the fiscal crisis emanate from the system of capitalist economic growth itself. We can take public workers and service recipients off the defensive by stressing the importance of certain items.

1. Socialization of the costs of production: monopoly corporations use state fiscal policies to transfer their costs of doing business onto the general public while maintaining private control over profit.
2. Capital flight: business moves away, frequently to the South or overseas, in search of higher profits, taking jobs and tax revenues with them.
3. Technological unemployment: human labor is replaced by machines in the interest of higher profit, thereby reducing

Mary Jo Hetzel is a member of the Public Sector Crisis Reader collective and teaches social sciences in Clark University's adult program; she is active politically in the Boston People's Organization. John Brouder has taught political science at the University of Lowell and Suffolk University in Massachusetts; a founder of Taxpayers Against Proposition 2 1/2, he is active in a range of public sector organizing activities.

taxable income and raising government spending for the jobless.

4. International capitalist crisis: U.S. dominance within the world-wide political economy has been severely undermined; capital investment slowed in the 1970s, increasing unemployment, depressing wages, and drying up tax revenue at the same time that unemployed individuals and financially strapped corporations were seeking additional government assistance.

Thus, the fiscal crisis emerged as a result of capitalist growth processes that resulted in competing demands for state resources. Groups such as low-income Blacks or public workers, who have been held accountable for the fiscal crisis, are actually victims of capitalist economic growth.

As a result of the conflict engendered by the fiscal crisis the state and the democratic process are undergoing a process of demystification. The state is no longer viewed as a neutral and benevolent savior when times are rough. Rather, the systematic constraints on state action are becoming all too clear: business needs come first for conservative *and* liberal government officials alike; people's needs come second, if at all. In order to promote social and economic stability, the state has historically played a double, often contradictory role: helping to create the conditions for profitable business growth on the one hand, while aiding the victims of that economic growth on the other. With the advent of the fiscal crisis, these tensions between community needs and the requirements of profitable business growth have become nearly irreconcilable. It is these contradictory, irreconcilable demands being placed on the state—from the business and financial community, from the people desperately needing jobs and services, and from citizens seeking tax relief—that constitute the political drama of the crisis in the public sector.

The Conservative Social Vision

During periods of capitalist crisis the forces of class exploitation and sexual and racial oppression accentuate the social conflict both within and between the key social classes of American society. Status anxiety rises to a new height during such times of prolonged economic crisis, and politics loses its comfortable liberal flavor. As the better-off segments of the working class blindly ally with big business and conservative government leaders against minorities, liberals, the left, and the unemployed poor, the danger of neofascism rises to the surface. Such a popular rightist movement, the signs of which can be seen all around us in the form of tax revolts, attacks on women and gays, and open racist violence against Blacks, is gaining strength in the face of a discredited liberalism and the absence of a strong, articulate, left movement.

The New Right and "class conscious" corporate capital represent the two complementary strands of the conservative-capitalist ideology gaining dominance today in the wake of liberal failure. The holistic philosophy and boldly articulated goals of the right stand in sharp contrast to the mass of confusion and narrow range of issues presently being raised by most left-liberal groupings. The more "moderate" corporate view is well represented by the following selection from the 1975 Annual Report of New York's Morgan Guaranty Bank:

> We believe that over the long run the validity of the investment process depends on the willingness of societies and their governments to recognize practical limits on the speed with which they attain certain social goals. . . . We urge patience in the pursuit of full employment, the availability of universal health care, quality education, clean air and water, and support for the needy. If we put humanitarian values before economic reality, then consumption will take the high ground over production. Capital for production is the highest goal.

This philosophy is shared by the vast majority of American corporate, financial, and political leaders.

While both moderate capital and the New Right give priority to the private sector over the public sector, the New Right also capitalizes upon the fears and anxieties arising from a wide range of social issues, including the crumbling of the patriarchal family, ethnic community ties, and the traditional work ethic. In the area of sexuality, their antagonism to gay rights, free choice of abortion, and public and paternal day care, are all related to the desire to preserve the superior masculine power position within the sexual division of labor. They espouse "white power," oppose affirmative action, and engage in vigilante action to protect their own from attempts by Blacks and other minorities to achieve equal housing, educational, and employment opportunities. Finally, they advocate a return to the days of "rugged individualism," which in the 1980s means freezing inequality through an attack on social spending and celebrating the private consumer culture as the true source of social status and moral worth.

The entire right wing sees its political task as twofold: to cut the public, social budget in order to increase aid to the private sector, and in the process to demoralize and frighten people into acquiescing to the new climate of fiscal and social conservatism. The main difference between class-conscious corporate capital and the New Right is that the former would like to redirect governmental social and economic policy toward the profit needs of major business. They "regret" the need to neglect pressing social problems out of "economic necessity." The New Right has no such regrets. They have launched an all-out attack on those people below them on the social scale. They seek to stop all progressive change that threatens their tenuous position of privilege and security within the work force, the community, and the home.

To sum up, in the conservative social vision it's "every man for himself" in the private marketplace; women should take care of children, be loyal wives, and if necessary earn "supplementary" wages in the low-wage clerical and service sector of the economy; public and private unions should defer to the requirements of profitable business growth; the poor should quietly disappear. For the conservatives, it is the survival of the fittest, or the most advantaged, in the 1980s.

Two Currents on the Left

There are two partially overlapping political tendencies on the left today. One, the left-liberal network composed of citizen-action, public-interest groups, tends to organize among the better-off segments of the working class and represent the forces of liberal reform against corporate power and wealth. Left-liberal groups work within the established political system in order to humanize capitalism, tame the corporations, and curb their greed for power and profit. They call for greater public or governmental involvement in corporate decisions to protect the consumer from exhorbitant prices, the worker from loss of jobs and wages, and the taxpayer from rising taxes. These groups focus on consumer rights and economic issues over other, more controversial social issues as a way, they say, to cut across all barriers of race, sex, class, and political ideology in order to unite a populist democratic majority against the priviliged few. It is a movement that has been built from the top by established liberal leaders within progressive labor bureaucracies and the Democratic Party, and by professional organizers and academics.

The other, more grass-roots tendency is composed of an array of low-wage workers and welfare-rights organizations, ad hoc groups fighting cutbacks in needed community services, rank-and-file progressive caucuses and militant union locals, grass-roots women's collectives, Black united fronts, and a handful of explicitly socialist, community-based organizations. The grass-roots groups seek to build a truly community-based, ground-up approach to change, in which the needs of the poor and national minorities are addressed and ties are sought with better-off segments of the working class. Working through conventional channels, and developing semicooperative relations with established political elites have been less tempting to grass-roots groups, since such methods have won them few concessions. Rather, mass action from below and militant disruption of sedate state offices, public-service agencies, and meetings have gained them far more.

The commitment of the people who give so much of their time and energy to both the left-liberal and the grass-roots movements is unquestionable. These two movements overlap at many points in terms of issues, membership, and tactics, and they frequently have a great deal in common both philosophically and practically. Both movements, moreover, are in such constant flux that positions taken one day can easily change in several months. But the grassroots groups appear to be moving in a more progressive direction than the left-liberal movement. We can hope that as the grassroots movement grows in strength it will come to have greater influence over the directions taken by the left-liberal movement. Significant differences are likely to persist between these two currents for some time. A strong class response to austerity policies, however, will require communication and cooperation between both movements.

Differences in the Two Movements

Grass-roots demands often focus on the very things that would require both an enlargement and a transformation of the public sector at the expense of private capital. The liberal network seeks

demands which can be more easily met within a capitalist framework, such as lower auto insurance rates and more equitable property taxes. While grass-roots groups participate in many of the same
consumer-taxpayer campaigns initiated by the liberal reform network, they push, in addition, for social needs such as public health
care, housing, education, day care, decent minimum incomes, and
expanded public-service employment. In so doing grass-roots
groups are pressing for an enlargement of those arenas in which
people are collectively engaged in work of genuine social value to
their communities, rather than in work promoting the goals of
private business.

Many women, racial minorities, and nonprofessional workers
have felt personally degraded in their dealings with public-service
bureaucracies. As a result, their criticisms of the state frequently
go deeper than those of the left-liberal network. Liberal public
sector unions, for example, strive to increase their own funding,
but resist grass-roots demands for community accountability and
participation in policymaking. For the left to become a strong class-
based force for change, it must deal with the racial, sexual, and
class antagonisms that exist between left-liberals in the public sector
unions and citizens' organizations and the lower-income grass-roots
communities.

Grass-roots groups tend to see governmental policies and business priorities as clearly intertwined, while the liberal network
frequently says the problem is big business not big government—
without clearly showing the connections between the two. More
importantly, grass-roots groups tend to press an explicitly antiprofit
perspective, in contrast to the left-liberal emphasis upon curbing
undue corporate privilege. Yet it has become clear in recent years
that it is precisely the *profit* needs of the real estate and health-
care industries, and financial and business elites that have motivated cuts in social spending across the board and that have had
such a directly exploitative impact upon poor and working people.

Socialist organizations such as Detroit Alliance for a Rational
Economy (DARE), among the most advanced segments of the grass-
roots movement, have begun to develop an overall strategy to deal
with the fiscal crisis. Left-liberal groups have taken a more ambivalent stance with regard to the fiscal crisis and imposed austerity.
Some have accepted the need for cost containment and tax reduction on business terms so long as their own program areas are
not cut back. Grass-roots socialist groups, on the other hand, defend

a wider range of social programs and place the blame for the fiscal crisis squarely on capitalism itself and on government fiscal policies that favor business interests.

Grass-roots groups are also an important progressive force because they are more willing to deal with the social issues currently on the organizing agenda of the New Right. They are compelled to do so since they have been more directly victimized by the New Right's ideological and political offensive. In response to the impotence felt by working people in the face of huge government bureaucracy, grass-roots groups support taking over and transforming that bureaucracy to meet community needs. Instead of quietly accepting the demands for cuts in human services, as some left-liberal groups have tended to do, grass-roots organizations argue that decent welfare and public-service jobs and the fight against racism and sexism improve the wages of all workers and the general political environment for left-wing organizing. While the left-liberal network downplays matters of racial and sexual oppression, exhorting Blacks and women to focus on the more "basic" and less divisive economic or union concerns, the grass-roots groups tend to fight on class, race, and sex fronts all at once. Finally, while left-liberals stress the need for a core of professionals to guide political action, the grass-roots groups develop the average citizen's capacity to act and participate in decision making.

The Left-Liberal Network

Citizen-Action Groups

Citizen-action groups have organized constituencies in the better-off segments of the working class. These professional organizations tend to focus on narrowly gauged consumer and taxpayer issues in order to galvanize the largest possible anticorporate coalition. The professional organizers, many of whom have their roots in the militant movements of the 1960s, have adjusted to the more conservative leanings of their new constituencies. They steer clear of many touchy social issues to avoid alienating their largely middle- and lower-middle-income working-class constituencies.

The organizing strategy of these citizen-action groups can be traced back to the pragmatic approach developed by Saul Alinsky in the 1950s. In this view, the task of organizers is not to deepen political and social conciousness but to give people the organizational tools they need to fight for their own interests. This pragmatic style of organizing brings mixed results. Their strategy is progressive, because people are encouraged to see unrestrained corporate power as a major source of their problems. However, it is potentially regressive—or defensively self-protective—because it does not foster an alliance with those below them on the economic and social scale. Nevertheless, grass-roots and left-wing groups support these citizen-action coalitions because of the anticorporate stance built into their campaigns to cut utility, telephone, and auto insurance rates and to redistribute the tax burden.

These groups have achieved some notable successes. For example, Fair Share won its campaign to tax residential properties at a lower rate than business properties and is now organizing two important campaigns to lower home heating-oil costs and prevent runaway shops. This last initiative is one of the most progressive to date, since it is a first step toward social control over corporate investment policy. There is, however, the danger that citizen-action groups will stay on the plane of consumer-rights activism, dealing with corporate abuses in piecemeal fashion. While membership organizations are being built in the process, their political direction and goals remain unclear.

The problems we face cannot be simply summed up as that of unbridled corporate power, as these groups suggest. This kind of liberal populism does not get at the question of class domination and the need for worker control over the means of production to release resources for social needs. When Tom Hayden and the leaders of citizen-action groups speak of their new philosophy as economic democracy, yet carefully distinguish it from the principles and practices of democratic socialist control over all the institutions of American life, they imply that capital can be cut down to size, the profit imperative significantly curbed, and people's needs met within the overall framework of state-aided private enterprise. In so doing, they impede the development of class conciousness and instead direct social discontent onto a treadmill of marginal liberal reform within established political channels.

These citizen-action organizations are often reluctant to deal with the wide range of social issues of greatest concern to low-income people, many women, and minorities. This has the effect of isolating these groups and depriving them of much-needed political support in the face of an antagonistic New Right. The deep schism that persists between the better-off segments of the working class and the disproportionately Black and female underclass has not been directly confronted by these citizen-action groups, despite the fact that no serious anticorporate movement for economic justice can succeed if these groupings within the working class remain divided.

Many of the issues that have not been dealt with by liberal groups have fueled the New Right. Fair Share, for example, refused to support the struggle of welfare recipients against Governor King's right-wing administration for fear of alienating some of their constituents. Confronting these traditionally emotionally divisive issues is not easy, but they must be dealt with in a clear and sensitive way that develops a concrete basis for unity between welfare recipients and working-class taxpayers. Likewise, when a Fair Share staff person was asked how the organization dealt with problems of racism, she responded that "race just doesn't come up. It's not an issue. We deal with the kind of economic and consumer issues that cross all such lines." A race war has simmered under the surface in Boston for decades and the largest progressive organization in the state has nothing to say or do about it.

It is impossible not to respect the energy and commitment of citizen-action organizations in attempting to develop an anticorporate working-class movement. However, by focusing too narrowly on a range of private consumer concerns, while evading the highly emotional tensions within the working class over issues of sex, race, and status, such groups leave the New Right free to dominate this terrain by default.

The Democratic Socialist Organizing Committee

Unlike many of the populist groups described above, DSOC concentrates on political education and tries to deliver an explicitly socialist message. To popularize this generally taboo concept, DSOC works from the top, within the Democratic Party, progressive trade unions, and the anticorporate coalitions such as the Progressive Alliance, the Citizen/Labor Energy Coalition, and Citizens Opposed to Inflation in Necessities (COIN).

Exactly how DSOC's brand of socialist practice differs from reform liberalism is not altogether clear. For example, despite the failure of the original Humphrey-Hawkins full-employment bill, a

DSOC staff person said there has been no reassessment of their strategy of seeking reforms through conventional political channels. Their gradualistic top-down approach to change keeps DSOC somewhat cut off from grass-roots struggles, which remain the foundation for any powerful left-wing movement in the United States. Without gaining a closer working relationship with less responsible groups— Black, feminist, welfare rights, and rank-and-file labor— DSOC and their organizational allies, will remain primarily middle income in orientation, reformist in philosophy, and top-heavy in structure.

Professional Elitism within the Left-Liberal Network

The mass membership of the left-liberal groups does not appear to have the same level of self-confidence or self-activation as the earlier civil-rights or welfare-rights movements. While this is partly because of the slightly more secure nature of these constituencies, and the more conservative nature of the national political climate (which makes action of any kind difficult), a third consideration is the atmosphere of liberal professionalism infusing these organizations. Fair Share, for example, is a relatively high-powered bureacracy, staffed by nearly a hundred mainly white, middle-class, college-educated, professional activists and administrators. A great amount of energy is poured into research to develop legislation, referendums, lobbying campaigns, and presentations before local boards and commissions. Disruptive tactics are generally discouraged and conventional legal channels are relied upon, in keeping with Fair Share's intention to maintain an air of respectability.

This reliance upon professional expertise may act as a deterrent to the more active involvement of everyday people in setting a group's political agenda. Although many of the leaders of these organizations are private socialists in theory, they tend to underestimate the ability of others to achieve the same level of political conciousness. Thus, top leadership tends to push a strategy of fairly narrow self-interest on the assumption that this is the only language that people can understand. How to avoid political domination from the top and encourage deeper political awareness and initiative from below should be a key focus for debate within such organizations, unions, and emerging left-wing coalitions.

The Pivotal Role of the Public Sector

In the absence of a significant socialist presence, many public unions have fallen prey to the same problems that historically have weakened private sector unions.

1. Economism, which emphasizes wage and benefit demands to the exclusion of control of the work process and the improvement of service delivery.
2. Racism, best exemplified by Shanker's AFT and their positions against community control of the schools and affirmative action.
3. Liberalism, underscored by the degree to which local and national unions fall over themselves in the scramble to endorse liberal candidates who, when in office, ignore (or harm) these unions under business pressure and fiscal constraints.
4. Bureaucratic elitism, in which union leaders stifle rank-and-file insurgency, in keeping with the premises of contractual bargaining, and promote a brand of professionalism, which makes alliances with lower-status groups difficult to achieve.
5. Class collaboration, as in New York City, where public unions cooperated in implementing the austerity strategies proposed by the city's financial elite. Rather than forging an alliance between rank-and-file workers and grass-roots community groups to fight the banker-business offensive, the union leadership, capitulated. They chose a junior-level partnership in which all of the agreements worked to the disadvantage of their members and the working-class people they served.

Many public-employee organizations are beginning to confront these contradictions. On a national level Citizens for Tax Justice (CTJ) is heavily subsidized by public unions. They have organized a broad, progressive coalition and have explicitly identified the New Right as their enemy. CTJ is prepared to spend millions of dollars to defeat tax-cut measures across the country. In California many locals of the Service Employees International Union (SEIU) spearheaded the grass-roots effort against Proposition 13 and have been instrumental in the creation of client-provider alliances in Alameda County and other parts of the state. In Massachusetts, some public employees, especially those in SEIU Local 880 and SEIU Local 509, have been involved with service recipients in efforts to improve services. A recent struggle on Cape Cod for quality health care was a joint project of SEIU Local 880 and the local Community Action Program (CAP). SEIU Local 509 has been active in opposing the state's workfare program and both SEIU Local 509 and SEIU Local 880 have assisted Fair Share in its battle for tax reform. In addition, a number of progressive rank-and-file caucuses, even within the most conservative public unions such as the AFT, are fighting the policies of their leadership.

Historically, public sector unions have cultivated friendships with state legislators and executives to serve their members' economic needs. This mode of liberal interest-group politics has proven ineffective in an era of fiscal conservatism, forcing these unions to look for a new political approach. Without a concious effort to the contrary, public workers could fall into the social-control role encouraged by the state policies of retrenchment and repression in the 1980s. However, public sector workers are in a pivotal position to help move this country to the left (or the right) politically. They have the organizational strength to establish common linkages with private sector unions, citizen-taxpayer associations, and the poor whom they often serve. The public-service nature of the work they perform makes public employees the natural allies of working-class and poor communities in promoting collective social programs to meet pressing community needs. Because the public sector work force contains a higher percentage of minorities and women than the private sector work force, public unions can seek the cooperation of private sector unions to support the concerns of minorities, women, and low-income people.

The Grass-Roots Movement

Citizen-Action Groups

The second type of citizen-action organization is well represented by the Association of Community Organizations for Reform Now (ACORN), an array of low-wage employee groups, welfare-rights organizations, and hundreds of neighborhood groups. ACORN has a large national presence and is affiliated with Carolina Action, Georgia Action, and California's Citizen Action League.

While these groups share the nonideological approach (which translated, means militant liberal reformism) of the citizen-action organizations discussed earlier, they differ in their choice of constituencies, issues, and manner of operation. ACORN's overall political goal is to increase the power of low- and moderate-income people by building strong local organizations that can serve as the base for citywide, statewide, and national networks. ACORN has initiated campaigns for property-tax equalization and an end to the sales tax on food and medicine. They have fought for welfare entitlements, public-service jobs, affirmative action, public health services, public transit in low-income areas, rent control, and relocation assistance in urban redevelopment areas. So far, ACORN has achieved considerable organizational success. In September 1979, ACORN had over 27,000 member families of which 55 percent were Black, 40 percent were white, and 5 percent were Chicano. They have offices in forty-five cities and nineteen states. ACORN'S organizing strategy clearly moves in the direction of working-class unity. A number of ACORN organizers used to work for Fair Share but left because they felt that organization was "going down the wrong chute."

ACORN is attempting to develop a long-term strategy to guide their political practice. Their people's platform has become a useful tool that details a set of demands and goals in the areas of energy, housing, health care, jobs, affirmative action, income, agriculture/food, community development, taxes, banking policy, and democratic representation in decision making, both public and private. ACORN is using this platform, which stresses the needs of people over the profits of business, as a way of pressuring both the Democratic and Republican Party candidates before (and after) the elections to pay attention to the needs of their constituents. Given their growing national presence it is possible that ACORN might be the base of a viable, populist third party in the next decade.

Grass-Roots Feminists Organizations

Some of the most promising grass-roots efforts have developed from the women's movement. While the liberal-feminist campaign for the ERA has experienced setbacks, local organizing on a collective basis has grown and prospered. Of particular importance for the future of progressive politics in the public sector has been the establishment of a wide-ranging network of centers for battered women and children, rape crisis centers, institutions for women in transition, and reproductive rights groups. Many of these groups are part of the National Coalition Against Domestic Violence and statewide networks, such as the Coalition of Battered Women Service Groups in Massachusetts. The grass-roots feminists are making a serious attempt to involve Black, Hispanic, and white working-class women in their movement. Many of these groups have also developed an explicitly anticapitalist approach. These efforts have arisen in response to the increase in sexual and racist assaults on women in a time of social and economic crisis.

The women's movement has countered the evident disinterest and inability of public sector service institutions to deal with the physical terror and desperate economic insecurity felt by increasing numbers of women by setting up their own collectives and networks to support and politicize their constituents. Unfortunately, many of these grass-roots feminist efforts have not received the full support of other progressive organizations. In addition, while some inroads have been made, the feminist organizations have yet to make a full impact on government-spending priorities and social policy in the areas of welfare, day care, job training, police protection, and counseling. These two problems are connected. Raising the level of struggle to influence the way public services are organized to meet the needs of working-class women would require the united strength of a left-wing movement including labor, citizens, and minority organizations. Only when these other movements begin to make feminist issues a central part of their overall program can they claim to be speaking for the American majority.

The grass-roots women's movement also has a great deal to offer the left-liberal network, particularly in their ability to establish egalitarian and collective forms of struggle. They rely less upon high-powered professionals to develop technical proposals for lobbying purposes. Instead, they have focused their effort on building the awareness and capabilities of all women by encouraging active and committed participation in all parts of organizational work.

Socialist Organizations

A number of explicitly socialist organizations have an impressive record of work within working-class communities across the country. Most of these organizations acknowledge the need to eventually develop a national labor and community party based upon socialist and participatory politics to confront the power of capital and the state. At present they perceive the work they do locally as the necessary foundation for building regional and national networks of organizations like their own.

Detroit's DARE is an explicitly socialist, multiracial working-class organization operating citywide. Its roots are in the working-class neighborhoods of Detroit, and DARE attempts at every turn to defend the interests of working people against the business-oriented policies of Detroit's public officials. DARE has publicized redevelopment strategies that use local tax money and federal Community Development Block Grant funds to benefit wealthy downtown commercial interests and real estate developers while ignoring the housing needs of working-class residents. They have led opposition to tax abatements for developers that would have decreased tax revenues available to support needed community services. They have fought the right of corporations to abandon communities at will, sought public control over utility companies, opposed public hospital closings, police brutality, funding cuts, and layoffs.

DARE actively participates in many of the campaigns and conferences directed by the left-liberal network without soft-pedaling their socialist politics. They support populist struggles wherever they occur and use such campaigns to deepen people's political and social conciousness. In left-liberal conferences DARE helps to clarify the limits of liberal reform and to remind people of the eventual need for socialized control over production to meet the needs of working-class people. Because socialism is DARE's long-term goal, their immediate work for reforms has added meaning and direction. DARE's leadership realizes that most of their Black and white working-class constituents are not socialists, but they think people will move in that direction if socialist ideas are presented in a way that makes sense to people's experience. DARE has also vowed to engage in a "relentless campaign against all manifestations of racism." DARE sees fighting racism as essential to building a class-conscious movement because racism has been so divisive to working-class unity in the past. DARE supports affirmative action as well as the expansion of public service jobs as an important interim step for building their movement.

DARE's electoral strategy has given it added momentum. They have already gained a city council seat and a judgeship and hope to win a city council majority and eventually elect Ken Cockerel or another DARE member as mayor of Detroit. Their electoral strategy is highly progressive because the people elected to office have a base in the city's working-class, grass-roots movement.

DARE officials are accountable to the people in those movements and are in a position to vigorously oppose the class interests of Detroit's financial elite. This is quite a different situation from that which exists in other cities where Black mayors who are not connected to a grass-roots movement have been constrained by the power and needs of the business community to act "responsibly" by implementing the austerity policies of the last decade.

What Kind of Alliances?

Our discussion has noted the development of two partially overlapping tendencies growing in importance on the left today. The first, the left-liberal network, is organized generally from the top-down and seeks reforms of a populist nature, primarily focusing on limiting corporate power. The second tendency is less well known (with some exceptions), but is having an increasingly important impact. It is a nonprofessional grass-roots movement, which stresses a wider range of political issues than the left-liberal network. This article is addressed primarily to people presently supporting the left-liberal tendency. We have hoped to show that changing political conditions in the United States require a more class-oriented political perspective. Such a strategy assumes that the needs of women, minorities, and the poor are as important as the needs of the traditional white working class. There is an enormous potential in the 1980s for people to develop an effective alternative to the austerity strategy of the New Right and the corporations. *This can be accomplished* from the grass-roots, if the progressive movement can achieve certain objectives.

A Class-Conscious Movement

Organizing at both the base and coalition levels should be guided by a class perspective. Programs and demands can be formulated that do not favor better-off segments of the working class at the expense of the underclass. This cannot be done by specific interest groups sitting down in isolation to draw up programs that speak primarily to the needs of their constituents alone. Only through direct social and political communication between groups that generally have little to say to one another can we create potentially successful programs of action.

The key social divisions that undermine the development of a class-based progressive struggle within the public sector include antagonisms between the better-off segments of the working class and the underclass, and between both of these class fragments and the potentially progressive professionals within state bureaucracies and left organizations. These schisms have deep social roots and cannot be glossed over in the interest of developing a superficial unity. The task of socialists today is to help find ways of breaking down these divisions.

Militant Opposition to State Policies Favoring Capitalist Class Interests

A working-class movement must oppose all attempts by business and the state to impose austerity measures. The American ruling class is the wealthiest in history. Their standard of living is not falling. Their income or quality of their services is not decreasing. The belt-tightening of the 1980s will not be applied to them.

The working-class movement must demand new and better services, even as it works to improve those that already exist. Money to provide these services should not come from the working class in the form of ever-higher taxes, but rather from corporate profits. Service bureaucracies can be democratized by public workers and professionals joining with recipients to bring control back to those people actually involved in the programs. In turn, the general public can help the public unions resist efficiency measures and productivity schemes designed to centralize state control in non-accountable bureacracies or private delivery institutions. Feminist issues in the area of reproductive rights, day care, affirmative action, and expanded public-service jobs for the underemployed are crucial issues to be supported. The racist and anti-working-class character of national urban policy, which encouraged the deterioration of inner-city housing, schools, health, and safety, can be fought in strong class terms.

Only militant and potentially disruptive pressure upon the institutions of capital and the state (not just lobbying) will bring the necessary gains. If present liberal leaders weaken the class struggle by collaborating as junior partners with business leaders and established politicians, then other activists can censure such politics of accommodation and pose demands that shift the burden of the fiscal crisis off the working class, backed by the threat of mass action. Even when short-term losses and compromises are necessary, political education can still be carried on, demonstrating how the profit orientation of the banking and business community and the housing, health-care, or nursing home industries inevitably obstruct any concerted response to pressing social needs.

Many progressive leaders urge their constituents to avoid militant confrontation at this time. They stress the weakness of the left wing and hold out the promise of increased rewards when the country's economic situation improves. However, progressives who urge political restraint today in hopes of getting a bigger piece of tomorrow's expanding pie simply do not understand the nature of the current economic crisis. The golden era of American capitalism has passed and the struggle over our society's goods and services will only become more acute in the 1980s. Only class struggle can transform the American political economy into a system that uses the huge economic surplus to fulfill social needs that the present profit-oriented system ignores.

Participation of Nonexperts

In mounting such a class struggle, any deference to the elite authority or technical expertise of leftist professionals can only be counterproductive. Issues with which the leadership grapples should become a matter of debate throughout the movement, with the goal that all workers and citizens achieve a deeper level of political conciousness and participate in decision making. Hierarchy and mental versus manual divisions of labor within political organizational work should be avoided in order to encourage widespread mutual development and an intensified spirit of commitment.

Conclusion

Critics of our views feel that we are out of touch with political reality. They maintain that people are not ready to entertain socialist ideas, whites are not ready to support Black struggles, the American working class is not willing to deal with feminist issues, and the voters are not willing to consider an alternative to Democratic and Republican Party politics. We disagree. We think people are torn in a number of different directions. For example, massive alienation from traditional democratic forms (such as elections) indicates that many people are questioning the effectiveness of traditional liberal and conservative approaches and are seeking a political orientation that makes sense in the 1980s. In the wake of further liberal failure to deal with people's needs and anxieties, the right will consolidate its control over our social and political institutions. Given the close political interaction and ideological unity between the right and the major corporations, it is clear that the real beneficiaries of this conservative "realism" would be the nation's current corporate elite. The public sector will remain a key area for conflict in this century. In the near future, the left must make the issue of who the state serves—capital or the *entire* working class—its Number One priority.

Available from URPE

U.S. Capitalism in Crisis—A radical analysis of the current economic crisis. Includes over thirty articles, tables, and notes for further reading. Some of the topics covered are: theory of the economic crisis, work and jobs, banks, energy, food, women, cities, housing, the family, unions, government, and "Where do we go from here?" $4.00

Taxes for the Rich and the Rest—Shows how the middle income groups pay and why they protest. Explanation of how specific taxes and the total tax system relate to income and wealth. $2.50

How to Research a Corporation—Questions and answers for the corporate opponent. All new material compiled by URPE members. $3.50

RRPE Abstracts and Subjects Index—A complete listing of over one hundred articles and book reviews published in the *Review of Radical Political Economics* 1969–1979. $3.00

Special Issues of the Review of Radical Political Economics

Women

Vol. 12 No. 2—Women and the Economy—Articles on the sexual division of labor and the working-class family, women's household production for the market, Iran and Iranian women, patriarchy in colonial New England, women's liberation and socialism. $4.00

Vol. 9 No. 3—Women and the Economy—Articles on Marxism and Feminism, teaching economics to women, the family and the state. $4.00

Vol. 8 No. 1—Women and the Economy—Articles on housework, subsistence production, Spain, China, rape and prostitution, Inez Garcia, and the Depression. $4.00

Health

Vol. 9 No. 1—The Political Economy of Health—Articles on stress-related mortality, political ecology of disease, the state, malaria, the health care industry, ideology, and China. $4.00

Development

Vol. 10 No. 3—Uneven Regional Development—Special 150 page issue on the sources and characteristics of regional differences internal to the dominant capitalist nations. $4.00

Racism

Vol. 7 No. 3—Perspectives on the Political Economy of Racism— Articles on economic discrimination against Blacks in the U.S. working class, racial biases in the property tax system, capital theory and racism, history and the intelligence of the disinherited, ideological presuppositions of "Time on the Cross," selection from "Roll Jordan Roll." $4.00

Economic History

Vol. 6 No. 2—Radical Interpretations of Economic History— Articles on what bosses do, origins of job structures in the steel industry, Marx on enclosures, social stratification in Boston. $4.00

Imperialism

Vol. 11 No. 4—Imperialism & The Crisis of World Capitalism— Articles on unequal exchange, mode of production and accumulation of capital, export-led industrialization, internationalization of capital, U.S. hegemony and third world thesis, Lenin-Kautsky, and the unity/rivalry debate; Puerto Rico. $4.00

Women's Work Project Pamphlets

Women in the Economic Crisis—Women's work roles in the household and labor force, relationship of women's work to the overall economic crisis, organizational strategies. $.50

Women in Health—Description and analysis of factors influencing women's positions in health occupations, organizing women in the health professions. $.50

Separate and Unequal—Discrimination against women workers after World War II (The UAW 1944–1954). $1.00

Women Organizing the Office—72 page survey of clerical work—its history, problems, and organizing efforts. $2.00

$.50 postage and handling for each issued

Send to:
URPE, 41 Union Square West, Room 901, New York, N.Y. 10003.

Tel: 212-691-5722